1989

Mastering the Message

LAUREN KESSLER and DUNCAN McDONALD

School of Journalism, University of Oregon

Mastering the Message

Media Writing with Substance and Style

WADSWORTH PUBLISHING COMPANY

Belmont, California   *A Division of Wadsworth, Inc.*

Communication Editor: Kristine Clerkin
Editorial Assistant: Melissa Harris
Production Editor: Vicki Friedberg
Managing Designer: Carolyn Deacy
Print Buyer: Randy Hurst
Permissions Editor: Robert M. Kauser
Designer: Adriane Bosworth
Copy Editor: Noel Deeley
Compositor: Weimer Typesetting
Cover: Mark McGeoch
Signing Representative: Tamy Stenquist

Acknowledgments are listed on page 319.

Printed in the United States of America   49

1 2 3 4 5 6 7 8 9 10—93 92 91 90 89

LIBRARY OF CONGRESS
Library of Congress Cataloging-in-Publication Data
Kessler, Lauren.
    Mastering the message: media writing with substance and style /
Lauren Kessler, Duncan McDonald.
      p.   cm.
    Includes index.
    ISBN 0-534-09678-6
    1. Mass Media—Authorship.   I. McDonald, Duncan.   II. Title.
P96.A86K47 1989
808′.066001—dc19   88-18122
                                                            CIP

To that newest communicator, Zane—and to our supportive host of veteran ones: Jane, Tom, Vanessa and Jackson. Salute!

Contents

Preface

We are a nation of communicators. We speak, sign—even sing—to get our message across. We routinely argue, reason, plead and bluster. And when our conventional language can't do the job, we use body signals to convey feelings we may find difficult to express.

As if this interpersonal mode of communication wasn't complicated enough, we also employ mechanical and electronic servants to give voice to our writing. The mass media—a socio/economic/political complex both heralded and cursed for its investigations and invasions—bombard our citizens with news, opinions, pleas and bargains.

In reading this book, you have demonstrated an interest in writing for the mass media. It is a profession, an industry, that grows daily as the demand for information, analysis and persuasion increases. In responding to this interest and to the need for clear, accurate mass communication, we have organized a body of thought we believe goes beyond a vocational or how-to manual.

Mastering the Message examines and explains the writing process. It focuses on what makes written expression both effective and creative. While it acknowledges differences in media forms, *Mastering the Message* explores the similarities that form the foundation of all good writing.

Mastering the Message is the third (and last) book in a series we have created for Wadsworth. Our first two books (*When Words Collide* and *Uncovering the News*) have examined the language skills and information-gathering tools that support good writing. With the publication of *Mastering the Message*, we believe we have completed a comprehensive introduction to the basic techniques of mass communication.

As teachers and professional journalists, we urge you to pursue the goal of effective writing with energy and enthusiasm. Our society depends on clear, concise and honest communication; unless you master language skills, information gathering, organization and style, your work will fall short of what society needs. With focus and practice, you can master the skills a professional communicator needs.

We wish you success!

Acknowledgments

As we wrap up work on our third book for Wadsworth, we continue to marvel at the dedication, enthusiasm and professionalism of the company's staff. We especially remember when we first worked with senior editor Becky Hayden, who created such a friendly atmosphere in all our dealings. It continues to be a professional and personal pleasure to work with Wadsworth; for this work, we especially want to thank our production editor, Vicki Friedberg, our editor, Kris Clerkin, and our designer, Carolyn Deacy.

Special thanks to the following manuscript reviewers who gave us many helpful comments and observations: R. Thomas Berner, The Pennsylvania State University; Walter B. Jaehnig, Southern Illinois University; William McKeen, University of Florida; Robert M. Ours, West Virginia University; Carl Sessions Stepp, University of Maryland; James W. Tankard Jr., University of Texas at Austin; John H. Vivian, Winona State University; Lee Wilkins, University of Colorado; and Eugenia Zerbinos, University of Maryland.

Lauren Kessler
Duncan McDonald
Eugene, Oregon

Mastering the Message

The Common Core

We all recognize good media writing when we read or hear it. It's the crisply written news story that informs and clarifies, the well-paced magazine article that rivets our attention, the dramatic advertisement that captures our interest. What do these diverse forms of writing have in common? What makes good writing *good*?

That's what this first section is about. Of course, newspaper stories, broadcast reports, magazine articles, advertising copy and public relations writing have obvious differences. They are written for different purposes and directed to different audiences. They appear in different media and necessarily take different forms.

These are important differences, but they shouldn't blind us to some startling similarities. Good media writing, no matter where it appears, shares important characteristics: It is honest, accurate and fair. It is based on solid information. Its language is clear, precise and correct. Its presentation is original and lively.

The following six chapters will explore these similarities. Chapter 1 presents a portrait of today's mass media and the opportunities for writers. Chapter 2 discusses the reigning—but nonetheless wrong-headed—journalistic philosophy of objectivity and the achievable goals that should replace it. Chapter 3 explores the most basic skill necessary to good media writing: gathering good information. Chapter 4 reviews common grammatical problems that can stand in the way of effective communication. Chapter 5 presents the components of clear writing, and Chapter 6 explores writing with style. Let's concentrate on these important basics. They form the common core of good media writing.

CHAPTER 1

Writing for the Mass Media

Time doesn't stand still, especially for a deadline. Neither does information—or the public's craving for it. Every day, countless information sources feed a media dynamo that tirelessly generates facts, opinions and entertainment for our use.

This information flows through efficient but fallible corporate organizations that depend on public acceptance for their survival. Successful dissemination to the public is dependent on two factors: complete, accurate information gathering and clear, concise presentation of that information.

Mastering the Message focuses on *writing*—its organization, structure and style. This chapter looks at the mass media's writing industry: the characteristics of its writing, its professional demands and its job opportunities. Most important, this chapter discusses a general approach to media writing and examines areas of expertise common to good writing.

The massive media writing machine

To appreciate the volume and variety of writing within our mass media, we must look beyond what traditionally has been called journalism. True, we do depend upon our daily "news fix" to orient ourselves to our various environments, but our media generate more information than how many car bombs exploded today in Beirut, who won the election for state treasurer or what some movie critic thought of "Rambo VIII." Our media provide much more than stories—they bombard us almost relentlessly with *messages,* ranging from a drop in stock market prices to a direct mail promotion for a magazine sweepstakes. These messages are channeled through many media industries:

— more than 1,600 daily newspapers

— almost 8,000 weekly newspapers

— more than 1,200 television stations and a growing number of specialized cable services

— almost 10,000 radio stations (with nearly 25 percent of them categorized in the news format)

— depending on the manner of tabulation, between 25,000 and 60,000 magazines issued at least monthly

— newsletters that defy an accurate count

— more than 2,000 advertising agencies with annual billings in excess of $1 million

— almost 2,000 public relations agencies

Media output doesn't stop there.

Consider, for example, that book publishers annually produce more than 35,000 titles, including trade, text and professional books. Consider also the explosion in technical writing positions. (Suffer through a poorly written computer software manual, and you'll appreciate the skill of a good technical writer.) Add to this media mix a growing number of television and film documentary scripts, and you'll begin to see the image of a media machine tireless in its prodigious output.

All of these media produce messages of varying quality, quantity and style. This is because the people who write for mass communications operate within a multitude of environments, audience demands and economic constraints. Their common link, however, is simple: They all write. They communicate. They research information, evaluate it, organize it and then present it in specified formats and varying styles. All effective messages are the products of processes with a common heritage.

Characteristics of media writing

One of the major premises of this book is that the writing *process* is not substantially different from one medium to the next. Now this may come as a surprise to some newspaper writers who feel that their writing is vastly different from that of a TV news writer. It may be shocking to the newsmagazine staffer who believes that magazine writing has more depth and color than any other medium. And it may amuse the advertising copywriter who thinks that ad writing is a creature unto itself. However, these writers may be reacting to obvious differences in style, message intent and special requirements of various media. Stripped of these embellishments, the common characteristic of all media writing is the process of its creation.

In addition, all media writing shares similar attributes: clarity, precision, flow, transition and detail. Let's examine writing excerpts from selected media industries to discover some common characteristics.

Newspapers

BAHRAIN—An Iraqi jet fired two Exocet missiles at the USS Stark Sunday night in the Persian Gulf, killing 37 sailors aboard the guided missile frigate.

The Stark, which was on patrol in these international waters, apparently did not think the French-made Mirage jet would fire on it, although the ship reportedly had twice warned the fighter to stay away.

(This preceding is an example of the classic summary approach to newswriting. In this format the writer attempts to pack as much information as possible, according to fact importance, in limited space.)

DALTON, Ga.—In a gigantic laundry here, a flotilla of washing machines makes the kind of rumble that would alarm a Maytag repairman.

Suddenly, one of the mammoth machines tilts forward. Out tumble 48 pairs of Lee jeans. Plus 50 pounds of pumice stones. A team of workers moves in quickly to shake pumice fragments from the damp jeans.

This is standard operating procedure at 20 laundries where the Lee Division of VF Corp. beats the bejabbers out of blue jeans, using a process known as "stonewashing." Nowadays Lee and its rivals can't churn out these battered denims fast enough.

Consumers love the look that manufacturers euphemistically call "used and abused" or "distressed." The worse the jeans look, the more they cost, especially if they have holes in the right places, such as the knees. To the wearers of New Waif couture, tattered is beautiful.

(This front-page Wall Street Journal *story has a classic magazine style. It is more relaxed, colorful and longer than a typical newspaper story. Although the* Journal *is a daily newspaper, it showcases one or two front-page stories daily in this style. Note the play on "New Wave" in the last sentence of this example.)*

Magazines Matadi, ZAIRE—Two vast legs of steel stand in the water of the mighty Congo River, and from them hangs Africa's longest suspension bridge. The new bridge, opened in 1984, boasts two decks, one for automobiles and one for trains. But there isn't any railroad here. The railroad deck runs into a solid rock cliff. A smoothly paved road crosses the river on the upper deck and runs past a granite inscription with the name "President Mobutu Sese Seko Suspension Bridge." Then the road disappears around a bend and turns into gravel and broken blacktop. During the first six months the bridge was open, an average of 53 vehicles a day passed over it.

When African nations gained independence 25 years ago, they desperately needed sensible development to secure their economic future. Too often they received white elephant projects like Zaire's bridge to nowhere. . . .

(This excerpt from The New Republic *magazine demonstrates the descriptive approach so common in magazine writing. It has an opening paragraph longer than that in a traditional newspaper story. However, its style is not markedly different from a* Wall Street Journal *special feature. Interestingly, this article was written by a former WSJ reporter.)*

Taxpayers in the Northeast pay the biggest bucks to put juvenile delinquents in the slammer. Locking up a young criminal costs the taxpayers $39,900 annually in the Northeast. The Midwest follows with a cost of $26,100; the West, $22,900; and the South, $22,700.

(Magazines aren't tied to a grand, flowing and leisurely style. With brevity and directness, this opening paragraph from an American Demographics *magazine story bears a similarity to what some consider newspaper style. The treatment is fairly straightforward, but an air of informality makes such information more welcome.)*

Broadcasting

ANNOUNCER (0:30)
    MORE ARSON IN TOLEDO. . . .
    WEARY FIREFIGHTERS RESPONDED TO A THREE-ALARM BLAZE EARLY THIS MORNING IN THE CITY'S WAREHOUSE DISTRICT, THE SCENE OF THREE OTHER ARSON-CAUSED FIRES IN AS MANY DAYS.
    THE CAUSE OF THE FIRE THAT DESTROYED THE TOFUTTI ICE CREAM DISTRIBUTION CENTER HAS BEEN LISTED AS ARSON.
    AS KIM MARTINEZ REPORTS, CITY OFFICIALS FEAR THAT THE ARSONIST'S

CAMPAIGN IS FAR FROM OVER.
MARTINEZ (2:30). . . .

(Although broadcasting uses "sound bites" [portions of recorded interviews] and videotape to complete its presentation, the stories that are prepared still require clear, concise—and easy to understand—writing to reach the audience.)

Advertising

Help us celebrate our best sales year ever!

It's the GMC truck celebration cash-in . . . with $500 rebates and Value Option Package savings available now on the full-size Sierra Pickup, S-15 Pickup, S-15 Jimmy, and full-size Rally and Vandura Vans. . . .

(The role of many advertisements is that of a super-efficient pitchmaker—to aggressively promote products and services in a highly competitive economy. This announcement of a truck sale must attract the attention of the intended audience. It works well in either a print or broadcast form. Some advertisements, however, promote important issues, as in the next example.)

Millions of acres of Central American rainforest are destroyed so U.S. hamburger chains and pet food companies can get cheap meat.

It's called rainforest beef. Which means it comes from marginal grazing land in what used to be rainforest.

Before the rainforest was bulldozed and burned, it was home to thousands of rare and exotic species. After the cattle have come and gone, it's an eroded wasteland practically empty of life. . . .

(This activist, no-punches-pulled advertisement contains the serious tone and persuasiveness seen in some newspaper editorials. In urging a boycott of U.S. hamburger chains that buy this beef, the advertisement promotes a course of action—which often is the aim of an editorial. Its style, however, is more like an ad.)

Public relations (the company magazine)

Like Sylvester Stallone's boxer protagonist in the "Rocky" films, Chevron USA's El Segundo Refinery has had to absorb its share of punches, often square on the chin. But lately, like Rocky, the refinery is also showing an ability to scrape itself off the canvas, shake off the blows and charge back into action.

(This excerpt is from Chevron Focus, *an oil company's monthly magazine for employees and a specially targeted audience. Although the article predictably sings the praises of a refinery and its tenacious management coping with environmental concerns, its style is common to both newspapers and magazines.)*

What characteristics do all these media excerpts share? They all present a message as clearly and precisely as possible. Their information is organized to eliminate conflict of points and images. When a new thought is offered, its way is paved by effective transition. Crisp detail is important. When appropriate, color and descriptions are used to enhance the message.

Such writing is not easily created.

Good writing requires more than imagination and a good vocabulary. Among other things, it demands training and discipline. It doesn't exist in the absence of clear thinking. Let's examine these requirements.

What is expected of a media writer?

"**P**roven talent and exceptional writing skills that demonstrate originality, organization and clarity."

Is this a line from an ad seeking a writer for a newspaper or a magazine? No, but it easily could be. It's from a flier for a computer software company looking for technical writers.

Consider this observation:

Good writers come in all sizes, shapes and ages. What they all seem to have in common is the ability to hear, to listen, to understand—and to distill what they hear and learn into something that's human and persuasive.

This could be a description of the qualities needed in a broadcast or print journalist, but Jay Chiat, co-founder of the advertising agency

Chiat/Day, was discussing qualities that breed success in the advertising industry.

Noted syndicated newspaper columnist James J. Kilpatrick champions good writing and bemoans weak, confused and inarticulate attempts at mass communication. This is his view, as expressed in his book *The Writer's Art*:

We want to amuse, to persuade, to arouse, to delight, to describe, and we want to do an effective job of amusing, persuading, arousing, delighting, and describing. We aspire to more than merely writing clearly; we aspire now to write gracefully, or literately, or wittily, or perceptively. We have built a sufficiency of chicken coops and would try our hand at the art of the cabinetmaker instead.

Let's consider these statements as we examine what is expected of media writers:

1. *A writer must have keen senses.* Good writers *feel* the world around them; they often *sense* what may not be openly expressed. They are open to life, but they receive its rush of fact and emotion with a quiet reflection that belies the creative energy it takes to process such overwhelming input.

2. *A writer must be organized.* Lack of attention to detail and an inability to determine the priority of different kinds of information will damage the most creative of efforts. Proper organization demands that a writer be able to construct a logical framework of information.

3. *A writer must gather information quickly and thoroughly.* Good writers know their way around the information jungle. They use research and organizational skills to find critical materials for their messages. (See Chapter 3.)

4. *A writer must understand language.* Writers who haven't mastered grammar, word use and spelling place themselves in a hostile environment when they try to communicate. When they violate rules of agreement, punctuation, meaning and spelling, they pay a terrible price: Their writing is devalued, misunderstood—and perhaps scorned. (See Chapter 4.)

5. *A writer must be clear and precise.* Good writers don't permit the force of their information and creativity to gush out like torrents of water from a collapsed dam; they deliver their output in measured doses to ensure understanding from their audience. Clarity and precision are the closest allies of creative writing. (See Chapter 5.)

6. *A writer must have style.* As Kilpatrick says, good writers want to go beyond the chicken coop. They want more than a technically proficient *craft*; they want *art*. Style, however, requires more than the ability to use colorful words and to pace effectively; it demands more than a knack for snappy metaphors and appropriate analogies. Style must be the original reflection and expression of a writer who says: "This is what I see. This is what I feel." (See Chapter 6.)

7. *A writer must be responsible.* Good writers have a duty to their audience. They should inform without misleading. They should persuade without demagoguery. They should be fair and direct. These responsibilities lead naturally to the topic of objectivity (see Chapter 2).

Media writing is difficult, demanding work. It requires training, discipline and constant practice. Some people have gone so far as to say that a good writer must sweat blood before producing effective communication. That's a thought-provoking image, but it isn't necessarily so. Regular sweat will do just fine.

What media jobs are out there?

Our society is well into the so-called Information Age. We live in a period in which information industries are outpacing the manufacturing sector in employment. City newspapers create national editions by transmitting facsimiles of their pages by satellite to regional printing plants. Our information gathering has moved out of the traditional library and into the world of the computer database. It is an exciting and challenging time to work in the mass media.

Let's examine some career possibilities in media writing and the opportunity to cross over from one media industry to another.

Newspapers

As recently as 20 years ago, a means of entry to a reporting job was to become a copyboy or copygirl—a "gofer" of sorts who would deliver copy from reporter to editor and from editor to typesetter, get coffee, pick up needed photographs, occasionally take a dictated story over the phone, and wait for the opportunity to "break" a big story. Today many daily newspapers have a position called *news aide*. Aides take routine information over the phone, compile listings of coming events (such as public meetings), do fact checking and write small, uncomplicated stories.

However, most college graduates who have had a summer internship that provided reporting and writing experience are able to secure an entry-level job as a reporter. It is not unusual for a reporter to spend a lifetime in a writing career, although some choose to move into editing and management.

Because of the time required for story research, interviewing and organization, it is difficult for a daily newspaper reporter to write more than two stories a day. Writing load and work pace, however, vary according to a publication's circulation and purpose. Small-circulation newspapers (below 25,000) often require a greater volume of writing, as do weekly newspapers, which are usually understaffed. Regardless of circulation size, however, newspapers demand the ability to organize and write quickly and accurately. It is not a skill quickly learned. Once learned, however, this skill is easily transferable to magazines and broadcasting.

Magazines

Many general-circulation magazines (those without highly specialized content) prefer that their staff writers have previous media experience, especially with newspapers. A number of specialized magazines (science, computers, business) prefer writers with training in the magazine's specialty. And many trade magazines (dealing with such topics as forest products and wholesale groceries, for example) often hire young graduates with a minimum of media experience. But many magazines are showing increasing dependence on freelance submissions. This means that writers with good story ideas, an understanding of a magazine's audience and the ability to write in-depth can work with a variety of publications without being tied to them as employees. Magazines certainly present the most encouraging opportunity to get into print.

Broadcasting

Radio and television, more than any other media industry, must consider the needs and uses of technology in the writing process. Writers and producers must consider the interviews done on audio and video when organizing stories; broadcast writing involves what the announcer is to say, as well as what will be included as an *actuality* (the radio tape) or the *bite* (the television equivalent). Because of this noticeable difference from print in the writing process, many people go directly into careers in broadcasting. However, the news-gathering function varies little between broadcasting and print. Considering that more competition exists between broadcast outlets than between newspapers, the job market for competent, creative writers in the electronic media looks very strong.

Public relations

A hard-working public relations person is hounded by a single task: to communicate. Usually that communication is written. It could take the form of a news release to the print and broadcast media; it could be a speech to be delivered by a company president; it could be a position paper to be presented to a state legislative committee; it could be a public service announcement to be broadcast nationally. A good public relations practitioner must be a creative and convincing writer. People with that ability don't just walk in off the street—they've probably had significant media experience elsewhere before moving into PR. This media experience is crucial because public relations is an important supplier of news and information to the media.

Advertising

Advertising agencies hire creative people to develop campaign concepts and to write the advertising copy to sustain these campaigns and make them flourish. People with good ideas and the talent to express them can be successful in this media industry, which trades in both information and persuasion. Good writers are valued in this profession, and they are honored annually in the Clio award competition. The first step in a creative career in advertising is to become an advertising copywriter.

This glimpse of writing careers in mass media industries reveals a broad and growing field. As we move deeper into the Information Age, the growth of mass communications industries shows no indication of abating.

Cross-media movement

Mass communications is dynamic not only because it involves fast-moving and rapidly changing information, but also because it is open to a variety of career changes.

Perhaps that is one of the attractions of this field. A newspaper writer may one day be a magazine editor or the director of corporate communications for a large industrial firm. An advertising copywriter may later pursue a successful career as a magazine writer and then publish several non-fiction books. A television newscaster may work later for a newspaper and broadcast wire service and still later edit a corporate magazine and write speeches for company executives.

Such crossovers are not unusual.

A former student recently related her job route since graduation. She began as an overworked and underpaid reporter/photographer at a small daily newspaper. Three years later she became a writer for Associated Press, writing for both the newspaper and broadcast wires. Two years later she moved to a large Eastern city, where she now receives regular and lucrative free-lance assignments from several prominent national magazines. What does she want to do after that? Public relations, she thinks, especially in finance, because she has developed a writing specialty in that area.

Freedom of movement is not as easy in some other professions. Think about career moves within dentistry or personnel management. Writing for the media provides glamour and challenge and variety that don't exist in other occupations.

A generic view
of media writing

Writing is an acquired skill. (A few "naturals" probably are out there, as in many professions, but most of us need hard work, concentration and practice to develop our skills.) We believe that good media writers reveal themselves long before they start a media career. Here are some of their important qualities:

— a healthy appetite for reading

— a natural curiosity, a desire to investigate

— an ability to write simply and directly, be it a letter, a book report or an essay

With these qualities as a foundation, students can gradually develop the skills to write effectively for the media. However, we believe that beginning with the broadest view of media writing—rather than assuming that the most appropriate foundation is newspaper reporting, for example—will reveal the common threads of the media fabric and will ease media career crossover.

With this intention in mind, *Mastering the Message* looks at issues of objectivity, information gathering, correct language use, clarity and style before addressing these three core areas of media writing:

1. *The news burst.* Timely information that is succinctly communicated exists in a variety of media contexts: a wire service story about a killer tornado in West Texas, a public relations release about a company's fight against a corporate takeover, or a health update in *American Baby* magazine. Speed and urgency are important characteristics of these "bursts" of news. Such news cannot be treated in depth at its most explosive moment; other media forms can provide needed context and correlation. Four chapters in this text examine how news is evaluated and written for print, broadcast and public relations.

2. *Depth and context.* Not all media messages are brief explosions of timely facts. An audience also wants in-depth treatment of people, events and issues. Magazines aren't the only medium to use analytical and descriptive writing. It is often found in newspapers, too. Broadcasting showcases it, as do film documentaries.

3. *Persuasion.* Advertising, broadcasting and newspapers share an important function in our culture: They promote products and concepts through persuasion and advocacy. Writing to persuade is difficult; it requires much more than a popular topic and smooth talk. Mounting an effective, winning argument is a critical skill.

Mastering the Message offers the broadest possible approach to media writing. In a sense, it provides a survey of the range of media messages. You will learn their similarities and become sensitive to their differences. But most important, you will travel to the core of effective mass communication: organization, focus, clarity and style.

Like food and shelter, information is a basic need of society. Like food and shelter, information needs skilled people to cultivate and construct it.

Can you master the message?

Objectivity

Media writers are constantly under attack for the way they practice their craft. What they write, says everyone from their bosses to their audience, is either too boring or too sensational, too flowery or too spare, too controversial or too bland, too shallow or too complex. But the strongest condemnation of all, the worst insult that can be thrown at most media writers, is lack of objectivity.

— "Your story isn't objective," yells an editor to a reporter.

— "This newscast obviously lacks objectivity," comments a disgusted TV viewer.

— "This press release is not objective at all," complains a reporter.

— "There isn't a hint of objectivity in that advertising claim," snorts a magazine reader.

Just what is objectivity, and what does it have to do with the way media writers do their jobs? Why is it a concept, an attitude and a series of techniques all media writers should think hard about?

What is objectivity?

Objectivity has been one of the fundamental philosophies of the news media since the 1920s. It is seen by many professionals as both a guiding principle that helps direct their daily activities and a lofty ideal to be doggedly—although sometimes not successfully—pursued. In a broad sense, objectivity is a way of trying to understand reality based on the collection of observable, verifiable facts.

By this definition, many professions claim to embrace and practice objectivity: the physician who observes symptoms and verifies findings with tests and instruments, the attorney who pieces together material evidence and looks for legal precedents, the scientist who constructs experiments and observes the outcome. These professionals claim to be impartial observers who gather, process and present information untainted by preconceptions or personal bias.

When media professionals claim they are being objective, they mean all or some of the following:

— They gather and present material without prejudice or partisanship.

— They act as impartial witnesses to events.

— Their work is not affected by their preconceived notions and ideas.

— Their work is uninfluenced by emotion.

— They keep personal opinions and judgments out of their messages.

— The information they present is neutral and nonjudgmental.

— Their messages are the sum of independently verifiable facts.

Compared with the long history of mass communication in this country, objectivity is a new concept. For more than two centuries, the U.S. press operated without concern for objectivity, frequently reveling in—and celebrated for—its biased, opinionated stances. But for the past 60 years, objectivity has reigned supreme. Why has it become such a popular principle?

Some say it's because objectivity provides a good defense against the manipulation of news by others. Not wanting to be seen as a pawn of any special interest group or a mouthpiece for any institution, the news media adopted a stance of objectivity to protect themselves against being used. Others say the news media embraced objectivity to make themselves an ideal advertising vehicle. If it were no longer overtly partisan, the news would be palatable to just about anyone. Because this large audience was attractive to advertisers, objective news organizations could bring in far greater advertising revenue than opinionated, partisan organizations. Still others say the answer lies with media professionals themselves. Objectivity is enormously popular with professionals because it serves to separate them from the rest of us, making them appear special and specially qualified.

Objectivity, say others, protects media professionals from the risks of the trade: libel suits, reprimands from superiors, barbs from outside critics. It is a shield that allows those in the profession to deflect criticism. "Attacked for controversial presentation of 'facts,' [media professionals] invoke their objectivity almost the way a Mediterranean peasant might wear a clove of garlic," writes sociologist Gaye Tuchman.

Objectivity and writing for the media

Striving for objectivity influences how media writers do their jobs. It affects the way mass media messages are constructed, from the choice of individual words to the structure of the entire message. To achieve their goal of objectivity, media writers practice the following techniques:

— *Use specific, verifiable, factual detail rather than general judgments.* A journalist who writes "Jones is a gifted writer" can be accused of lack of objectivity. *Gifted* is a judgment. In the context of the sentence, it appears to be the journalist's personal opinion. If that journalist instead writes "Jones has twice won the National Book

Award," the journalist can claim objectivity. The message contains factual detail that can be independently verified. An advertising copywriter who writes "Brand X is the best toothpaste for your kids" obviously cannot claim objectivity. But if the advertisement reads "In government laboratory tests, brand X proved to be three times as effective in preventing cavities in children as any of the other brands," then the copywriter can claim objectivity.

— *Use quotations.* To distance themselves from the statements of others and clearly indicate that opinions stated are not theirs, media writers frequently quote others. This practice is called attribution. Suppose the journalist had written " 'Jones is a gifted writer,' says the president of Random House publishers." By attributing this judgment to a source, the journalist maintains an objective stance. Suppose the copywriter had written " 'Brand X is the best toothpaste for kids,' says the president of the American Dental Association." Again, the use of quotation for a matter of opinion protects the media writer from accusations of lack of objectivity.

— *Use officially titled experts as sources of information.* Because they themselves are often not experts on the subjects they write about, media writers almost always depend on others for information. But even when they are experts—the trained economist writing on economic issues, for example—they hold back their own opinions and analyses to avoid what would be considered overt bias. (Column writers and reviewers, of course, are exceptions. They specialize in expressing their own opinions.) Most media writers depend on people who, by virtue of their position or job title, are generally accepted experts. For example, the PR writer constructing a press release on National Book Award winner Jones wants to quote someone about Jones' talent. The writer goes to the president of a major publishing company—an officially titled expert. It's possible (in fact, more than likely) that someone else, let's say an unknown assistant editor at an obscure literary magazine, might actually be better qualified to comment on Jones' talent. Ironically, however, depending on sources who lack official stature exposes the writer to accusations of the lack of objectivity.

— *Present both sides of the issue.* In an effort to avoid overt bias, media writers often attempt to balance conflicting claims of truth expressed by sources. This frequently shows up in media messages as "On the one hand . . . On the other hand . . . ," implying that both claims have equal weight and that either (or neither) can be true. This balancing act can actually get in the way of the truth.

For example, consider a story on the potential health hazards of cigarette smoke to non-smokers. A story based solely on information supplied by the American Cancer Society could be accused of being biased. But suppose the reporter wrote "On the one hand, the American Cancer Society claims the danger is real. On the other hand, the Tobacco Institute of America says the studies are inconclusive." This balancing act, which can be seen in public relations and editorial writing as well as news journalism, is one of the mainstays of journalistic objectivity.

— *Structure messages according to accepted convention*. One way to look at objectivity is to say that the fewer personal, individual decisions the writer has to make about constructing the message, the better the chance of achieving objectivity. One major decision that faces media writers every time they sit down to write is the arrangement of information. How should the message begin? In what order should the information be presented? Where should it end? Presumably, left to their own devices, writers would make individual decisions about order and structure based on personal judgment and past experience. Would those decisions be objective? By definition, they would not. But suppose public relations writers and print and broadcast reporters all agreed to structure their stories in similar ways? Suppose they agreed to relate information in descending order of importance? This would take some of the individual guesswork out of constructing a story and increase its chances of being objective.

Objectivity and the differing goals of media writing

The concept of objectivity is considered important for all media writers but in different ways. One obvious difference among media writers that affects their practice of objectivity is the *intent* of their message. Messages constructed to inform—news reports in the print and broadcast media, for example—consciously strive for neutral presentation of verifiable facts. Messages constructed to persuade—editorials and advertisements, for example—may be designed to be overtly biased. An editorial urging the election of candidate X will attempt to make the best possible case for candidate X rather than neutrally presenting all the candidates. An advertisement designed to persuade a consumer to try brand Y will be expressly biased in favor of brand Y.

It is true that advertising copywriters, public relations writers and editorial columnists do not often construct their messages with an eye toward objectivity. But objectivity, in some form, is highly prized in all the media industries. Public relations practitioners, explains one veteran consultant, "need to *have* objectivity but not necessarily display it. They have to *be* objective in their research and planning but *act* for the client." In public relations, objectivity is seen as a valuable concept when applied to gathering and evaluating information but not when presenting it to the public. Much the same can be said for the interpretation of objectivity in the advertising industry. "We look at the competition objectively to determine strengths and weaknesses," says an award-winning copywriter. "We evaluate studies on the product objectively. But, of course, we're not paid to write objective copy."

Whether they claim to practice unbiased information gathering, unbiased evaluation of information or unbiased presentation of information, all media writers claim objectivity in some way.

They are all wrong.

Why objectivity isn't possible

In 1906 a Virginia physician published a long, scientific article comparing the brains of American blacks and whites. Using scientific methods, he measured a structure within the brain thought to be linked to higher intelligence. In every case (he measured more than 100 brains), the scientist found that in blacks' brains the structure was smaller than the same structure in whites. From this objective measurement, he concluded that whites were intellectually superior to blacks, a finding that conveniently meshed with his own racist beliefs.

But one of the physician's colleagues was suspicious. The numbers were just too perfect. The colleague repeated the measuring procedure, using some of the brains from the original experiment, but with one important difference: He made sure he didn't know which brains were from whites and which from blacks until after he finished measuring. The outcome? The second scientist found no difference between blacks and whites. Author, teacher and biologist Stephen Jay Gould, who tells this anecdote in *The Mismeasure of Man,* concludes:

"Prior prejudice, not copious documentation, dictates conclusions." But it was more than that. Prior prejudice dictated what the first scientist actually *saw*. The scientific calibrations themselves were affected by his bias.

This may be an extreme case, and we may have learned some important lessons in the ensuing 80 years. But it illustrates a fundamental point about the impossibility of objectivity: Who we are and what we believe color what we see.

We're only human

Media writers, like scientists, are human beings. They are the sum of their experiences, and their experiences differ. An Asian-American female growing up in San Francisco experiences the world differently from a rural Minnesotan male with a Scandinavian background. Both become media writers. Both conscientiously keep their opinions out of what they write. But the fact is, they see the world differently; they ask different questions, see and choose different details, use different vocabularies, care about different issues. That's good—diversity is vital to a democratic media—but it's not objective.

As the experiments of the two brain-measuring scientists show, "objective fact" can change according to who is recording it. Each of us processes the experiences of everyday life through our individual "filters," which are determined in large part by our age, gender, race, education, socio-economic background, religion, personal philosophy and life experiences.

Consider the case of two journalists who traveled to Alaska to discover what was at the heart of America's last frontier. Both were after the truth, and both observed reality to get it. After thousands of miles, months of research and hundreds of interviews, one journalist painted a picture of rampant drinking, divorce, human disintegration and oil-inspired greed. The other wrote a story detailing pioneer spirit, self-sufficiency and human ingenuity. The first journalist, Joe McGinniss, is the younger man, the product of a more cynical time. Born and educated in New York City, he is on his second marriage. The second journalist, John McPhee, is a middle-aged, Princeton-educated outdoorsman. Who these journalists are determined what they saw, how they interpreted what they saw and what they chose to write about. Their stories couldn't be more different, yet both were based on verifiable, "objective" fact.

The observer and the observed

Media professionals may think of themselves as neutral witnesses of reality, but in fact, the act of observing often changes what is being observed. Put yourself in the place of a person being observed by a journalist. Let's say a magazine writer calls you one day and asks for an interview. On the day of the interview, you dress with far more care than you normally do. When you arrive at your office, you quickly clear your desk of its habitual mess. The writer arrives to find a well-dressed interview subject seated behind a clean desk. The mere presence of the journalist has affected reality.

This seems particularly true in the presence of television journalists and their equipment. Some people play to the cameras, say veteran TV correspondents. The presence of the camera transforms them from mere information sources to actors on display. Conversely, the camera may so intimidate some people that they become far less articulate than they usually are. In either case people become something they are not because the camera is trained on them. The audience accepts the image as an accurate representation of reality.

Selection and subjectivity

The process of writing a media message, be it a diaper commercial or a disaster story, is a process of selection. Faced with choices—from what information to highlight to which words to use—individual writers make individual choices. Choosing one set of "objective" facts over another, something that all writers must do in the course of putting together virtually every piece of communication, is a subjective act.

The selection process begins immediately as the writer sorts through numerous possibilities concerning the overall direction and content of the message. The diaper commercial, for example, can be geared to new parents, experienced parents, fathers only or mothers only. The message can stress health, convenience, comfort or cost. These decisions can be affected by the client's desires, group input and the copywriter's ideas. Each time the writer makes a decision, or follows a decision made by others, he or she travels down a particular, subjective road. The news reporter could interview six people but only has time to talk with two. Who is chosen? The interviews take two hours, but the reporter has space for only five quotations. Which are chosen? Who the writer is affects what choices he or she makes.

The nature of mass communication

The very nature of mass communication makes objectivity impossible. First, consider the content of mass media messages: It is almost entirely dependent on information gleaned from sources. These sources—clients or government representatives, industry reports or official documents—are themselves biased. Sometimes the bias is easy to detect. Consider the political campaign manager who has only wonderful things to say about the candidate. But sometimes the bias is more subtle—for example, a rosy government report on declining unemployment that doesn't factor in teen-age joblessness. The point is that all sources, to some degree and at some time, act out of self-interest. Thus the very information that media writers have to work with is not objective.

Second, consider the function of media writers. It is *not* to judge the correctness, accuracy or truth of information gleaned from sources. Most media writers are not experts in the field they are writing about and would not be capable of independently assessing the quality of the information they receive. More than that, allowing the media writer to make independent judgments about information would be considered the epitome of bias. Thus the self-interested information obtained from sources goes unchallenged (except by other self-interested sources) and passes for objective reality.

Third, consider the background of media writers. Is there anything in their training that prepares them to be objective? Physicians, for example, are trained to look at the disease, not the person. This detachment allows them to function professionally in an often highly charged emotional atmosphere. They are taught to concentrate on the tumor, not the distraught, despairing patient. Attorneys are trained to distinguish legal from moral questions. Scientists are taught scientific method and inductive reasoning.

What are would-be media writers taught? "Be objective," they are told by their teachers. But they are never told how. If there is special training that can help an individual first recognize the full complexity of his or her personal filter and then somehow perceive and select information independent of that filter, it certainly isn't given in journalism schools. "Keep your bias to yourself," say teachers and bosses. But how exactly is this accomplished? Certainly, objectivity means more than *not* inserting overt personal opinion in a message.

What should be the media writer's goals?

If objectivity is a false and impossible ideal, what goals should you aim for as you gather, assess and present information?

— *Honesty.* Be honest with yourself first. Recognize that who you are determines what you see and what you select. You can remove overt bias from your dealings with others and from your presentation of material, but you often cannot recognize, let alone overcome, the deep-seated personal biases in your character. Therefore, consistently question your own approach. Scrutinize what you select and how you select it. Continue to enlarge the kind of experience with ideas, issues and people that will challenge your own stereotypes. Be honest in your relations with others as well. Open and truthful communication between media writers and their bosses, sources and clients must be the norm.

— *Fairness.* Strive for principled, decent, fair-minded, professional conduct throughout your professional life. Play fair with all people you come into contact with. Operate on high moral and legal planes while serving the interests of the public or the client. All media industries have developed codes of ethics to help guide practitioners. But most of these codes have no enforcement machinery—they are self-regulations.

— *Accuracy.* Aim for the highest degree of accuracy in the information you select and present. Accuracy is directly tied to the information-gathering skills at the core of every media writer's job (see Chapter 3). Accuracy also is tied to the selection process underlying all media writing. By choosing representative details from the vast amount of information you have gathered, you create a realistic picture. Finally, accuracy is tied to your own sense of pride in what you do, the internal force that will not allow you to assume correctness without checking it.

— *Completeness.* For those who write messages to inform and educate, completeness of information is an important goal. This means much more than presenting opposing arguments in the "on the one hand . . . on the other hand" format. It means gathering and presenting the fullest, most comprehensive information possible at the time. For media writers intending to persuade with their messages, completeness may mean gathering and assessing—but not necessarily presenting—complete information. In all cases completeness is a goal in some part of the process.

— *Complexity.* Within the constraints of time and space, recognize the complexity of the issues, ideas, people, institutions or products you are trying to present. Discover that complexity through solid information gathering. Ask, pursue and answer the questions that will most help your audience gain knowledge, perspective and understanding.

These are lofty goals, and from time to time they may be difficult to achieve. But they *are* attainable. And they are at the center of the mass media professions. With these goals in mind, let's explore the skills shared by all media writers.

Information
Gathering

When Los Angeles copywriter Ann Keding took on the assignment to create an ad campaign for the L.A. Commission on Assaults Against Women, she had a lot of questions: How widespread was abuse in the area? Was there a typical abused woman? If so, what kind of person was she? How did the hotline function? Who used it? Why wasn't it used more often?

Keding looked at federal and state statistics. She read local crime reports. She talked with members of the Commission and representatives from other concerned groups. She interviewed hotline personnel. She listened to actual calls to the hotline. Only then was she ready to begin thinking about constructing the message. The ad itself consisted of only three sentences (see page 32), but each one was the result of thorough research. "By the time I sat down to write," she remembers, "I knew my audience."

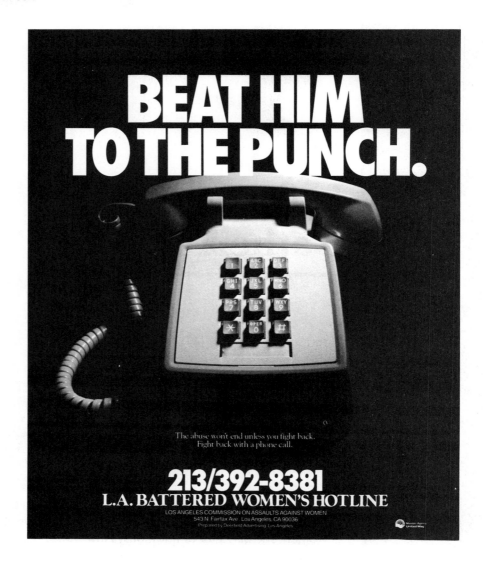

Keding's research revealed the following:

— Battered women felt powerless (thus the "empowering" headline: "Beat him to the punch").

— Although these women believed their abusers' promises to stop, the battering continued (thus the second line: "The abuse won't end unless you fight back").

— These women thought there was nothing they could do to help themselves (thus the third line: "Fight back with a phone call").

Every line of the message Keding created was guided by well-focused research. Information gathering was at the heart of her effort, and it paid off handsomely: Hotline use increased; the campaign won two prestigious national awards and a special citation from the governor of California.

Information: The heart of all messages

Accurate, complete, timely information is at the core of all successful mass media messages. The search for that information is an activity common to all media writers. But because information seeking is a behind-the-scenes activity and information presentation is a visible, public one, those outside the media professions (including students) can vastly underestimate the importance of research to the process of creating messages.

People outside the advertising industry, for example, have an image of copywriters as creative wizards who grab terrific ideas from thin air. Creative wizards they may be, but as we have seen, solid research stimulates their creativity. Casual watchers of television may erroneously think that all broadcast reporters do is stick a microphone in someone's face. What they don't realize is how much behind-the-scenes research went into deciding whose face to stick the microphone in and what questions to ask. Those outside the public relations industry have no notion of how much time and money is spent trying to determine exactly what to communicate and to whom.

The medium may differ. The intent and style of the message may vary. The audience may change. But all messages consist of information, and all message writers must also be expert information gatherers. In fact, the search for information normally involves far more time than the actual writing of the message, be it a three-line ad or a 3,000-word magazine story.

Successful media writers spend that time. They know, often by painful experience, how lack of solid information can cause writing problems. Attempting to write about something not fully understood leads to vague, foggy language. Attempting to write without the benefit of all the facts leads to poor organization. Attempting to write around holes in information leads to disturbing jumps in logic. The quality of writing suffers when the message is constructed without complete information. When quality suffers, the ability of the message to communicate also suffers. But what suffer most are the integrity and professionalism of the media writer.

Information-gathering strategies

"**R**esearch is endlessly seductive," writes distinguished American historian Barbara Tuchman. She should know. The two-time Pulitzer Prize winner is internationally acclaimed for her vibrantly written, meticulously researched ("I don't invent anything, even the weather") historical narratives.

Many media writers would agree. The information-gathering process can be an active, exciting time of discovery and learning. It can bring into play the traits that seem most common to media writers: curiosity, resourcefulness and imagination. Good information gatherers are careful, logical, analytical and persevering, but they are also imaginative and original.

For those unlucky souls who don't know how to approach the information-gathering process and aren't familiar with all the sources at their disposal, research can be a frustrating, tedious experience. But for those who learn the ropes of research, the problem is to make themselves stop digging long enough to sit in front of the keyboard and start writing. This chapter won't tell you all there is to know about information gathering, but it will get you started and get you thinking.*

---

*To enhance your information-gathering skills, delve into any or all of these books: Lois Horowitz, *A Writer's Guide to Research,* Cincinnati: Writer's Digest Books, 1986; Lauren Kessler and Duncan McDonald, *Uncovering the News: A Journalist's Search for Information,* Belmont, Calif.: Wadsworth, 1987; William Rivers, *Finding Facts,* Englewood Cliffs, N.J.: Prentice-Hall, 1975; Alden Todd, *Finding Facts Fast,* Berkeley, Calif.: Ten Speed Press, 1979; Jean Ward and Kathleen Hansen, *Search Strategies in Mass Communications,* White Plains, N.Y.: Longman, 1987.

The most important part of the information-gathering process, the plotting of a search strategy, takes place before you dash to the library, pick up a phone or punch in a keyword. Let's examine this strategy step by step.

1. *Find the focus.* The key question is: What is this information search about? Without defining and narrowing the focus, you cannot hope to search for information efficiently and successfully. Most students have had experience with this process in planning term papers. You begin with a general interest in a subject, then carefully refine that interest into a manageable topic big enough to be significant but small enough to be practical for the time and space you have to devote to it. This is just what media writers do when they begin their information searches.

2. *Define the key issues.* Once you've established the focus of the search, the next step is to define the key issues or the component parts of the topic. Here is where the media writer's curiosity, imagination and sense of audience come into play. What does my audience need or want to know about this topic? What information would most help my audience understand or appreciate this topic? What am *I* most curious about? These are some of the questions the media writer asks to establish the key issues.

3. *Brainstorm specific questions that emerge from each key issue.* The key issues provide smaller focal points for the search. Within each key issue, there are precise questions that need to be answered. By taking the time to brainstorm these questions, you are moving a giant step closer to efficient information gathering.

4. *Question by question, brainstorm likely sources.* Now that you have divided the original topic into a series of precise questions, it is time to use both logic and your knowledge of information sources. Question by question, you pinpoint the most likely sources for the information you need. First, establish the general category of source you think is most likely to have the answer to the question. Consider these three general categories:

   — individuals

   — institutions and organizations

   — written or published material

Once you've established the category, begin brainstorming specific sources within that category. The more precise you can be, the more efficient your search will be. Keep in mind that it's common to use sources in all three categories in any given information search.

5. *Gather the information.* If you've faithfully followed the preceding steps, the actual information gathering should be productive, economical—and fun. You know what you're looking for and you have a fair idea where the information might be. One of the joys of the process, of course, is that you're often surprised. The information trail takes a turn you hadn't predicted. A source you had thought of leads you to a source you hadn't—and to important information that enhances the message. An important part of the gathering process is the ongoing evaluation of information. As you discover answers, you attempt to clarify and evaluate them, testing (and retesting) their validity with other sources as you go along.

6. *Select appropriate information.* At the end of the gathering process, the idea is to have more information than you need to create the message. You should be in the position of selecting among relevant details—not attempting to mask holes in your knowledge. But you don't want to have so much information to choose from that the selection process itself is tedious and time-consuming. Too much information means you didn't narrow your focus sufficiently or you didn't pay attention to the boundaries you set for yourself. Of course, it can also mean that you were having so much fun discovering and learning that you couldn't stop yourself. (Fortunately or unfortunately, most deadline-pressured media writers can't indulge themselves like this.)

7. *Organize the information.* Media messages differ widely in their organization: the top-heavy news summaries of the "news burst" form, the slowly unraveling narratives of depth-and-context writing, the punchy repetition of persuasive messages. Here in step 7, the differences among forms become important. The intent of the message, the medium used and the audience appealed to are vital concerns here. Now you are ready to write—and rewrite—until the message is crisp, clear and understandable.

Let's see how this step-by-step strategy works by tracking a real search. We will follow a university public relations writer as she gathers information for a lengthy press release to be sent to a variety of newspapers. Here's the story: A West Coast university has invited a graduate of the class of 1942 to participate in the commencement ceremonies she was barred from 45 years before. The student, a Japanese-American, was not allowed to participate because of the post–Pearl Harbor hysteria that swept the West Coast. Her visit is seen as an event of considerable human interest that could garner extensive press coverage for the university.

1. *Find the focus:* This story is *not* a history of the treatment of Japanese-Americans. It is *not* a look backward at Japanese-American students on campus or an investigation of policies and procedures at the time. It *is* a small, human story about one person and her experiences, particularly as they relate to the university. At the story's center are an individual and an institution.

2. *Define the key issues:* The major components of this story are *biographical* (the woman herself and her experiences), *institutional* (the part played by the university then and now) and *historical* (the context in which it occurred).

3. *Brainstorm specific questions:* The following list is far from exhaustive, but it will provide a beginning. Concerning the biographical issue: Where was she from? What kind of a student was she? What did she major in? What experiences did she have on campus before and after Pearl Harbor? What happened to her after she was barred from the graduation ceremonies? What does she do now? How does she feel about what happened 45 years ago? Concerning the institutional issue: What was the university's involvement in all of this 45 years ago? How do today's officials feel about what happened? How did her story come to light? What is the university doing now? Concerning the historical issue: What policy, procedure or decision barred her from participating in the ceremonies? What was happening to Japanese-Americans on the West Coast during that time? What was happening on campus?

4. *Brainstorm sources:* Looking at the biographical questions, it's clear that the woman herself will be the best source. Some answers may also be found in university records. Her campus friends at the time also may be worth contacting. The answers to the institutional questions reside both with individuals and in documents. Current and past administrators can be asked to comment. University correspondence and records kept in the institution's

archives will be a major source. The historical questions can be answered by straightforward library research, including relevant books and newspaper and magazine articles.

Our public relations writer is now ready to gather information. She knows what she's looking for and generally where to find it. Her search will be focused and efficient. This search actually took place. The writer consulted all the sources mentioned here (and more). The story that emerged was published widely and picked up by a variety of newspapers, several national magazines and a television network. The university public relations bureau won several awards for the story.

Tracking facts

Media writers usually need to find facts fast. At noon a TV reporter is assigned to cover the just-announced visit of Steven Spielberg to one of the city's movie theaters. The reporter needs complete and accurate biographical background on the famous director—fast. A magazine journalist writing a story on men who fail to pay court-ordered child support needs to check on the latest divorce statistics. A PR writer gathering information for a special booklet celebrating the company's silver anniversary needs a quick summary of what was going on in the world 25 years ago.

Such facts are rarely in the possession of individuals. To track facts quickly and accurately, media writers depend on a variety of published reference sources. Becoming familiar with these sources is an ongoing process that begins with discovering where the local repositories of information are. Depending on where the media writer works, some or all of the following will be available:

— public library

— university library

— government documents library (often found within a university library)

— law library (connected to a law school or part of a major firm's resources)

— medical library (connected to a medical school or a good-sized hospital)

— association and trade group libraries

— newspaper libraries (often called morgues)

A competent media writer quickly discovers which of these resources are locally available and, over time, becomes increasingly familiar with what they contain, how they are organized and who runs them.

Not even the most experienced, highly trained reference librarians always know where to go for a piece of information, so media writers certainly can't hope to. But they can work toward becoming familiar with commonly used sources, and they can strive to understand the organizing principles basic to reference material.

Basic organizing principles

ONE-STEP OR TWO-STEP.   Reference sources are either *one-step* or *two-step* guides. One-step guides are direct sources of information. You come to the source with a question and it offers you an answer. How do you spell *embarrassment*? A dictionary, the media writer's most common one-step source, tells you the answer. What is the capital of Bulgaria? An encyclopedia tells you it's Sofia. What percentage of registered voters in your state voted in the last presidential election? An almanac tells you.

Two-step sources don't tell you the information itself but rather where the information can be found. These sources are generally organized as indexes. You want background on the skyrocketing costs of malpractice insurance. The *Business Periodicals Index* guides you to articles on that subject published in insurance journals. You need information about insanity as a legal defense. The *Index to Legal Periodicals* guides you to articles published in more than 300 legal journals.

INTERNAL ORGANIZATION.   How are reference guides organized? A writer who understands the basic principles of organization can use references quickly and efficiently. *Alphabetical organization* is one of the most common forms. Phone books, dictionaries and encyclopedias use it. *Organization by category* is also a popular method. Indexes to newspapers and periodicals are constructed this way. Using them well means learning to think like an indexer, brainstorming categories until you hit upon the one the indexers used. *Chronological organization* is another form. Guides to events in recent or past history are often constructed this way. Other guides are organized according to the *origin of the information*—for example, an author, agency or organization.

UPDATES.   How often and in what form is the source of information updated? Media writers in search of the most current information need to know. Some database sources (see page 47) are updated almost immediately. Some microform sources (microfilm and microfiche) are updated weekly or monthly. Other printed sources may be updated quarterly or annually. Using these sources efficiently often depends on knowing how current the information is.

FORM.   Today information exists in many forms, from books to strips of microfilm to digitized blips. Using library resources efficiently means knowing what form to look for.

Commonly used sources

No single chapter in a book—in fact, no entire book— can introduce you to the enormous scope of published reference sources commonly available in the library. The following list is designed to give you a basic overview:

— Dictionaries, common reference tools for all writers, come in sizes from pocket to multivolume. They also reflect a wide range of topics. English language dictionaries help writers check spelling, meaning, pronunciation, syllabication and word origin. Lesser-known specialty dictionaries define and explain the jargon of various professions from architecture to zoology. Biographical dictionaries are quick sources of background data on people with noteworthy accomplishments in a variety of fields.

— Encyclopedias contain brief articles on an unbelievably wide scope of subjects. Most people are aware of general encyclopedias like the excellent *Encyclopaedia Britannica,* but few are aware of the many specialized encyclopedias containing background information on subjects as diverse as dance, engineering, economics and psychiatry.

— Almanacs are good sources for facts and figures. The popular *Information Please Almanac* and *World Almanac and Book of Facts*, like most almanacs, are issued annually. Undoubtedly the most important single almanac is the *Statistical Abstract of the United States*, a digest of data collected by the federal government's statistical agencies.

— Directories are among the least-used but most valuable sources on the reference shelves. There are so many of them that they have their own directory, *The Directory of Directories*. These books can pinpoint associations, organizations, agencies, businesses and individuals. The telephone book is the one directory everyone knows and every media writer depends on.

— Indexes are two-step guides that tell you where to find information. Major newspapers like the *New York Times, Washington Post, Christian Science Monitor* and *Wall Street Journal* publish their own indexes. *Newsbank* is a monthly index to articles from more than 100 of the nation's largest dailies. Consumer magazines are indexed in the microfilm *Magazine Index* and the familiar *Reader's Guide to Periodical Literature*. Every specialty area you can imagine—the arts, business, health, education, science, technology, politics—has one or more indexes that will lead you to articles published on the subject.

— Government documents are a vital source. The U.S. federal government is the world's most prolific publisher. Agencies and departments within this enormous bureaucracy produce books, magazines, newsletters, brochures, pamphlets, reports, bulletins, manuals, studies, proceedings, bills, laws and more—at the rate of almost 70,000 publications a year, according to the government's own estimates. All media writers should have working familiarity with the government documents sections of their nearby libraries. Indexes are the key. Your documents librarian can walk you through their use. Here are a few of the most important ones:

— *Monthly Catalog of U.S. Government Publications* is the government's official index to its publications. Organized in seven indexes either alphabetically or numerically according to author, keyword, title, subject, report number, stock number or classification number, the catalog is issued monthly and cumulates annually.

— *CIS/Index* indexes and abstracts most documents generated by Congress. Issued monthly, it cumulates first quarterly, then annually, then every four or five years. The indexing system is similar to the *Monthly Catalog,* but broader in scope.

— *American Statistics Index* is the most comprehensive guide to statistical material generated or collected by the federal government. It is issued monthly and cumulates quarterly and annually.

— *Congressional Record Index* is the guide to the daily proceedings of the House and Senate, including both verbatim debate on the floor and material inserted later.

Finding experts

The L.A. copywriter whom we mentioned earlier was not an expert on battered women. The university public relations writer was not an expert on the treatment of Japanese-Americans during World War II. A news reporter assigned to cover a teachers' strike is probably not an expert on the educational system or labor relations. Most media writers are not authorities in the areas they write about. But good media writers *are* expert at finding and talking to experts.

People as sources

Whether it's a TV journalist interviewing a rescue worker on camera or an ad copywriter quizzing a client during a conference, media writers are often engaged in conversation with those who have specialized information. Individuals are good sources for comments, re-actions, opinions, rebuttals and denials. They can offer analysis and recount personal experience. They can help explain complexities to the media writer and to the intended audience. They can point the media writer to other sources of information, or they themselves can be at the heart of the story, as in a newspaper, magazine or broadcast profile.

However, depending on people as sources of *factual* information has its pitfalls. All media writers ought to be wary of these potential problems:

— *People may not know.* Many facts a media writer might want to discover are not likely to be carried in the head of any particular individual. Suppose you wanted to know the comparative employment rate of men and women in network TV during the past 10 years. This kind of detailed numerical material rarely is on the tip of someone's tongue. You are far more likely to find it in a report or study.

— *People may think they know but don't.* A confident, but ignorant or misinformed, source is worse than no source at all. People who think they know, but don't, put the information gatherer at a terrible disadvantage. If you don't check the validity of the information before using it, you are just as liable for spreading incorrect information as your source is for communicating it in the first place. Let's say an insider tells you, with great confidence, that network X has the industry's best record of hiring women. The network's rate of employing women has increased sharply during the past 10 years, the source says. You use that information in a story, an editorial or a speech. The problem is, it isn't true.

— *People may know but don't want to tell.* For all sorts of reasons, both valid and invalid, a person might not want to give information to a media representative. Although some information is legally public, individuals are under no particular obligation to answer your questions about other information. In our example, network X is a publicly owned corporation, so various business and employment records would be public information. But a particular network official would be under no obligation to discuss specific personnel decisions.

— *People may tell you only selected bits of information.* Everyone has his or her own agenda working at certain times. Everyone acts out of self-interest at one time or another. A network X executive tells you that women's employment at the network has increased 80 percent during the past 10 years. The executive *doesn't* tell you most of this increase was a major expansion of the secretarial pool.

— *People may lie or misrepresent the facts.* To project a certain image or to protect themselves, their reputations or their businesses, some sources may deliberately give you erroneous information. That's one reason a vital part of the research process is corroborating information and validating its authenticity. Let's say the network X executive in charge of top-level hiring tells you the network has made great strides in employing women. That makes the executive look good and the network appear pleasantly progressive. But by checking public documents and talking with others, you discover this just isn't so.

Despite all these problems, people are still vital sources of information. Let's discuss how to quickly locate a needed expert.

Where are the experts?

Experts are everywhere. Finding them involves some basic knowledge of institutions and how they are organized. It involves familiarity with important directories. And, not incidentally, it involves creative and logical thinking. Let's look at three institutions where media writers are likely to find expert sources: government, industry and the university.

GOVERNMENT. The federal government employs more than 700,000 information specialists within its scores of agencies, bureaus, commissions and departments. On subjects ranging from peanut farming to pernicious anemia, the government is a major source of both current and historical data. To tap this vast and important resource, you need to understand how the government is structured, and you need to be aware of several indispensable directories.

The *United States Government Manual*, the basic guide to the federal government, describes the responsibilities and activities of the various agencies within the three branches and includes telephone numbers, addresses and top officials' names. More specific guides can point you directly to information sources below the top layer of officialdom. *Congressional Quarterly's Washington Information Directory* lists 5,000 information specialists in the legislative and executive branches. *Congressional Quarterly's Federal Regulatory Directory* offers extensive profiles of government regulatory agencies with names and numbers of key contacts. *The Congressional Staff Directory* is a guide to the thousands of people who work in the House and Senate. *The Federal Staff Directory* lists 27,000 decision-makers in the executive branch. *The Washington Monitor's Congressional Yellow Book* and *Federal Yellow Book* are loose-leaf directories of government officials and their staffs. All of these important, easy-to-use guides are commonly found in the documents section of libraries.

State and local governments are also prime places to find people knowledgeable about a range of issues as wide as the scope of government itself. Most states publish directories (called bluebooks) that describe the responsibilities of their agencies, departments and committees, listing officials and their phone numbers. City and county governments often do the same on a smaller scale. Public information officers employed by governments or government agencies can help locate experts for you.

INDUSTRY. Much of what media writers are concerned with—from the political reporter working on a story about illegal campaign contributions to the advertising copywriter researching the gourmet ice cream market—has a business component. Industry experts are thus often vital sources of information. If you need to pinpoint a particular company or corporation before you search for an individual, reference works in your nearby library will help you. Standbys like *Poor's Register of Corporations, Moody's Manuals* and various Dun & Bradstreet publications are readily available and easy to use.

Often used for background research, trade publications and business magazines can be excellent places to look for the names of industry experts. Trade associations (listed in the *Encyclopedia of Associations*) can also be helpful, as can various hotlines run by industry groups. Many are toll-free numbers that can be found by looking in an 800 directory or calling 800-555-1212. Finally, public relations specialists in corporations often can help locate expert sources.

THE UNIVERSITY. Where else can you find hundreds of men and women who devote their lives to becoming experts? They study for years to become knowledgeable in their fields. They spend their days reading, writing, researching and talking about their specialties. They are accustomed to explaining complexities to nonexperts; they are committed to the free flow of ideas. It sounds like an information gatherer's paradise—and it can be. Academic experts may be the best, least-tapped sources around.

University catalogs and phone directories may help you locate the expert you need. So may a quick call to the head of the relevant academic department. Many universities have news bureaus or public information departments designed to make the expert-hunter's job easier.

Of course, many potentially valuable sources lie outside the institutions of government, industry and academia. But often experts within these institutions can point the way. A government expert may refer you to a citizen's lobby; an industry expert may know of a consumer group; a university expert may point you to a non-profit organization. Referrals, whether from experts themselves or from experienced colleagues and friends, are the mainstay of the source-hunting process.

Dealing with experts

You've located the names and phone numbers of the experts you need. Now what do you do? Before you rush over to an office or pick up a phone, you do your homework: You background yourself. You should know enough about your subject to ask intelligent and incisive questions. You should know enough to understand the answers to these questions and not be easily fooled or misled. The key to a successful interview is thorough (or as thorough as time allows) research. Without it, communication is difficult and the interview itself is, at best, inefficient. Many of the sources described in the "Tracking Facts" section of this chapter can be used to prepare yourself for an interview.

Your style as an interviewer is far less important to the success of the conversation than is your preparation. But that doesn't mean interviewing technique is unimportant. Asking straightforward questions, listening well and responding flexibly are essential skills. You must know when to probe, when to ease off and how to establish a basic rapport with an interview subject. But none of this is possible without solid backgrounding.

The interview, under the best of circumstances, is an intelligent, directed conversation that neither loses its sense of purpose nor becomes too rigid to allow for potentially important tangents and digressions. A good interview, be it a two-minute phone call or a two-hour face-to-face conversation, cuts to the heart of the matter and yields material you cannot find elsewhere.

Moving into the electronic age

Computers are changing the way media professionals do their jobs. In fact, no invention since the telephone has so affected the working life of media writers. One part of this revolution is the use of computers to write and edit. As everyone knows who has moved from typewriter to computer keyboard, editing and revising become easier, more efficient and even more enjoyable. But the computer revolution cuts deeper than this. It now affects the most important component of the media writer's job: access to information.

The digitization of information

Information—from local police reports to the entire *Encyclopaedia Britannica,* from stock market quotations to Supreme Court decisions—can be digitized and stored electronically. The information housed in a good-sized library can now be stored in a computer smaller than a phone booth. These electronic libraries of information are called *databases,* and they are changing forever how media writers gather information.

Now a television reporter in San Francisco can have immediate access to government documents in Washington that would have taken weeks to arrive through the mail. An ad copywriter in Atlanta can have immediate access to a market research report filed in Denver. A newspaper reporter in Denver can have immediate access to last month's *Los Angeles Times.* In an important sense, the digitization of information means that big-city media writers have no advantage over their small-town counterparts. All have equal access to important information.

Digitization also means that the information is always available. There are no more problems with articles ripped out of magazines, journals sitting at the bindery or books missing from the shelves. There is no more waiting for the library to open or the mail to come. Geography and time—formerly the obstacles to rapid, thorough research—become unimportant. When information is housed in a publicly accessible database, anyone with a computer, a communications hookup, a password and the price of access time can dig in.

Databases

Today there are almost 2,000 public databases, hundreds of which contain information relevant to media writers. These electronic storehouses range in size from a few hundred to many million items and come in two basic forms: bibliographic and full-text. A bibliographic database is an index (or set of indexes) that provides the information necessary to locate the actual material. MEDLINE, for example, is a database that includes the complete contents of three enormous, multivolume medical indexes. The information in the database tells you exactly where to find articles in hundreds of medical, dental and nursing journals. A full-text database provides the entire contents of selected magazines, newspapers, books, reports and documents. LEXIS, a virtual law library in computer form, contains the full texts of court decisions, statutes, regulations and other legal materials.

Specialized databases contain everything from current corporate information on 8,800 publicly owned companies (Disclosure II) to the full text of the *New York Times* (NEXIS). Some databases are directories, like ENERGYNET, an up-to-date list of almost 3,000 organizations and 8,000 individuals in energy-related fields, or the Electronic Yellow Pages, a digitized compilation of 5,000 telephone books. Others contain vital market research; ADTRACK, for example, is an index of all advertisements of at least one-quarter page appearing in 148 major U.S. magazines. The federal government is computerizing many of its important indexes for easier use.

The computerized information industry is so dynamic that keeping track of new, expanded and discontinued databases is often difficult. A few commercial publishers have created annual directories to help. These are available in the computer sections of large bookstores. Some companies, called on-line vendors, lease the rights to a variety of databases and publish directories to their offerings. Virtually all university libraries and a growing number of newspapers, magazines and ad agencies subscribe to the services of on-line vendors.

Getting started

Gaining access to databases is an information-gathering skill that involves working knowledge of a computer, familiarity with database commands and an understanding of how indexers' minds work. All these come with practice and with diligent reading of manuals and directories. If you are a free-lance media writer or if you work for a small organization, you may be developing these skills yourself. Your own desktop computer can be converted easily and inexpensively into an information-gathering machine with the addition of a modem (a device that allows computers to converse over telephone lines) and special communications software.

If a good library is nearby, you can depend on the expertise of librarians specially trained in database research. An increasing number of major news organizations are hiring their own specialized librarians. It will soon be common for the larger newspapers, magazines, broadcast stations, PR groups and ad agencies to employ their own in-house computer searchers.

Information gathering, whether it's digging at the library, interviewing a source or logging on to a database, is one of the activities common to all media writers. All media writers must share a commitment to thoroughness and accuracy. They must think both logically and creatively about what information they need and where it is likely to be found. They must be aware of at least some of the vast resources available to them.

Good Grammar

Mention the word *grammar,* and some people panic. They think of rigid rules and rote learning, incomprehensible exceptions and suffocating restrictions. Good writers know better, of course. They know that grammar is a generally sensible system that establishes relationships between words and builds logical patterns. They know that grammar brings order to language and that its guidelines are mainly reasonable and coherent. Most important, they know that grammar is the most practical and necessary of skills because it makes communication possible.

Good grammar and good writing

Whether you're writing a speech, a magazine article, a news story or an advertising message, good grammar is a constant in good writing. Regardless of the medium or the purpose, word use and sentence construction must be correct and coherent. All writers must know and respect the language. Knowing grammar means knowing the possibilities of that language and being able to use its variety and richness.

"But I can always write around a grammatical problem," insist some novices. "I can find another way of saying it so I don't have to worry about the rule." The pros know better. They have learned that writing around problems limits what they can do with the language. Variety suffers. Awkwardness creeps in. Grammatical ignorance imposes limits on writers and prevents them from developing a unique style.

Because what they write is often read or heard by millions of people, media writers must be aware of the power of their grammatical standards. Their mistakes, when printed or broadcast, can become entrenched in the language. By the same token, their careful use of language can help preserve its clarity throughout society. Media writers are today's guardians of the language.

That's a high-minded reason to learn grammar. Here's a practical one: It's the skill employers value most. A recent study asked the editors of America's largest daily newspapers to recommend college classes for students majoring in journalism. The first choice of almost three-quarters of the editors was a course in grammar and usage.

This chapter won't teach you all you need to know to use the language accurately and correctly. That is a job for a much longer work.* But the chapter will highlight the thorniest parts of six important grammatical concerns: subject-verb agreement, antecedent agreement, case agreement, gender agreement, restrictive and nonrestrictive clauses and comma use. These are the most common grammatical problems.

Subject-verb agreement

The rule is simple: The verb must agree with the intended number of the subject.

Following the rule is a two-step process. First, you must identify the real subject of the sentence. Second, you must determine whether

---

*We have written a book on grammar for journalists called *When Words Collide: A Journalist's Guide to Grammar and Style*, 2d ed., Wadsworth, 1988.

the subject's meaning is singular or plural. Often, these steps are easily accomplished, as in

The computers are arriving tomorrow.

The subject is *computers;* its meaning is clearly plural. The verb choice is *are,* a plural form. But identifying the subject is not always that easy. Other sentence parts may confuse you. Remember that a subject is not just any noun or pronoun in the sentence. It is not the object of a preposition. Nor is it a noun found in a parenthetical phrase or the expletives *here* or *there.*

Once you identify the *real* subject of the sentence, you must determine whether it is singular or plural. Many English nouns are clearly singular or plural by their endings (table/tables, man/men) and present few problems. But certain pronouns and nouns can cause problems. Briefly, here is an overview of some of the toughest calls:

Pronouns

— When used as subjects, the following pronouns always take the singular verb: *each, either, neither, anyone, everyone, much, nobody, no one, nothing, someone, it.* Think of *each* as "each single one," *nothing* as "no one single thing" and the singular meaning is clear. For example:

Everyone is invited.

— When *each, either, every* and *neither* are used as adjectives, the nouns they modify take singular verbs. For example:

Each computer is hardwired to the mainframe.

— When used as subjects, *both, few, many* and *several* always take plural verbs. For example:

Many are called; few are chosen.

— Pronouns such as *any* and *some* take singular verbs if they refer to a unit or general quantity and plural verbs if they refer to amount or individuals. For example:

Some of the work was sloppy.
(general quantity)

Some employees were disappointed.
(*individuals*)

— The indefinite pronoun *none* takes a singular verb when *none* means "no one" or "not one." When *none* means "no two," "no amount" or "no number," the verb is plural. For example:

None of the defendants was willing to grant an interview. (*"not one"*)

None of his clothes are suitable for this climate. (*"no amount"*)

Troublesome nouns

— Collective nouns, although they imply plural subjects, most often take singular verbs. That's not as confusing as it sounds if you remember this rule: If the individual members implied by the collective noun are acting as a unit, the noun takes a singular verb. In a far less common construction, if the individuals are acting as separate individuals, the noun takes a plural verb. For example:

The team is practicing.
The jury looks sympathetic.
The committee is debating the issue.

In all these sentences the collective nouns are acting as units. But in the following sentence the individuals implied by the collective noun are acting individually:

The herd of goats were running in several directions.

(*Most writers would rewrite this correct but awkward sentence as "The goats were running . . . ," dropping the unnecessary collective noun.*)

— Nouns ending with the suffix *-ics* (politics, athletics, graphics, acoustics) may look plural, but they can take either singular or plural verbs depending on their meaning. If the word refers to a general field, it is treated as singular. If the word refers to the practices and activities of that field, it takes a plural verb. For example:

> Although politics [the general field] is some-
> times a dirty business, his politics [practices
> and activities] are beyond reproach.

— Commonly used Latin and Greek words have singular and plural endings different from English words and can be confusing. *Media*, for example, is the plural form of *medium*; *criteria* is the plural of *criterion*. Short of taking crash courses in Latin and Greek, the way to deal with these words is to consult the dictionary or, better yet, memorize them.

Not-so-odd oddities

When you stop to consider the implied meaning in certain sentences, odd agreement rules become much more understandable.

— When *the number* is used as a subject, a definite, definable unit is implied. Thus, the subject takes a singular verb. When *a number* is used as a subject, the amount is some undefinable number more than one. Thus, the subject takes a plural verb. For example:

> The number of suicides is increasing.
> A number of suicides have been reported.

— This definable unit rule also holds true for plural words relating to time, money, distance, food, organizations and medical problems. For example, all the following take singular verbs:

> Six hours is a long time.
> Six dollars is not enough.
> The United Farm Workers is calling for a strike.
> Mumps is a serious disease in adulthood.

— As subjects, fractions or related words (*part, the rest*) are singular or plural depending on the nouns they refer to. Thus, in this exceptional case, the number of the object, not the subject, determines the verb form. For example:

> Half the magazine is advertisements.
> Half of the magazines are poorly printed.

Antecedent agreement

Here's the rule: A pronoun agrees in number with the noun or pronoun it refers to or substitutes for (called the antecedent of the pronoun).

In most cases, making nouns and pronouns agree is a simple task. Most nouns are obviously singular or plural by their endings. But the same few nouns that cause verb agreement problems can also cause pronoun troubles.

— Collective nouns usually denote single units and therefore require singular pronouns. Remember the rule: When the individuals implied in the collective noun are acting together as a unit (which is most often the case), the pronoun used to substitute for the noun must be singular. For example:

The committee submitted its report.

If the individuals are acting separately, the pronoun would be plural:

The jury were polled on their split verdict.

This last construction sounds awkward. In such cases the writer usually expresses it another way. For example:

The jurors [or the members of the jury] were
polled on their split verdict.

Collective nouns like *team, group, council, committee, board, jury* and *company* are common in media writing.

— Foreign nouns used in English cause problems because their singular and plural forms differ so much from English endings. Take care with these words, checking their number before you use a pronoun substitute. Examples:

The media increased their coverage of Central
America.

A medium must be true to its audience.

The alumni contributed to their university.

As an <u>alumna</u>, <u>she</u> participated in the festivities.

— Sometimes both the subject and its antecedent are pronouns. You must determine whether the first pronoun is singular or plural in order to bring the second pronoun into agreement. For example:

<u>Neither</u> of the men is responsible for <u>his</u> actions.

<u>Both</u> of the women carried <u>their</u> umbrellas.

Potentially troublesome pronouns like *each, either, anyone, everyone, someone, both, few, many, several, any, none* and *some* are explained in the previous section on subject-verb agreement.

Case agreement

Case refers to the form a pronoun (or noun) assumes in relation to other parts of the sentence. Pronouns come in the nominative, objective and possessive cases; nouns can be possessive. Probably the most troublesome area of case agreement is choosing between the nominative case pronoun *who* and the objective case pronoun *whom.*

The rule itself is straightforward: Use *who* when the sentence or clause needs a subject; use *whom* when the sentence or clause calls for an object.

Selecting correctly depends on your ability to divide a sentence into its component clauses. In each clause you ask yourself: Where is the subject? (Who or what is responsible for the action?) Where is the object? (To whom or to what is the action happening?) When a sentence has only one clause, choosing *who* or *whom* is usually simple, as in

<u>Who</u>/Whom will be the next president?

Without the first pronoun, this sentence has no subject. Because the pronoun must act as a subject, it must be in the nominative case. Now consider the following sentence:

Who/<u>Whom</u> did you vote for in 1988?

This sentence already has a subject (*you*). What is missing is the object (the person you voted for). Reordering the words in standard subject-verb-object form makes the choice of the objective case *whom* obvious: You did vote for whom in 1988.

Let's look at a few examples that present tougher choices.

— *A two-clause (or more) sentence.* When you divide a sentence into its clause components, look first for the subject, remembering that each clause needs its own subject. If the clause needs a subject, choose the nominative *who,* as in this sentence:

She is the candidate who/whom will campaign
the hardest.

Divide the sentence into its component clauses (She is the candidate . . . who will campaign the hardest). The second clause needs a subject; thus *who* is the correct choice. If the clause already has a subject, choose the objective *whom,* as in this sentence:

He is the man who/whom the party will
support.

The second clause (whom the party will support) already has a subject, *party. Whom* is the object of the verb *support.*

— *Subject separated from clause.* Sometimes clauses aren't clumped together neatly and aren't easily separated from one another. It takes a bit more work to find the component parts and discover whether they are missing subjects or objects. In the following sentence, the subject (*who*) is separated from its clause:

The senator who/whom the president said was
disloyal to the party was re-elected by a
landslide.

Whom is not the object of *president said.* Divide the sentence this way:

The senator was re-elected by a landslide
who was disloyal to the party
the president said   *(parenthetical attribution)*

— *Prepositions that don't take objects.* Normally, when we see a preposition, we expect a pronoun following it to be in the objective case, as in

The president is prepared to throw his support
to whomever the party nominates.

Here *whomever* is the correct choice because the second clause (whomever the party nominates) already has a subject (the party). *Whomever* is the object of the verb *nominates*. But the presence of a preposition does not automatically signal the choice of an object. Suppose the clause following the preposition requires a subject, as in

They explained the problem to whoever would
listen.

The second clause (whoever would listen) needs a subject. That's why the nominative *whoever* is the correct choice.

Gender agreement

The rule: Treat the sexes equally when you choose and use words. Don't presume maleness unless that presumption is warranted.

Writers encounter two basic problems in gender agreement, both of which can be easily solved. They are the "generic *he*" and masculine endings for words referring to both sexes.

The generic *he*

He, him and *his* are *masculine* pronouns and should substitute only for masculine nouns. For example:

The father and his children

Mike talks. He talks too much.

Many other languages assign gender to all nouns. In Spanish, *el pan* (bread) is masculine; in French, *la lune* (the moon) is feminine. But in English all but a few nouns (mother, father, aunt, uncle) are neither masculine nor feminine. To avoid sexism in your writing, do not use *he* to refer to a noun of unknown gender. Do not presume the maleness of the noun. For example:

A lawyer should act in <u>his</u> client's best
interests.

This sentence presumes that lawyers are men by substituting the sexually exclusive pronoun *his* for *a lawyer's*. Nouns like *author, journalist, artist, doctor, accountant, mayor, athlete* and *student* can and do refer to both sexes simultaneously. To be both grammatically correct and culturally accurate, you need to rewrite the previous sentence in either of two ways:

A lawyer should act in <u>his or her</u> client's best
interests.

<u>Lawyers</u> should act in <u>their</u> client's best
interests.

The second alternative—making the noun plural and using sexually inclusive plural pronouns like *their* and *them*—is generally the best way to handle gender agreement. The second sentence is clear, graceful and nonsexist.

The pronouns *everybody* and *everyone* create another problem with the generic *he*. The following sentence breaks the gender agreement rule and is culturally incorrect:

Everybody must take responsibility for <u>his</u>
actions.

On the other hand, it is grammatically incorrect to write

Everybody must take responsibility for <u>their</u>
actions

because *everybody* requires a singular pronoun. But it makes no sense to use the exclusive male pronoun. In fact, more than half of "everybody" is female. The sentence could be rewritten as

Everybody must take responsibility for <u>his or
her</u> actions.

Or, better yet,

<u>People</u> should take responsibility for <u>their</u>
actions.

Words with masculine endings

Words like *newsman, spokesman* and *chairman* make sense when referring to a male but are ludicrous when used to refer to a female, as in

Judy Woodruff is a fine newsman.

Eleanor Smeal was NOW's spokesman.

If you have trouble seeing how odd these sentences are, switch the sexes:

Bill Moyers is a fine newswoman.

Lee Iacocca is Chrysler's spokeswoman.

Using sexually exclusive terms when referring to members of the excluded sex is laughable. You have two acceptable alternatives when faced with words having a -*man* ending:

1. You can use the -*man* ending when the word refers to a male and use the -*woman* ending when the word refers to a female:

   Bill is an accomplished craftsman.

   Cynthia is an accomplished craftswoman.

2. You can use a non-gender-specific word (called a neuter) to refer to both men and women, as in

   Bill is an accomplished artisan.

   Cynthia is an accomplished artisan.

Similarly, newsmen and newswomen become *reporters* or *journalists;* anchormen and anchorwomen become *anchors;* chairmen and chairwomen become *chairs* or *chairers.* Finding an all-inclusive word means you won't have to contend with the lengthy and awkward-sounding -*persons* ending when you need a plural. Thus, Bill and Cynthia are referred to as *artisans,* a pleasant word, rather than *craftspersons,* something of a tongue twister. They are *co-chairs* of the county art council, not *co-chairpersons.*

Restrictive and non-restrictive clauses

Many writers have difficulty choosing between *that* and *which* to introduce clauses. *That* and *which* are not interchangeable, although spoken language often makes them so.

Here is the rule: In a choice between *that* and *which*, always choose *that* to introduce a restrictive clause; always choose *which* to introduce a non-restrictive clause.

A *restrictive clause* is essential to the meaning of the sentence. Without it, the sentence lacks definition. For example:

The bus that she normally takes is late today.

Without the restrictive clause (underlined) the meaning of the sentence is unclear. *That* is always the choice when introducing a clause necessary to sentence meaning. Note that the clause, because it is an integral part of the sentence, is *not* set off by commas. (Note also that the word *that* can be omitted without harm to the sentence.)

A *non-restrictive clause* is not essential to the meaning of the sentence. It adds information that elaborates, but it is not vital to the understanding of the sentence. For example:

The bus, which is enjoying a rebirth in urban transportation, is an energy-efficient way to commute.

The non-restrictive clause (underlined) introduced by *which* offers additional, non-essential information. Note that the clause *is* set off by commas.

Of course, you always choose *who* to introduce a clause referring to people, regardless of whether the clause is restrictive or non-restrictive.

The woman who led the strike was injured. *(restrictive)*

Donna Simmons, who led the strike, was injured. *(non-restrictive)*

The comma

$\mathbf{O}$f all forms of punctuation, the comma seems to cause the most problems. Commas are distinct grammatical signals with specific functions. Let's briefly review some of them:

— Commas separate items in a series.

> Their leader was vain, vile, vicious and villainous.

Note that in journalistic writing, the final comma in the series is normally dropped.

— Commas separate two independent clauses connected by a coordinating conjunction.

> Firefighters battled the blaze all day, but it spread throughout the city's posh residential district.

If the clauses are internally punctuated by commas, use semicolons to separate the clauses.

— Commas set off long introductory clauses and phrases as well as short ones that would be confusing without the comma.

> While the city's posh residential district burned, nine firefighters collapsed from heat prostration.

> To Bob, Jean is a walking success story.

— Commas set off non-restrictive clauses and phrases (see preceding section).

> Smith, who started her own agency three years ago, won the international competition.

— Commas separate descriptive modifiers of equal rank. If you can use the modifiers interchangeably and can insert the conjunction *and* between them, use a comma.

Smith created a bold, innovative concept for
the campaign.

— Commas set off participial phrases that modify part of the independent clause.

The Senate adjourned today, having successfully defeated the filibuster.

It's also important to know when *not* to use a comma. Beware of these two common misuses:

— Using commas to link two independent clauses in the absence of a coordinating conjunction (known as the comma splice). The comma is too weak to make the connection. Use a semicolon, create two separate sentences or add a coordinating conjunction.

The prime rate plummeted two points, the
home mortgage rate didn't budge. *(incorrect)*

The prime rate plummeted; the home mortgage rate didn't budge. *(correct)*

The prime rate plummeted. The home mortgage rate didn't budge. *(correct)*

The prime rate plummeted, but the home mortgage rate didn't budge. *(correct)*

— Using a comma to introduce a dependent clause. This happens most often with subordinating conjunctions such as *because*, which do not join clauses of equal rank. Of course, if the clause begins the sentence, use a comma to set it off as you would any long introductory clause or phrase.

The scientists visited the Soviet Union, because they were interested in working for world peace. *(incorrect)*

The scientists visited the Soviet Union because they were interested in working for world peace. *(correct)*

Because they were interested in working for world peace, the scientists visited the Soviet Union. *(correct)*

There are many other important grammatical concerns. This chapter offers only a summary of some of the more difficult usage problems writers face. If your own mastery of the language is somewhat less than masterful, you owe it to yourself and your future audience to gain grammatical competence. As you will see in the next two chapters, clarity of expression depends on it, and style emerges directly from it.

Clarity

At this point in time we are going to commence to discuss a situation in which a writer utilizes numerous words and certain kinds of construction and presentation factors in regards to sentences in order to attempt to maximize the communication process; but it should be pointed out that instead of optimization of this particular type of process, the utilization of these various techniques instead erects a large number of barrier-type obstacles to the true lucidity of communication.

What??? Here's the translation:

Now let's consider how clutter, murky construction and confusing presentation interfere with clear communication.

As that purposely awful first paragraph illustrates, writers can get caught in such a tangle of words that both they and their audience are left struggling for meaning and sense. Clarity is the issue here. Let's explore it.

What is clarity?

To our 17th-century ancestors *clarity* meant "brilliance, glory and divine luster." Although 20th-century writers may hope to achieve these lofty goals with their words, today *clarity* simply means "clearness." Writing with clarity means using language precisely, succinctly and logically. It means simplicity, order and clear-headedness. It means prose—for whatever purpose, in whatever medium—that is easily understood. Because shared understanding is at the heart of communication, clarity of expression must be the writer's primary goal.

But before they can write clearly, writers must first think clearly. And before thinking of words, they must think of ideas. "What am I trying to say? What do I know? What do I want to communicate?" writers must ask themselves. In other words, writers must know *what* they are going to write about before they consider *how* they are going to write it. Thus, the foundations of clear, understandable prose are solid information and clear focus. Much of murky writing is an attempt to "write around" holes in the story. Much of what masquerades as "writer's block" actually is lack of information, poor direction and fuzzy focus.

Another precondition for clear writing is a firm grasp of grammar. Without a good working knowledge of the basics of the language, writers cannot hope to choose and use words correctly and coherently. Clear writing is rarely intuitive or accidental. It is, instead, the result of a parade of purposeful decisions, determining the choice of individual words.

Let's examine how to defeat three formidable enemies of clarity: cluttered language, murky construction and faulty presentation.

Cluttered language

"Fighting clutter is like fighting weeds—the writer is always slightly behind," writes William Zinsser in his crisply written, clutterless book *On Writing Well*. Unfortunately, lean prose does not usually flow from writers' minds to the page. That's why editing and revising are such vital parts of the writing process. It is then that writers remove all the weeds they can find. But how do you know which is weed and which is grass? Three identifiable varieties of weeds are poor word choice, wordiness and jargon.

Word choice

VERBS.   Verbs move sentences, giving them life, power and authority. Strong, well-chosen verbs are major contributors to vitality; imprecise or overmodified verbs can quickly sap a sentence of its strength. When you write—and especially when you edit—pay particular attention to verb choice. Here are some guidelines:

— Choose a verb that means precisely what you intend. Our language has thousands of strong, exact verbs that capture subtleties of meaning. Don't settle for a general word like *talk*, when what you mean is *chatter* or *yammer*. If you mean *stride* or *saunter*, don't settle for *walk*. Think clearly about the picture your words will create. A crisp, in-focus picture often depends on a well-chosen verb. For example:

He walked to the mirror and looked at his face. *(weak)*

He shuffled to the mirror and peered at his face. *(stronger)*

— Choose simple, straightforward verbs. In your search for precise verbs, don't let a dictionary or thesaurus lead you to lifeless, windy concoctions like *palliate* (excuse), *consternate* (scare) or *desiccate* (parch). When possible, choose generally familiar, relatively short words.

— Don't modify a verb when instead you should be searching for a better verb. Adverbs are useful parts of speech, but they shouldn't be used to bolster weak or inexact verbs. Descriptive phrases and clauses have their place, but it's not to prop up sagging verbs. Instead of saddling an imprecise verb with a load of modifiers, search for the one word that will do the job. For example:

Instead of talk wildly, rave

Instead of talk very fast, chatter

Instead of talk on and on about trivial things,
blather

— Once you find a strong, precise verb, trust it to do its job. Don't weaken it by overmodifying. If, for example, *rave* means "to be delirious, to talk wildly," it only weakens the verb to write *rave wildly*. If *glide* implies a graceful walking movement, then *glide gracefully* just robs the verb of its power. It restates what is already a vital part of the meaning of the word.

INTENSIFIERS. Our spoken language is laced with words like *very, really, truly, pretty, totally, completely, positively, perfectly* and *so*. We *really* use them *pretty* thoughtlessly *so* much of the time that they can easily creep into our written language. Intensifiers often serve no purpose other than to clutter a writer's prose. Before you use one, ask yourself the following questions:

— Are you intensifying a weak or vague word when you should be searching for a more precise word? For example:

Instead of very tired, exhausted

Instead of look at really carefully, scrutinize

— Are you overintensifying an already powerful word when you should be trusting the word to do its job? For example:

Not totally despondent but despondent

Not completely elated but elated

— Are you creating a redundancy by intensifying? If you understand and value the meanings of words, you will not write *perfectly correct*. *Correct* is, by definition, perfectly correct. The addition of the intensifier adds only clutter. *Completely destroyed, absolutely deserted, totally foresaken* are all redundancies.

FANCY WORDS. Nothing robs vitality from writing like using stodgy, multisyllabic words. Some writers mistakenly believe that fancy words impress an audience. More likely, they depress an audience by casting a pall over the prose, deadening the ideas with heavy language. As you search for precise words and work to improve your vocabulary, don't let the dictionary lead you astray into the land of *facilitate* (instead of *ease*), *fractionalize* (instead of *split*), *fabrication* (instead of *lie*) and *precipitation* (instead of *rain*). Increase your vocabulary with words like *drudge*, *clout*, *parch* and *gird*, not *salubrious*, *lachrymous* and *pertinacious*.

MADE-UP WORDS. Language must be dynamic to keep pace with changes in society. But that doesn't mean writers should create un-pleasant-sounding new words serving no distinct purpose. The habit of adding the suffix *-ize* to nouns to change them to verbs gives us such contrivances as *respectablize, concretize* and the ubiquitous *prioritize*. Worse yet is to take these *-ize* verbs and convert them back to nouns by adding *-ation*. For example:

signal
signalize
signalization

In many cases, the *-ization* word means just what the original, undoctored word meant. The only difference is that the new word is longer and uglier.

Of course, there are many legitimate *-ize/ization* words. When you are deciding which words to weed out, ask yourself these questions:

1. Is the word listed in the dictionary?

2. Does it have a unique meaning?

3. Does it have a pleasant sound?

If the word passes all three tests, use it. If not, don't *awkwardize* your prose. Find another word.

Another troublesome suffix is *-wise*. Our language contains acceptable words like *clockwise* and *crosswise*, but that doesn't mean *-wise* can be tacked on any word to add "with reference to" to its meaning as in

Timewise, we're running ahead of schedule.

Or, as Revolutionary War pamphleteer Tom Paine could have—but mercifully didn't—write:

Soulwise, these are trying times for men.

CONFUSING WORD PAIRS. English is full of word pairs that cause confusion. Some sound alike and are spelled similarly but have different meanings; others are distinct words that are often incorrectly interchanged. Clear word choice depends on your understanding of these troublesome pairs. Remember: Clutter is any excess baggage, including ill-chosen words that don't do the job you intend them to. Here are some of the more common confusing word pairs with meanings in parentheses:

adverse (unfavorable)	*averse* (reluctant)
affect (to influence)	*effect* (result)
allude (to refer indirectly)	*elude* (to avoid detection)
anxious (fearful)	*eager* (enthusiastic, impatient)
censor (to prohibit)	*censure* (to condemn)
complement (finishing touch)	*compliment* (praise)
continual (repeated)	*continuous* (unbroken)
disinterested (impartial)	*uninterested* (indifferent)
enormity (wickedness)	*enormousness* (largeness)
farther (physical distance)	*further* (more)
imply (to suggest)	*infer* (to deduce)
invoke (to appeal to)	*evoke* (to produce, to reawaken)
principal (first-rank person)	*principle* (doctrine)
reluctant (unwilling)	*reticent* (reserved)

Of course, there are many other confusing word pairs. To avoid misusing the language and creating clutter, be sure of the meanings of words before you use them. Keep a dictionary handy.

Wordiness

REDUNDANCY. Redundancy is unnecessary repetition that clutters prose with superfluous words. Calling someone an incumbent officeholder is redundant because the definition of *incumbent* is "officeholder." Writing that someone suffered a fatal strangulation death is doubly redundant. *Fatal* means "causing death"; strangulation always results in death. Dubbing a product the most unique on the market is redundant. *Unique* means "one of a kind." Redundancy comes from a lack of understanding of the true meanings of words. To achieve clear, concise language, writers must attack the tendency to be redundant, both in the writing process and, more important, in the editing and revising stage.

CIRCUMLOCUTIONS.   From the Latin "to speak around," *circumlocution* means the use of indirect or roundabout language. It's when the dentist says "You may find yourself experiencing some pain" instead of "This is going to hurt." It's when the TV weather reporter forecasts "increased precipitation activity" instead of "more rain." By definition circumlocutions are clutter: They take up space without adding meaning. A major foe of clear writing, they obscure meaning rather than clarify it. Tough editing is the cure. Make every word pull its own weight. For starters, here are several all-too-common circumlocutions and their translations:

at the present time (now)
at this point in time (now)
during the course of (during)
due to the fact that (because)
despite the fact that (although)
the reason is because (because)
notwithstanding that (however)

SPACE FILLERS.   Certain words or phrases do nothing but take up space. Any time you catch yourself using the following words, stop and evaluate whether they add meaning to the sentence. In most cases, they do not. These weeds should be pulled:

kind of
sort of
type of
variety of
aspect
element
situation
factor

Jargon

Jargon is the specialized or technical language used by a profession or trade. "Stet graf 2, and give me another take," the editor yells at the reporter. Translation: Leave the second paragraph as it is, and write an additional page. "The essay itself is inseparable from the heteroglot apperception of it," writes an English professor in a scholarly journal. Translation: You can't evaluate the essay without also considering various interpretations of it. "I wanted to give the president a future window of tenable deniability," testifies a government official. Translation: Later, the president would be able to deny it.

Jargon can be convenient shorthand for those within a group. But it is also a linguistic barrier that insulates the group from the outside world, making it difficult for outsiders to understand insiders. Because one of the media writer's most important jobs is to act as a conduit between insiders (the experts with the information) and outsiders (the curious audience), jargon has no place in media writing.

Others may use jargon to obscure ideas or to make ordinary ideas sound important. They may use it unconsciously because they are accustomed to speaking that way. But in writing for a general audience, the media writer must translate jargon into clear, understandable language. If you don't understand a piece of jargon, don't pass it along. If you do understand it, realize that most of your audience won't.

Murky construction

Careful word choice is only the first step toward clear writing. Clarity also depends on crisp construction and proper word placement. Let's consider four major contributors to murky construction: backing in, using expletives, splitting parts and misplacing modifiers.

Backing in

In most media writing, getting to the point quickly is paramount. Readers, listeners and viewers have little patience with messages that take a long time to reveal themselves. They don't want to dig for what's important—and they won't. It's the writer's job to present the vital information succinctly and straightforwardly. *Backing in* means creating a sentence that makes the audience wait unnecessarily for the most important information. The front of the sentence is weighed down with details that would best be left until after the main point is expressed. Long introductory clauses and phrases are the common danger signs of backing in. For example:

Because she believed she had exhausted all
legal avenues and had no other alternative,

Smith shot her husband three times in the
stomach.

From a journalistic point of view, the core of the sentence begins with
"Smith shot." By backing in with a long clause, the writer has made
the audience wait through 16 words before getting to the point. For
clarity, the main clause with the main idea should come first:

Smith shot her husband three times in the
stomach, claiming that she had no alternative
after exhausting all legal avenues.

Double clauses or combinations of clauses and phrases create even
murkier sentences, like this one:

When he was only 20, while suffering from
painful shinsplints, which seemed to affect his
stride during the final four miles, Smith won the
Boston Marathon.

In most cases media writers keep introductory clauses and phrases
short and rarely begin sentences with a string of clauses or phrases.
The spotlight is on the main idea, clearly expressed.

At 20, Smith won the Boston Marathon although painful shinsplints seemed to affect his
stride during the final four miles.

Using expletives

You may know one definition of *expletive*—a profanity or obscenity, as
in "expletive deleted"—but grammarians have an additional definition: Expletives are certain words added to a sentence to change its
syntax, or word order. *There* and *it* are expletives in the following
sentences:

There was a strike by the local teachers' union
today.

It is the union's plan to attract national
attention.

What's wrong with these two sentences? *There* and *it* add no meaning. They not only take up space, they also deaden the sentences they introduce by shifting the emphasis away from what could have been strong verbs. By deleting the expletives, changing these poor constructions and rescuing the hidden verbs, clearer, more concise sentences emerge:

The local teachers' union struck today.

The union plans to attract national attention.

In most cases, *there is/there are* and *it is* constructions should be weeded out of your prose.

Splitting parts

VERB PARTS.   Split verbs often dull clarity. In most cases, you should place auxiliary verbs next to main verbs and avoid splitting infinitives. Consider how the coherence of the following sentence suffers because of a split verb:

The hearings have been for more than five days focusing on the constitutionality issue.

Keeping all parts of the verb together makes the sentence more immediately understandable:

The hearings have been focusing on the constitutionality issue for more than five days.

Occasionally, it is acceptable, even preferable, to interrupt a multipart verb when you use a single word to add emphasis. The word is almost always an adverb, as in this sentence:

The hearings have always been conducted behind closed doors.

Also avoid splitting infinitives (*to* plus a verb—for example, *to play*). In most cases, keeping the infinitive intact promotes sentence clarity. But when it doesn't, forget the rule, and choose the clearest structure. Splitting the infinitive in the following sentence aids clarity:

Suburban New York real estate prices are expected to more than triple during the next five years.

Keeping the infinitive intact would interfere with coherence:

Suburban New York real estate prices are expected more than to triple during the next five years.

SUBJECT AND VERB. To ensure clarity, keep the subject and verb as close as possible. The essence of most sentences, especially journalistic ones, is *who* (subject) *is doing what* (verb) *to whom* or *to what* (object). A sentence construction that makes your readers or listeners wait too long to find out hinders clear communication instead of enhancing it. For example:

The commission, by a 4–3 margin with Jones abstaining and Smith absent because of health problems, approved the downtown revitalization plan.

Here 14 words stand between the subject and its verb. A simple rewrite solves the problem:

The commission approved the downtown revitalization plan by a 4–3 margin, with Jones abstaining and Smith absent.

VERB AND COMPLEMENT. Splitting the verb from its complements (object, adverb, descriptive phrase) also interferes with clarity. Again, the concern is with maintaining the simple, easy-to-understand subject-verb-object construction. Note what happens to coherence and readability when 14 words stand between the verb and its direct object:

The commission approved by a 4–3 margin, with Jones abstaining and Smith absent because of health problems, the downtown revitalization plan.

Communication is sharper with two sentences:

The commission approved the downtown revitalization plan by a 4–3 margin. Jones ab-
stained, and Smith was absent.

Misplacing modifiers

MISPLACED ADVERBS.   In careful sentence construction, modifiers
point directly to what they are supposed to describe. With careless
construction the reader must reread for clarity; the listener may be
permanently misinformed or confused. Adverbs are a particular problem. We tend to be somewhat devil-may-care about their placement,
yet *placement determines meaning.* Look at how the meaning of these
sentences changes as the adverb moves:

The committee almost rejected every new
application.

*(No applications were actually rejected, but it was
a close call.)*

The committee rejected almost every new
application.

(Just about every application was rejected.)

To ensure that the meaning you intend comes through clearly, place
the adverb next to the word it modifies.

MISPLACED PHRASES AND CLAUSES.   Varying the placement of
phrases and clauses adds diversity to writing. But remember: Placement affects meaning. When you construct sentences, place phrases
and clauses as close as possible to what you intend them to modify.
Again, consider how phrase placement affects meaning:

The brownout throughout the Northeast interfered with all government operations.

*(The brownout was regional; the effect was
national.)*

The brownout interfered with all government
operations throughout the Northeast.

*(We don't know how widespread the brownout was,
but the effect was regional.)*

Here is a clause that changes the meaning of its sentence as it
moves from one place to another:

The book that the publisher is considering will
affect the new marketing strategy.

The book will affect the new marketing strategy that the publisher is considering.

In the first sentence, the *book* is under consideration; in the second,
the *marketing strategy* is under consideration.

Sometimes a misplaced phrase or clause causes confusion, ambi-
guity or unintentionally hilarious results as in this example from
Strunk and White's *Elements of Style:*

New York's first commercial human-sperm
bank opened Friday with semen samples from
18 men frozen in a stainless steel tank.

DANGLING MODIFIERS. A particular variety of misplaced modifier,
a dangling modifier "dangles" because what it is supposed to modify
is nowhere in the sentence. This placement error causes confusion
and interferes with meaning.

While going to school, a part-time job became
available.

"While going to school" dangles because it does not modify anything
in the sentence. The only word it could modify is "job," but the sentence makes no sense read this way. A job doesn't go to school. The
cure for dangling modifiers is always a rewrite. The modifier must
refer to a word in the sentence, and the closer the referent is, the
better.

While going to school, she heard about a part-
time job.

Faulty presentation

Clarity depends on straightforward, understandable presentation. Well-chosen words carefully placed are not enough. Writers must work on balance and symmetry by creating *parallel structure*. They must strive for directness by avoiding *passive voice*. They must present ideas clearly by shunning *fragments* and *run-ons*. Let's examine these four concerns more closely.

Parallel structure

When you place like ideas in like grammatical patterns, you create parallel structure. The result is not just good grammar; it's clear, emphatic expression. Lining up related ideas and offering them to your audience through the repetition of grammatical elements creates order, symmetry and, ultimately, power. The ideas may be single words:

With shampoo X, your hair will be <u>clean</u>, <u>shiny</u> and <u>manageable</u>.

(Parallel traits expressed in parallel adjective form.)

With shampoo X, your hair will be clean, have shine and can be easily managed.

(Lack of parallel structure makes this sentence awkward and ruins its rhythm.)

Any repeated grammatical pattern—single words, compound modifiers, phrases, clauses, even whole sentences—can be used to create parallel structure. In the following examples, note how the lucid, rhythmic, predictable patterns help set up each idea and promote easy understanding:

Now is not a time <u>for words</u>. It is a time <u>for</u> <u>ideas</u> and <u>for action</u>.

(Note both the repetition of the prepositional phrases and the repetition of basic sentence structure.)

When your eyes are <u>red</u>, your ears are <u>clogged</u> and your nose is <u>runny</u>, you know spring is here.

(Note both the repetition of clauses and of the single modifiers.)

Parallel structure is commonly used to set up complementary, contrasting or sequential ideas. Sometimes the relationship between the ideas is implied; other times writers guide the audience through the relationship with words such as *not only/but also, both/and, either/or, neither/nor, first/second/third.*

<u>Both</u> solid research <u>and</u> clear thinking are necessary for good writing.

<u>Either</u> you write with clarity <u>or</u> you risk being misunderstood.

<u>First</u>, choose words well; <u>second</u>, place them correctly; <u>third</u>, create clear constructions.

Passive voice

Nothing can obscure ideas and deaden prose quite like passive voice. It twists a clear, straightforward, active-voice construction (who does what to whom) into a wordy, awkward, reverse presentation (who is having what done to it by whom).

The new software was experimented with by the writer.

(passive: What is having what done with it by whom.)

The writer experimented with the new software.

(active: Who did what.)

Passive voice adds words while it takes away clarity. It can make a sentence unnecessarily awkward. It can create stilted, falsely formal writing. And that's not all:

— Passive voice can rob the verb of its power by replacing direct presentation of action with an indirect construction.

Rows of strawberries were stooped over by them. *(passive)*

They stooped over rows of strawberries. *(active)*

— Passive voice can bury the real verb of the sentence, sapping vitality from expression.

The investigation of the misappropriation of funds is being conducted by the subcommittee. *(passive)*

The subcommittee is investigating the misappropriation of funds. *(active)*

— Passive voice may obscure who or what is responsible for the action. In reverse presentation, it is all too easy to eliminate the back end of the sentence, the part that includes who or what is responsible.

The investigation of the misappropriation of funds is being conducted.

Who is responsible for the investigation? Obscuring the responsible parties is not just bad sentence construction; it is bad journalism.

With all its serious disadvantages, passive voice would seem to have no place in clear, direct writing. That's almost, but not quite, true. Most of the time passive voice hurts clarity and demands a rewrite. But in two special cases, writers may use it in good conscience, despite all its failings:

— Because passive voice reverses sentence order, it is a useful device when the *who* or *what* responsible for the action is not as important as the *recipient* of that action, as in

The Statue of Liberty was restored by hundreds of artisans.

The mayor was robbed by three men in masks.

— Passive voice is useful when the *who* or *what* responsible for the action is unknown or difficult to identify, as in

The unsigned ransom note was sent Federal Express.

The painting was damaged during transport.

Although passive voice is allowable in these cases, it is still not preferred. If you can reconstruct the sentence without harming its meaning, do so:

The restored Statue of Liberty reflects the work of hundreds of artisans.

Regard passive voice as a last resort.

To resuscitate passive-voice sentences, first find the verb. Then, ask yourself who or what is performing the action of the verb. Finally, reconstruct the sentence so that the responsible party directly performs the action. For example:

The house was struck by lightning. *(passive)*

Verb: was struck

Who or what struck: lightning

Lightning struck the house. *(active)*

Sentence fragments

A fragment is an unfinished chunk of a sentence, a group of words lacking a subject, a verb or a complete thought. Grammatically, it cannot and should not stand alone (although stylistically, it sometimes does, as Chapter 6 will discuss).

Fragments can be single words, brief phrases or lengthy dependent clauses. The number of words is irrelevant. What matters is that the words don't work together as a sentence. A common mistake is to look only for a subject and verb and, having found them, think you have written a complete sentence. Remember, a sentence must express a finished thought.

Whenever he traveled overseas

contains a subject (*he*) and a verb (*traveled*) but does not express a complete thought. It is a fragment—a dependent clause, not a sentence.

To listening audiences, fragments can be choppy and disorienting. Readers have a different problem: Their eyes are trained to regard a capital letter as the beginning of a sentence and a period as the end. In between they have come to expect a complete thought. A fragment doesn't deliver. It can therefore confuse and frustrate a reader, hindering coherence and clarity.

The concert was rescheduled for July 19. Because of rain.

Is the meaning clear in this example? Perhaps the writer meant

Because of rain the concert was rescheduled for July 19.

But maybe the writer intended no such connection. Perhaps the fragment was supposed to signal the beginning of a new idea.

The concert was rescheduled for July 19. Because of rain it was moved indoors.

Offer your readers clear, complete thoughts. Write full sentences.

Run-on sentences

A run-on sentence is actually two, three or any number of complete sentences strung together without proper punctuation. Run-ons tend to offer too much information too fast. Breathlessly rushing forward, these out-of-control sentences fail to establish strong links between ideas. The necessary words or symbols that create these links are missing. The result is confusion and lack of clarity. (For specialized, stylistic use of run-ons, see Chapter 6.)

The following example illustrates the most common run-on error writers make: using only a comma to separate complete thoughts. Called a comma splice, this faulty construction muddies the connection between complete thoughts.

The state's dependence on migrant workers hit home yesterday, federal immigration reforms created massive worker shortages, berry harvests were thrown into chaos.

Commas are meant to signal brief pauses within one continuous idea. Readers or listeners expect that what follows one of these pauses will complement or augment what comes before it. When there is no such relationship, coherence suffers. A simple rewrite can establish clear links between main ideas.

> The state's dependence on migrant workers hit home yesterday <u>when</u> federal immigration reforms created massive worker shortages <u>and</u> threw berry harvests into chaos.

Writers can also create run-ons by using a linking word without proper punctuation, by using a linking word where no such linkage is meant or by neglecting to use any punctuation.

Whatever the cause, the cure is the same: Create a clear, explicit relationship between ideas. You can do so by one of these methods:

— Change the run-on sentence into two or more complete sentences with the necessary periods and capital letters.

— Use a comma followed by a coordinating conjunction to connect two complete, related ideas.

— Subordinate one idea to the other, rewriting the run-on in independent and dependent clause form.

— Use a semicolon to link two complete, related ideas. (Because of the semicolon's formality and the risk of creating an overly long sentence, this option is the least desirable.)

Remember, run-ons are as confusing to listeners as they are to readers. Audiences are left dazed by the rush of words whipping by. Broadcasters are left gasping for breath. No one is left with a clear understanding of what has been said.

Striving for clarity

Media writers have different purposes when they compose their messages. The broadcast or print news writer may merely seek to signal the occurrence of an event. The public relations writer may intend to set a general tone. The editorial writer may want to rabble-rouse. The advertising copywriter may want to persuade. The magazine writer may want to analyze.

But before any of these media professionals can achieve their separate goals, they must all achieve the same goal: lucid presentation of ideas. Based on clear thinking and solid research, clarity of expression evolves from careful, precise, purposeful use of the language. It is the foundation of all effective public communication.

Style

"Young writers often suppose that style is a garnish for the meat of prose, a sauce by which a dull dish is made palatable," writes E. B. White in *The Elements of Style*. But style is no garnish, no spicy condiment added to bring zip to bland writing. It is an integral part of a piece of writing that reflects the writer's way of seeing, thinking and using language. Your style is inseparable from who you are. It is your unique vision—and your lively, original expression of that vision—that keeps the audience's attention riveted to the message. It is the product of purposeful choices, the culmination of many things done well, the result of sheer hard work.

Novice writers, and some experienced ones as well, harbor several misconceptions about style: They believe if they write lean, clutterless prose, their writing will lack style. They think style has something to do with verbal gaudiness and ornamental language. They think that style is mysterious and unattainable.

They're wrong.

First, style and lean prose are absolutely complementary. In fact, one of the big lessons writers learn—often after years of working at their craft—is how strongly style is tied to simple, direct expression and clear, precise language use. It's not just that stylish writing must build on a foundation of crisp, clear expression. It's that stylish writing is itself often simple, direct expression. There's nothing fancy, but everything stylish, about this opening sentence from a Judy Bachrach story in the *Washington Post:*

> Six hundred pounds of Haystacks Calhoun rises to its full height of 6 feet 4 inches, lumbers outside his hotel on downtown H Street and blocks out the afternoon sun.

Second, style has little to do with ostentatious language use, verbal ornamentation, fancy tricks or self-conscious flashiness. Style isn't showing off in print. It isn't, in William Zinsser's words, "gaudy similes" and "tinseled adjectives." In fact, overly fanciful writing that consciously strains for stylishness can be both deadening and confusing. Consider this sentence from a (later revised) first draft of a magazine story about an excursion to the North Pole. The writer has tried mightily to be stylish. The result is thick, confusing prose:

> For two months, the world watched and read and listened to news reports of their progress—or lack: of the first 120 miles, brutal, endless days of chopping through a war zone of pressure ridges crunched by shifting sea ice against frozen land, dwarfed in jumbled moonscapes of shattered white boulders, prying, jacking, muscling 1,500-pound sleds over jagged fissures and up icy spines—20 and 30 feet high—imperceptible movement on the maps, seemingly inconsequential effort in such desolation, in such incomprehensible cold.

Finally, style is *not* mysterious. It is not a bag of tricks given to some writers and not others. It is not a secret device you discover in a frenzy of inspiration. Of course, talent and inspiration play a part in all forms of expression. But stylish writing is much more likely to be the result of a series of hard-headed decisions than the product of some Muse whispering in your ear.

Stylish writing can be found everywhere in the mass media, from the brief news story to the lengthy magazine piece, from advertising copy to a broadcast report. But that doesn't mean it comes easy. Good writers struggle long and hard to write original, vigorous prose. They know that learning to write with flair is a lifelong process. Let's begin that process by examining several major components of style: precision, detail, word play, rhythm and sound.

Precision

Liveliness and originality, the hallmarks of stylish writing, come from precise language use. In Chapter 5 we discussed word choice as an important element of clarity. It is also an element of style.

Verb choice

Because it can be the most important word in any sentence, the verb has great style potential. A strong, precise verb can enliven a sentence like no other word. It can capture action and describe movement with originality and power. Consider the rush of well-chosen verbs in this opening paragraph from an article about skin:

We tingle, twitch, shiver, sweat, blush and blister. We itch, smart, prickle and quiver, feeling pain and pleasure as we react to the world around us. What enables us to do all this is the finely layered tissue that sheathes the bone and muscle—the resilient bag, paper thin, that holds us together: the skin.

Remember to use adverbs sparingly, searching instead for the one verb that precisely captures the meaning you intend.

Adjective choice

Writers choose adjectives to bring precision, specificity and life to nouns.

the man

the <u>slack-jawed</u>, <u>horse-toothed</u>, <u>squinty-eyed</u> man

But many adjectives can actually work *against* vivid expression. Let's examine two potential problems with adjective selection: judging versus describing and telling versus showing.

JUDGING VS. DESCRIBING. Certain adjectives stand in the way of vivid writing because they *judge*—that is, they offer the writer's judgment rather than a description. Adjectives like *tall, short, big, little, small, large, beautiful, ugly* and *intelligent* summarize what the writer has observed, translating it into a judgment meaningful only to the writer.

Let's say you're conducting an interview in the subject's home. It's a three-bedroom, two-bath, 3,000-square-foot Victorian. To you, a starving free-lancer living in a one-room apartment, this is a *big* house. The rooms are *large;* the furnishings are *luxurious.* But using these judgment adjectives doesn't help your audience *see* the house. In fact, you may be miscommunicating with members of your audience. To a reader living in an eight-bedroom mansion, a three-bedroom house is not large and luxurious. This reader imagines a far grander home when you use these words. Because you are prejudging the experience for your audience—and judging it on your own terms—your choice of adjectives obscures what you are trying to illuminate.

TELLING VS. SHOWING. When you *tell* instead of *show,* you summarize rather than describe in detail. A summarizing adjective obstructs audience involvement in the message by distancing your readers or listeners from the action. For example:

Smith was depressed.

The adjective *depressed* describes Smith, but does it add color and style to the sentence? No. Condensing Smith's actions into a bland summary robs the message of vitality.

Smith sat staring at the unplugged TV set for three days. He didn't sleep. He didn't talk. He didn't eat. Twice he composed suicide notes.

Now you have *shown* Smith's depression.

An adjective can tell rather than show in another sense. It can tell the audience something without showing meaning and context, without truly communicating. For example:

Alaska is 589,757 square miles with a population of 401,000 and a population density of 0.7 people per square mile.

The numbers *tell* facts about Alaska. But look at how journalist and author Joe McGinnis *shows* what they mean:

Alaska was so big that it contained four time zones; yet its population was smaller than Columbus, Ohio. . . . If Alaska's population density . . . were applied to New York City, the population of the borough of Manhattan would be fourteen.

Be cautious about selecting adjectives. Precise choices add meaning and color. Imprecise, judgmental or summarizing adjectives rarely do.

Wordiness

By definition, wordy prose lacks precision. Clutter not only hurts clarity, it also stands in the way of style. Let's briefly review the dos and don'ts:

— Don't depend on intensifiers; do search for one precise word. Use *very, really, so, truly, completely, absolutely* and so forth sparingly. Instead of intensifying a weak or vague word, search for one strong word: *exhausted* or *drained* rather than *very tired*. Instead of intensifying an already powerful word, leave it unadorned, trusting it to do its job: *exhausted*, not *really exhausted*.

— Do understand the meanings of words; don't create redundancies. Saying the same thing twice shows ignorance and lack of respect for the language, both powerful enemies of stylish writing. Forget *most unique, exactly parallel, mutual cooperation* and the like.

— Do translate jargon into vibrant, understandable prose; don't pass it along to your audience. For example:

Divided into two atria and two ventricles, the viscus of cardiac muscle maintains movement of the sangius through arterial and venus vessels. *(medical jargon)*

The heart is a four-chambered machine hooked into a vast network of tubing. *(translation)*

Direct expression

Contrary to the notion that style is something fancy, liveliness and originality often come from direct expression. One component of direct expression is *active voice,* the straightforward, who-did-what-to-whom ordering of a sentence. As Chapter 5 explained, active voice promotes sharp, clear, vigorous sentence construction. It also cuts clutter while adding power to the verb, two important elements of stylish writing.

Present tense, the simplest, most direct verb form, can also be a powerful contributor to stylish writing. Because it allows the audience to experience the story or message as it unfolds, present tense helps create audience involvement. Accomplished writers often choose present tense to tell anecdotes or offer descriptions. The urgency and immediacy of the present tense can enliven writing.

Detail

Detail—the controlled, creative use of vivid specifics—can make a scene or a person come alive. One of the mainstays of stylish writing, detail depends on keen observation. Writers cannot paint vivid pictures unless they first *see* (hear, smell) vivid pictures. This openly sensual way of experiencing the world cannot be taught, but it can be learned through repeated practice. You can train yourself to be alert to specifics: the catch in someone's voice, the feel of a plush carpet, the spot on someone's tie. Small details like this engage your audience by presenting a fresh mental picture.

Consider the clever detail in this excerpt from a Nora Ephron story about fashion designer Bill Blass:

One day not long ago, Bill Blass, who is tall, slender, and tawny and speaks with a cigarette dangling from his lower lip, was standing in his brown plaid Bill Blass suit ($175), his brown Bill Blass shirt ($22.50), his brown Bill Blass silk tie ($15) and brown Bill Blass buckled shoes ($50) in the center of the Bill Blass men's boutique at Bonwit Teller's.

The description begins with several ordinary observations (tall, slender, tawny) but then moves to wonderful detail as Ephron presents Blass' attire complete with retail prices. The repetition of "Bill Blass" before each item pokes mild fun at the designer-label mentality she explores in the rest of the article.

Far simpler but no less vivid is one writer's description of middle-aged ex–football hero Fran Tarkenton as "blazered, loafered, Rolexed." It is the precision of detail that makes this three-word gem work. To write that Tarkenton wore "a jacket, casual shoes and an expensive watch" also presents detail, but the picture it paints is flat and unoriginal.

Details can be simple, spare and adjective-free. See how the following scene comes alive through the author's use of unadorned specifics (television, refrigerator and so on). The writer, a *New York Times* reporter, covered freshman moving-in day at New York University.

It was either somewhere around the time he unloaded his color television and the refrigerator or while he was carrying his electric typewriter and telephone answering machine into New York University's Joe Weinstein Residence Hall that Bill Freiberger realized the one thing he had forgotten to bring from his home in Merrick, L.I., was his clothes.

Even basic, on-deadline news stories can contain rich detail. Note how the specifics in this *Los Angeles Times* news story bring the scene to life. A TV camera could not have done much better:

Former hostage David Jacobsen stepped from a white Lear jet into the arms of his aged father

Sunday afternoon at Orange County's John Wayne Airport, ending a journey that began 17 months ago when he was taken captive in Beirut.

The reader sees the white Lear jet and the aged father. The reader smiles at the specific reference to John Wayne Airport. The basic facts of a news story are enhanced by a few well-chosen details.

Visual details are probably the most common, but other senses can come into play when a writer observes and later puts observations into words. Here is a writer describing how Nobel laureate Linus Pauling speaks:

Pauling has a rolling, full voice, quavering a little and gravelly with age but full of expression, diving to a bass grumble at times, then rising to emphasize a point. The way he speaks says a lot about the way he thinks. Each syllable is sharp and distinct. His sentences are sparse but complete, packed with hard fact, uncluttered by "umms" and "aahs."

Detail is a key element in lively, original writing. But not just any details will do. The specifics you choose to highlight in print should be

— *Precise.* Remember the $50 Bill Blass shoes and Fran Tarkenton's Rolex? Observing a general detail—Bill Blass is dressed in his own designer clothes—is only the first step toward creating a sharply detailed portrait.

— *Original.* The freshness and novelty of a detail will enliven writing and bring a picture into clear focus. The *New York Times* reporter sees refrigerators, typewriters, answering machines, television sets—and later in the article, woks, yogurt makers, toaster ovens, word processors and popcorn poppers—not just boxes of belongings.

— *Multisensory.* All of the audience's senses can be engaged. A skillful, creative print writer can make a reader see, hear, smell and taste a scene. A TV reporter who relies on videotape to supply audiovisual details can further enhance the viewer's experience by writing about smell, texture and taste.

— *Meaningful.* Most important, the details chosen must be meaningful to the message as a whole. Novice writers sometimes go for details with a vengeance, describing everything from how a person parts her hair to what color socks she wears. Some details add meaning to the message because they say something beyond the detail itself. In the description of Linus Pauling's speech mannerisms, the details are interesting in themselves, but they also serve a larger purpose: He speaks as he thinks. Although someone you're writing about may be short, red-haired, freckled, mustached and bespectacled, none of these details may be particularly telling or meaningful in the context of the whole message. It may be that one single detail—the orange juice stain on his tie—tells more than a string of adjectives.

Word play

The reader or listener is moving through the message. Suddenly, there's a neat turn of phrase, an understated pun, a clever choice of words, a small verbal joke. The audience, charmed by the unexpected, is drawn into the message. For a moment at least—and perhaps for much longer—the message is memorable. By skillfully playing with words, the writer has succeeded in touching the reader and distinguishing this message from all others. When a stylistic technique does this, it can enhance both the effect of a piece of communication for the audience and the joy of communicating for the writer.

Word play, an important and frequently used stylistic technique, is directly tied to the writer's respect and love for the language. It comes from a good vocabulary, a strong sense of audience and the confidence to try something new, even under pressure of deadline. The writer can play with the meaning of an individual word, set up a series where items play against one another or construct an image or scene offering a unique verbal slant. Word play can be serious, funny or neither. Found in news, in-depth or persuasive writing, it can be used to educate, entertain or influence. Let's look at some examples and see how they work.

Writers often play with the meanings and sounds of individual words. This most common form of word play can add zest to prose.

The carefully constructed headline for a Campbell's chicken soup advertisement reads:

Tender Loving Fare

This simple play on the common phrase "tender loving care" merely replaces one word with another. Because of the rhyme (care/fare) and the commonness of the expression, the reader immediately understands the word play.

Writing on deadline the evening after a five-hour Grateful Dead/ Bob Dylan concert, a newspaper reporter refers to Grateful Dead aficionados as

tie-dyed-in-the-wool fans

By adding the word *tie* to the cliché "dyed-in-the-wool," the writer succeeds in creating an image of colorfully garbed concertgoers as he breathes new life into a trite expression. As a bonus, the phrase contains a nice rhyme.

In a magazine profile of a locally famous play-by-play basketball announcer, a writer offers this sentence:

As the game began, the normally unflappable
Schonley was flapped.

The surprising end to the sentence, with its play on the word *unflappable,* works because the writer is intentionally and humorously ungrammatical. The writer knows *unflappable* means "not easily upset," and he knows the adjective is *not* based on the verb *flap* (which means "to wave up and down"). The startling misuse grabs the reader's attention.

The following two sentences are both opening paragraphs for brief news stories. They were undoubtedly written on deadline.

Non-smokers celebrated clean air in restaurants Friday, but smokers fumed as a no-smoking law they perceive as a breach of civil rights took effect.

The makers of Dial soap are in a lather over a magazine ad for a liquid cleanser that showed disease-causing micro-organisms superimposed over a picture of a soap bar.

In the first example the word *fumed* transforms an ordinary sentence into a story opener with a bit of zip. The image of smokers fuming is wonderful. In the second example *lather* plays on the meaning of the word as soap foam and on the expression "in a lather" (agitated). Both plays on words are simple, straightforward and clever.

Not all word play aims at humor or light-heartedness. The following is a slogan for a radical environmental organization:

We stand for
what we stand on

The play on the two meanings of *stand* makes this sentence powerful, rhythmic and memorable.

Sometimes writers get a little fancier with their word play, as in this string of descriptive words from a *Harper's* article on what became of the 1960s' counterculture in the 1980s:

tough-talking, bottom-line, top-drawer, middle-
management ex-hippies

The "bottom/top/middle" play on words is witty. The rapid-fire litany has both rhythm and flair.

Occasionally writers have the time to develop more sophisticated word play. In an *Esquire* profile of a small-town New England businessman, the writer introduces his subject as

an example of the kind of men who, if they
didn't exactly build America, at least put in the
duct work.

The word play here doesn't focus on a particular word but rather on a twist of the cliché "they helped build America." The writer takes *build* literally and plays with the image. In the context of the story, the sentence is even more clever than it appears here: The man being profiled is a heating contractor who puts in duct work for a living.

Here's another sophisticated play on words and images, this time from a *Mother Jones* story about the tumultuous history of National Public Radio. With one sentence the writer sums up the six years during which free-spending Frank Mankiewicz headed NPR:

After the Mankiewicz party ended, what was
left of NPR's staff awoke with an incredible
hangover.

A hangover after a party is certainly not an original image. But characterizing the Mankiewicz era as a party and relating the unsteadiness of the staff after Mankiewicz to a hangover bring new life to the image.

Whether writers create a single-word pun or a more complex image, successful word play has several common characteristics. As the examples you've just read show, word play must be

— *Correct.* Much word play depends on twisting, manipulating, interchanging or substituting the meanings of words. Writers have to know those meanings and use them precisely and accurately; otherwise the result is confusion, not style.

— *Original.* Unfortunately, trite expressions, ideas and images come far more quickly to mind than original, imaginative word play. If writers recognize a cliché and play with it, that's style. If they don't recognize it and use it, that's bad writing.

— *Appropriate.* Word play must be consistent with the tone of the entire message and appropriate to the subject itself. It must involve a twist that the particular audience would be expected to understand and appreciate.

— *Understated.* When style is gaudy, it takes the spotlight away from *what* is being said and focuses it on *how* it is being said. In mass media the meaning of the message is paramount. If a play on words is so flashy that it distracts an audience from the message itself, the writer has damaged communication, not enhanced it.

Rhythm

Words march to a beat. Sentences have rhythm. Their pace can be fast or slow; their cadence, soothing or staccato. The skillful writer controls the dance of words by carefully manipulating the structure of sentences. Long sentences can flow gently, picking up momentum as they go. Short sentences can create a tense, insistent rhythm. Repetition can add accent and meter.

Rhythm can be a stylistic element for all writers, regardless of the media they write for or the purpose of their messages. Readers clearly hear the beat of sentences in their minds as they read. Listeners, of course, hear the beat out loud. That's why skillful writers for all media write for the ear. Let's examine four specific techniques for creating rhythmic construction: repetition and parallelism, sentence length, fragments and run-ons.

Repetition and parallelism

Deliberate repetition of words or phrases can add rhythm to writing and help create graceful transitions between ideas. Parallelism—the use of like grammatical patterns—can create emphasis and drama. Let's see how these techniques work.

Repetition is well-suited to advertising copy, as these first two paragraphs from a Rockport shoe ad illustrate:

It all started in a VW bus back in 1969. Out of the back of that bus, we started selling Rockports.

We sold them to back-packers. We sold them to sculptors. We sold them to just about everyone who spent long hard days on their feet and needed a pair of comfortable shoes.

The writer has created a rolling pace by repeating the phrase "we sold them" through the second paragraph. The insistent parallel structure creates a rhythm that pulls the reader through the copy—just the effect any writer strives for. Note that the writer sets up the repetition with the last clause in the first paragraph.

Magazine columnist, essayist and novelist Nora Ephron is known for her witty writing. In the following sentence from a magazine story on food writers, she uses repetition and parallelism to make a point:

In the beginning, just about the time the Food Establishment began to earn money and fight with each other and review each other's books and say nasty things about each other's recipes and feel rotten about each other's good fortune, just about that time, there came curry.

The insistent beat of the repeated *and*, and the parallel placement of the verbs (*earn, fight, review, say, feel*) create a breathless litany that pushes the sentence forward. Note how skillfully Ephron changes the rhythm at the end of the sentence, surprising the reader with an abrupt change.

Here is an example of parallelism without repetition of any single word. The author isn't a professional media writer; he's a "DWM" (divorced white male) advertising himself in the personals column of an urban newsweekly:

Passions: good fiction, bad movies, most music, few sports, all food, no tobacco, close
friends, distant places, short hikes, long
dances.

It's clear the writer has taken time to craft these words, setting his interests into parallel form with clever contrasts. The result is rhythmic prose with a sense of humor.

Parallelism is a basic element of clear expression (Chapter 5). But when it is employed obviously and insistently—and especially when it is coupled with repetition of words or phrases—it becomes an important stylistic technique as well. Like all stylistic devices, repetition should be used sparingly. Overuse of any technique decreases its power. Overuse of repetition can bore an audience.

Sentence length

Imagine: Something as ordinary as the length of a sentence can be a stylistic device. Short sentences deliver punch. Long sentences establish a more leisurely rhythm as they move forward somewhat breathlessly. Sentences can also play against each other, with a short sentence used for drama and emphasis after a string of longer sentences or a long sentence used to relieve the tension of a string of short ones. Let's examine a few examples.

Here are the first three paragraphs of a public service ad created by Gard & Lesh, a Portland, Oregon agency. Pay close attention to sentence length and its effect.

It hurts to grow up. Sometimes it hurts too
much. Too many kids in Oregon are abused—
physically, psychologically and sexually. Too
often the wounds never heal. They grow up
bitter and angry. We pay the price of their pain.

Do you hear the slow drum beat of these six medium-length sentences? The solemn, dramatic effect comes from stacking sentences of similar lengths. Because the dash breaks it in two, even the longer third sentence does not destroy the insistent rhythm. This is powerful writing.

Here is what a series of short, tightly constructed sentences can do. The author is Washington, D.C., journalist Sally Quinn; her subject is a TV anchorwoman who committed suicide on camera.

> Her right arm stiffened. "We bring you another first." Her voice was steady. She looked up again into the camera. Her eyes were dark, direct and challenging. "An attempted suicide." Her right hand came up from under the anchor desk. In it was a .38-caliber revolver. She pointed it at the lower back of her head and pulled the trigger. A loud crack was heard.

The effect of this string of simple, declarative sentences is understated drama. Their brevity creates tension and immediacy.

The following 77-word sentence opens a feature profile in *Esquire* magazine:

> It is 7:45 on a cold, steel-gray winter morning between the last out of the World Series and the first crack of the bat in spring training, and Michael Jack Schmidt, thirty-seven, three times the National League's Most Valuable Player, one of the pre-eminent home-run hitters in baseball history, ten times a Gold Glove third baseman for the Philadelphia Phillies, a virtual deity in the City of Brotherly Love, is sweating like a pig.

The rolling, leisurely rhythm of the sentence sets up the reader for the surprise ending. The singsong series of details lulls the reader. That's why the final incongruous words are so effective.

Fragments

A fragment—an unfinished piece of a sentence—is not good grammar. But sometimes a writer purposefully commits a grammatical error to create a special effect. Because they are usually short and clipped, fragments can create tension like a terse sentence. Used after a long sentence or string of sentences, a fragment can come as a dramatic surprise. Ad copywriters seem fragment-prone. Sometimes they overdo it, and the result is choppy, disorienting prose. But sometimes they use fragments well, as the following examples show.

Here is the copy for the opening two pages of a Nike shoe ad. The first page:

What does a 6'5", 270 lb. defensive lineman
do for a workout?

The reader turns the page for the answer:

Anything he wants.

The fragment is punchy, powerful and surprising. It's also funny.

Less dramatic but along the same lines is the fragment in this ad for Neutrogena soap:

Neutrogena does one thing and one thing well.
It cleans perfectly. What could be better than
that? Nothing.

Nothing, as a single word, is definite and emphatic.

The opening lines of this advertisement for the Range Rover refers to a large photograph of the truck above the copy. The fragment here has a different feel to it:

How can we call that mud-splattered vehicle
beautiful? Quite easily, actually.

This fragment is conversational and informal. It's not meant to deliver a wallop but rather to mimic dialogue.

Of course, copywriters are not the only ones to use fragments. Broadcast journalists often introduce stories with fragments that serve as punchy headlines. Speech writers use fragments for drama and emphasis. Magazine journalists play with fragments to manipulate the rhythm of paragraphs. The trick is using them for a specific, appropriate purpose—and using them sparingly.

Run-ons

Run-ons are two or more complete sentences incorrectly spliced together. Using them unconsciously is bad grammar. Using them consciously for effect can be style. Run-ons can quicken the pace with a giddy rush of words or slacken the pace with a languid, rolling motion. They are more dangerous to use than fragments because they demand heightened concentration from the audience. "Sit still and listen to all this," a run-on says to the audience. "There will be a payoff at the end." In other words, the writer has to make it worth the trouble. The writer has to deliver. Here's one who does, a *Washington Post* journalist beginning a story about a Marine drill sergeant:

> He is seething, he is rabid, he is wound up as tight as a golf ball with more adrenalin surging through his hypothalamus than a cornered slum rat, he is everything these Marine recruits with their heads shaved to dirty nubs have ever feared or even hoped a drill instructor might be. He is Staff Sgt. Douglas Berry.

The first sentence, actually four complete sentences strung together, zooms forward with frantic, nervous energy. Sentence structure reinforces and enhances the message.

Sound

Competent writers choose words for their precise meanings. Notable writers choose words for their meanings *and* their sounds. They know that sound communicates, whether words are spoken or silently repeated in readers' minds.

Our language is full of words that sound like what they mean. Onomatopoeic words like *crack, buzz, boom* and *clang* imitate the sound they describe. Some words are not actually onomatopoeic, but their sound enhances their meaning. The unpleasant hiss of the beginning *s* sound adds a touch of nastiness to *sneer* and *smirk* that the synonym *look askance* lacks. The forceful *p* and harsh *k* sounds in *pesky* make the word itself annoying. Sound adds an extra dimension. In addition to choosing individual words for their sounds, writers can play with two stylistic techniques often considered the private reserve of poets: alliteration and rhyme.

Alliteration

Alliteration is the repetition of consonant sounds to achieve a special effect. Consider this opening paragraph, written by a sports reporter:

> With 10 minutes left and the Los Angeles Lakers lollygagging their way to another riotous rout while the Boston Celtics starters sat stone-faced on the bench, the Forum fans began the inevitable chant.

The five *l* sounds at the beginning of the sentence laze languidly on the tongue. You can feel the Lakers taking it easy. The growling *r* sounds of *riotous rout* change the pace. The many *s* sounds hiss at the unfortunate Celtics. This is lively writing.

Sometimes the effect of alliteration is merely playful. This Associated Press writer is just having fun:

> Some downtown Seattle hotels are luring the locals with posh pampering at pared prices in order to keep rooms filled.

The alliteration sets a light tone for the story. It pulls the reader in with its playfulness.

As you can see, alliteration need not be limited to the repetition of only one sound. The effect of repeating a single sound can be quite dramatic, but it's harder to construct a passage with this alliterative consistency. Here is one written by master journalist Gay Talese:

> It was not quite spring, the silent season before the search for salmon, and all the old fishermen of San Francisco were either painting their boats or repairing their nets along the pier or sitting in the sun talking among themselves.

Note the soft, quiet mood achieved through the repetition of the *s* sounds.

Rhyme

Used sparingly and appropriately, rhyme can add verve to prose. It can create rhythm, quicken pace and inject humor. Rhyming lines tend to stick in readers' or listeners' minds. This makes rhyme a powerful device for advertising copywriters who want to create memorable slogans like these venerable ones:

See the USA in your Chevrolet

Winston tastes good like a cigarette should
(Note the terrible grammar.)

Oscar Mayer has a way with b-o-l-o-g-n-a

Other writers may experiment more delicately with rhyme. Consider the not-quite-rhymes in this line from a *Wall Street Journal* story about the tobacco habits of members of Congress:

Today's senators not only sniff no snuff; they
also eschew chewing tobacco.

By toying with the sounds of words, this journalist increases his readers' enjoyment of the story.

In this opening paragraph from an article on hair, the journalist creates several pleasant rhymes:

We twirl, curl, cut and pluck it. We shave,
brush, tint and wax it. We wash it, brush it,
braid and pomade it. We spend more than $2
billion a year pampering it and have more of it
per square inch than a chimpanzee. When it
begins to turn gray, we panic. When it begins
to recede, we have mid-life crises.

Note that rhyme doesn't have to be sustained. A few words here and there do the trick.

Striving for style

"**R**ich, ornate prose is hard to digest, generally unwholesome and sometimes nauseating," writes E. B. White in *The Elements of Style*. Lively, original, stylish writing, on the other hand, is a delicately seasoned dish you can't get enough of.

It's a dish that takes much practice to create. Writers spend their lives experimenting with and practicing the techniques of stylish writing. They toy with different devices. They make mistakes. They search for their "voice." If they love their craft, if they love the language—and if they work long and hard enough—they may become stylish writers. It is something experienced writers aspire to, not something novice writers should hope to attain quickly.

As you begin to learn what goes into writing media messages, look toward the goal of stylish writing. Like someone learning to play music, you will have to struggle first with scales and exercises. But as you struggle, know that ahead is the promise of a symphony.

The News Burst

News is at the heart of most information that media writers struggle to understand and present. It is the starting point for most media writing, whether the writing is intended for print, broadcast or public relations use.

We refer to news as "bursts" because of the very nature of news: It often "explodes" onto the scene, scattering information in all directions. The media writer must collect these pieces and arrange them for the audience in a faithful reproduction of the event.

For some people news is truly *new* information; for others it is *updated* information or a new wrinkle on a familiar theme. Most people, however, consider news any *break from normalcy*. The effective media writer must be able to recognize, evaluate and present such information.

Two important characteristics of the news are timeliness and prominence. That's hard to dispute, but we'd like you to consider two more attributes: breathlessness and economy.

Real news rushes at you, in the voice of a breathless messenger. Real news wastes neither words nor time in presenting the message. Such urgency signals the media writer that this information has real value; it creates a distinction between the somber reporting of the Challenger spacecraft explosion and the sensational tabloid storytelling of a man, crippled for 20 years, who "miraculously" walks after sitting on a porcupine.

Chapters 7–10 examine what we call the "news burst": how it develops, how media writers evaluate its worth, how it is organized and how it is written. The chapters focus on techniques common to newswriting, whether for print, broadcast or public relations use. They also analyze the differences in newswriting for various media industries.

Let's get down to business.

What Is the News Burst?

We are a nation of news hounds.

We *must* have the latest information, be it about triumph or disaster. We seem to have a vast capacity for media messages about the stock market, drought in Sudan and Ethiopia, a premature infant's struggle for life, a gruesome murder trial, production of a new sports car, arguments over seat belt legislation, a nurses' strike and, yes, even the sex life of a politician. But we also are a fickle audience, easily bored. Give us new and stimulating messages, we demand. Give us constant bursts of news.

As media writers, we must understand the seemingly insatiable appetites of our audiences—and their varied tastes. However, we must not overlook the universal characteristics of information we call news:

— It is *new* (or seems so). It has not happened before. It may come without warning, like a bridge collapse during rush-hour traffic.

There may have been some warning, as in the explosion of Mount St. Helens, but the deadly volcanic eruption was a new and historic event. Such news may come unexpectedly during a scheduled event, like a city council meeting in which the city manager announces her resignation.

— It is *urgent.* When President John F. Kennedy was assassinated in Dallas in 1963, the pressure for information was so great that regular broadcast programming was suspended and extra newspaper editions were issued. More than 20 years later, a nation mourned the deaths of astronauts killed in the explosion of a shuttle spacecraft. The media reaction was the same as that after the JFK assassination—even swifter because of improvements in technology. This tells us something about the "pecking order" of news events. News of less urgency, such as a house fire with no injuries, is placed lower on the list of "must run" stories than, for example, a report of the shooting death of a police officer during a convenience store robbery. Urgency does not have to have death or injury as its chief characteristic, but it must have the quality of breathlessness that speeds the information to the audience. That doesn't imply, however, that important context and background have to be sacrificed.

— It reports on *change.* Not all change is urgent, but some changes can have significant effects. For example, a dramatic increase in rates for medical care is a change that affects most of the population. Media writers must explain *what* these changes are and *why* they occurred.

— It involves *prominent people.* When a private plane crashes with the loss of four lives, that story may seem newsworthy but not particularly urgent. If the dead are unknown to the mass audience, information about the crash seems distant and abstract. However, if one of the dead is a movie star, the crash story becomes more important to more people because of audience association with a familiar name. Another example: It's not news when a golfer accidentally hits his companion with a golf ball, but if the errant golfer is former President Gerald Ford, his prominence attracts widespread media attention.

— It is *close to home.* We naturally pay more attention to what happens nearest to us. A rampaging flood that claims 50 lives in Afghanistan has less impact on a small U.S. community than does a house fire that kills three children in that community. The proximity factor cannot be overlooked when determining what information is of interest to your audience.

These characteristics of news reveal that an audience is bound together by common curiosity and environment. People want to know: What happened? What is going to happen? When, where, why and how? These common concerns of an audience reveal a more general characteristic of the news, which should never be overlooked, regardless of the media industry delivering the message:

— *It affects the lives and attitudes of your audience.* News of federal tax reform may affect consumer spending and saving habits. News of a radiation leak at a nuclear power plant may have an impact on attitudes about construction of a plant in a community. News of lower interest rates may stimulate home purchases. This is information that writers and editors present because it is "news you can use." As society becomes increasingly complex, people turn to clear and accessible information for guidance.

Some information, however, is packaged as news although it doesn't affect a wide audience, isn't particularly urgent, isn't close to home and doesn't involve a prominent person. Consider the opening paragraph of a story distributed through a nationwide news service:

An animal handler at the Fort Worth Zoo died today when a 4-ton elephant knocked him to the ground and stepped on his head.

Such information falls into the so-called "gee whiz" category of news. Although such information is definitely a break from normalcy, it gives people currency for conversation but little else. Of course, people involved with the Fort Worth Zoo and the family of the victim are affected; this shows how reactions to and uses of news vary.

How news functions in today's media

News is the power plant of our colossal information machine. The output of such power obviously is intended to inform and educate, but it also may persuade and entertain. It may account for only 30 percent of newspaper and magazine space and less than 20 percent of local broadcast programming, but it still holds a cherished place in our society because people want to know what has happened and what may or will happen. In this sense news provides social cohesion: It is a glue that binds a people together.

The media develop, acquire, produce and channel the news to an eager public. The media must determine when an event is newsworthy; they must also calculate how long such an event remains news. This is often referred to as the gatekeeping function of the media. Media gatekeepers know well what sociologist Michael Schudson means when he talks of the "continuous present tense" of news focus:

Events drop into the news media like pebbles in a pool of water. The first day, one sees only the immediate "plunk" into the pool. That plunk is what journalists imagine all journalism to be: hard, fast, new, breaking, well-defined, a story that any fool would recognize as news. But if the pebble sinks without a trace, no one will ever remember it. Stories that matter are stories that persist and take different turns over days or weeks or longer. With an important "plunk," as time passes, the story grows, the ripples spread out into the past and the future, the reverberations to past and future become the new context for the story.*

Most news follows a rather predictable process, which includes the following:

1. An event happens. Media writers receive signals of that event through their news-gathering process. They evaluate this information for its newsworthiness, deciding whether to follow up on the story and how much emphasis to give it.

2. By disseminating their information through traditional news channels, media writers signal the audience. Interest develops and heightens. Media stimulate that interest by giving more attention than usual to the story, enhancing their reputations as well as increasing readership and viewership.

---

*Michael Schudson, "What Time Means in a News Story," Occasional Paper No. 4, Aug. 1986, Gannett Center for Media Studies, Columbia University.

3. The action or "fallout" resulting from this event causes a reaction. Schudson's "ripple effect" is evident here. The story begins to branch out, and new events develop with a life of their own.

4. Some resolution is reached. The story closes, becomes history.

5. A look to the future may be needed. Some analysis of the event may be done.

Let's examine an obvious news event and see if it follows this process:

1. A DC-10 jumbo jet is forced to make a violent, twisting maneuver to avoid a twin-engine plane directly in its path over a metropolitan airport. Only minor injuries to jostled passengers are reported. Using interviews with airport officials, airline representatives and some airline passengers, media writers file their stories for print and broadcast use.

2. The audience learns of the story through traditional channels. Because a major tragedy was narrowly averted, interest in this story will remain high for longer than usual.

3. Two days after the incident, the jet pilot files a complaint. The Federal Aviation Administration launches an investigation. Several other airline pilots complain that they had similar incidents happen at this airport but that the FAA never made its investigations public. In addition, an air controller on medical leave because of job stress reveals that the control tower at the airport is dangerously understaffed. Reacting to the "ripple effect," the media communicate all these developments to their audiences.

4. Because no death, serious injury or financial loss occurred, the value of this story finally drops in the minds of the story editors. No new disclosures surface that would sustain interest in this near miss.

5. However, several stories that focus on illegal use of airline flight paths by small aircraft and on inadequate staffing and training of flight controllers appear in the media. Analyzing why near misses occur at this and other airports, these stories show how news goes beyond the burst stage and provides perspective and correlation of other information.

People often tire of certain news and seek new information and perspectives. That is why editors feel compelled to produce fresh news, as if a three-day-old story were taking on the look of wilted lettuce. This puts pressure on media writers to get new angles, fresh approaches, for their messages. Despite this pressure, however, the news does have a fairly standard format.

The common look of news

People who write the news usually do so with common purposes: to inform, to educate, to affect opinion and perhaps to stimulate some action. The quality of writing is central to these purposes; if the information is difficult to follow because of problems of organization, clarity and style, confusion will take the place of comprehension.

Let's examine a news event and see how various media industries present information about it.

Here are the facts:

— Tommy Anderson is a 5-year-old boy who must have open-heart surgery to repair a life-threatening valve defect.

— He lives in a low-income, single-parent household. His mother has a part-time job but must also care for Tommy and his two brothers. She receives some government assistance but has no medical insurance.

— The mother needs to raise money for medical bills, but she faces a more threatening problem: Tommy has the rarest of all eight blood groups: AB negative. The hospital says it must have 10 pints before the operation can take place.

What characteristics of this news will media outlets react to in organizing and presenting this information? Review the list at the beginning of this chapter, and you will see that the media likely will focus on *urgency*. The youngster may take on some prominence as his story becomes well-known, but now the focus is on a life-threatening situation, and the public will be asked to help.

The daily newspaper might begin with this approach:

Unless he receives donations of a rare blood type soon, 5-year-old Tommy Anderson will be unable to have the heart operation that may save his life.

Tommy needs at least 10 pints of AB negative blood available during the operation. That is the rarest of all blood groups, his doctors say.

Working with the PR representative of the blood bank, a radio station might create this public service announcement:

You've heard about 5-year-old Tommy Anderson. You know he needs our help. He needs our money for his open-heart surgery, and he desperately must have our blood.

Unfortunately, he must have the rare AB negative type. The Urban Blood Bank tells us that only one person in 167 has that type and that only 40 percent of that group may be eligible to donate.

If you have this blood type, won't you please call the Blood Bank at 686-7777 or this station at 484-1000?

Tommy's life may be depending on your call.

A television news account might show video interviews with Tommy and his mother, his doctors and the blood bank. This might be the lead-in to the story, spoken by the announcer on camera:

A 5-YEAR-OLD METROPOLIS BOY IS IN A RACE FOR HIS LIFE . . . TO FIND A RARE BLOOD TYPE NEEDED FOR HIS OPEN-HEART SURGERY.

AS HELEN MARSHALL REPORTS, PEOPLE ALL OVER THE COMMUNITY ARE WORKING TO HELP TOMMY ANDERSON WIN HIS RACE. . . .

All three examples focus on the obvious: the urgency of the child's plight. Money is an issue because of the lack of medical insurance, but that is not as urgent as the need for blood.

As this news story develops, the media will look for new angles. For example, have donors come forth? Do any of these donors have interesting stories? One donor, for example, may have traveled from another state to Metropolis to meet Tommy and donate blood.

Who writes the news?

People who write the news don't necessarily have similar training and perspectives. They are not all educated in schools of journalism; some have studied other disciplines but have received important on-the-job training. An internship is a valuable source of early training regardless of a writer's academic major, as is experience writing for campus publications and broadcast outlets.

Once on the job, all media writers recognize the value of speed. To be timely and to meet important deadlines, writers must organize and present their information quickly. People who write the news must constantly fight the jitters brought on by deadline pressures. Such anxiety applies to the newspaper reporter trying to organize and write a story about a major fire in less than an hour; to the television reporter, just back with video of violence between striking machinists and replacement workers, deciding what visuals and interviews to use while organizing announcer and reporter copy, all within 45 minutes; and to the public relations representative, who is "asked" by the company vice president to prepare an opening statement for a press conference to start in less than 30 minutes.

Sharing similar news values and organizing according to time-honored formats make it possible for writers to work quickly. Beginning media writers are given relatively simple assignments that they can research and organize quickly. The beginner finds that a story format focusing on the most important topic first and then dealing with others in descending importance is a valuable organizational tool. With this structure in place, the writer can fill in the blanks with information relevant to a particular story. The writer can present that information clearly and simply.

As writers master the simple news story, they are assigned topics of greater complexity. Speed remains a factor, but the writers' facility with organization and language assures they will meet deadlines.

Chapter 8 will deal with the simple approach—techniques basic to newswriting. Chapter 9 will deal with more complex newswriting techniques. Chapter 10 will review the similarities and differences between print, broadcast and public relations newswriting. By examining techniques and studying story examples in these chapters, you should soon understand the pattern and process of today's newswriting.

A word about style

Some newswriting students express fear that the "news style" will turn them into journalistic robots who depend on stock phrases and trite expressions to reach their audience. It is true that print space and air time limit the news burst to only the plain facts, clothed in direct, simple language. However, that is only the beginning. The basic news style is simply a technique for quickly getting into a body of information and announcing it to an audience. What happens *after* the news burst stage says a lot about a media writer.

Writers will always use the gift of language to create their own style. This style becomes a second signature to the byline or story credit. But style can vary according to the aim of the media outlet and the expectations of its audience. In the news burst, however, our style *must* be clear and succinct because audience interest may dwindle in the face of a rambling narrative.

Media writers must understand their audience as well as the mission of their media outlet when they make style decisions. As writing teacher Roy Peter Clark of the Poynter Institute says, "Good writers are concerned with the needs of the readers."

Don't let your style get in the way of your message. Let it carry the audience into the story, not away from it.

Writing the
News Burst

Take 1

May doesn't seem a likely month for a snowstorm.

But in western mountains, heavy snow driven by 60-mph winds isn't surprising, even in early June. So when 13 members of a high school climbing party failed to make their May 12 return from a one-day trek to the summit of Oregon's Mount Hood, concern about the group rapidly turned to fear.

A news story—about tragedy and heroic rescue—was beginning.

For the next three days, information would burst out between long periods of silence and anxiety.

— Two members of the climbing team descended the mountain the morning of May 13 to reveal that the others were trapped in a blinding snowstorm and took refuge.

— A search team found the bodies of three students at the 8,400-foot level of the mountain on May 14.

— On May 15, in the early evening—three days after the climbers were to have returned—searchers poking the snow with 8-foot probes discovered a snow cave containing eight people.

— The eight were flown to Portland hospitals. Six of them died; two survived, despite frozen limbs and dangerously weak heartbeats.

This story, reported by scores of newspapers, broadcast stations and magazines, met the important criteria of news: It was new, extremely urgent, and relevant to climbers and skiers; and because it involved many young people, it attracted attention beyond the region.

This was a *major* story. It meant working fast, sometimes almost automatically. Even seasoned writers sent out on this story depended on their early training, which taught them to write the most basic stories quickly and accurately. That training focused on these areas:

1. *Making news judgments.* This involves sorting through information and deciding what is necessary and appropriate to present to the audience as news.

2. *Choosing story focus.* After selecting the elements of news to include in the story, the writer must emphasize the most important element. That is the beginning of the story, what happens in that first breathless burst: "Hey! Guess what happened?"

3. *Writing the lead paragraph.* In straight newswriting, the lead works to bring the audience into the story. In the most basic of news stories, that opening summarizes information while emphasizing a key point.

4. *Organizing the body of the story.* Some novice writers think the rest of a story falls into place once the lead is fashioned. They're mistaken. There's a natural, logical sequence to each story. That sequence isn't chronological—it answers questions that naturally flow from the previous information.

This chapter examines these four areas, as well as techniques specific to print, broadcast and public relations writing. Chapter 9 will deal with more advanced writing techniques.

Learning news values

Not all the day's information that qualifies as news appears in a newspaper or a television newscast. One reason is that the sheer volume of news in a 24-hour period can't be accommodated; another is that the media present a lot more than news. Examine your daily newspaper, and you'll see a lot more advertisements than news. You'll see a lot of entertainment and advice, too. It's rare to have more than a five-minute newscast hourly on your local radio station, and you'll probably never see more than a one-hour local television newscast.

The media professionals who decide what's news do so under rigid time and space constraints. Therefore, it's not surprising that these pros depend on a fairly rigid formula for choosing what enters media channels as news. In Chapter 7 we discussed the universal characteristics of news. Those characteristics, or values, influence a formula based on a set of agreed-upon values that help define the news. These include time, proximity, prominence, conflict, consequence and human interest. Naturally, none of these news values stands alone. The *who, what, when, where, why* and *how* are usually important in a story; sometimes, however, the *what* may be more important than the *who*, the *when* more important than the *how*. Let's examine each and look at media writing that focuses on those values.

Time

The news is supposed to be *new*. The audience generally will be interested in the *what* of a story but will always want the *when* to be as current as possible. When people have current information, they can do something with it, as in this story excerpt:

A natural gas explosion this morning closed all lanes of State Highway 202 in downtown Circleville. No injuries were reported.

The 6 a.m. blast from the underground pipeline made a crater 10 feet deep and 40 feet wide. A highway official said two hours later that the four-lane road will be closed for at least two weeks.

The speed with which this news is brought to the audience is critical. Naturally, the broadcast media (especially radio) will be fastest with the information. The print media also will focus on the time element as a matter of record but will be able to spend more time on *why* this event happened. Consider another example:

For the first time in its 80-year history, the Mid-States Oil Company has declared an operating loss, the company treasurer announced today.

Sarah Kingsbury said that the normal $2-per-share dividend would not be issued on Friday.

The company suffered a loss of $28 million on $165 million in revenues, Kingsbury explained. "It may be two years before we can issue another dividend," she said.

Many people will be affected by this bad news. The two-year delay of new dividends will also affect new investments.

Proximity

We are a parochial people. We seem to be most interested in what is closest to us because we can identify most easily with it. Good media writers must be aware of this interest but also must be wary of pandering to such provincialism. For example, an audience in Wichita might not pay a lot of attention to this story:

QUITO, Ecuador—Eight workmen died when a three-story building collapsed on them, a government official announced this morning.

However, the Wichita audience would naturally be attracted to a story that takes place in their town:

Three members of a Wichita family, including a 3-month-old girl, died this morning when their mobile home exploded into flames.

Information that affects our community and people we may know obviously grabs our attention more firmly than does a story of tragedy thousands of miles away.

Prominence

People suddenly thrust into the media spotlight and those long accustomed to its glare are people we somehow seem to know. They are part of the cast of characters in our daily conversation—and they certainly are part of our media diet. Sometimes the glare is worldwide:

NEW YORK—Bernhard Goetz was found innocent today of all attempted murder charges but was convicted of illegally possessing the weapon he used to shoot four teenagers in a subway train 2½ years ago.

The intense media attention on the so-called subway vigilante made him a world figure for a time; we could not ignore his prominence. But lesser prominence can also team up with proximity to make local media take note of a well-known figure in their town:

Midville Mayor John Harris was among 80 passengers killed yesterday when a Trans-America jet crashed on takeoff from Cleveland's Hopkins Airport.

Although the 80 deaths make this a tragic story that would be covered by the media regardless of the prominence of the victims, local media will react more intensely if one of the dead is a prominent citizen of their community.

Conflict

Confrontation involving people and institutions is an important media staple because it tells us of discord and of a breakdown in society's machinery. It's not a break from normalcy when things are running well, but when the system starts to break down, the audience wants to be witness to the conflict:

Four members of the Fern Ridge School Board will be the subject of a recall election Nov. 4 as a result of a successful petition drive by members of a group calling itself "Parents for Better Education."

By focusing on the *what, how* and *why* of this conflict, the media help explain this breakdown and perhaps point the way toward resolution of the conflict. Sometimes, however, the media can only reflect the status of an on-going conflict:

Three striking Puyallup teachers were arrested this morning after they allegedly hit replacement teachers with rotten fruit.

A total of 15 teachers and aides have now been arrested during the 9-day-old strike, according to the Pierce County Sheriff's Department.

Consequence

It's not enough to report the bare facts of an event. People want to know the *effects* of that happening. The results, or consequences, can create a whole new set of events:

More than 50 senior citizens are homeless this morning in the aftermath of a fire that destroyed their low-income apartment complex in downtown Flint last night.

What will happen to these people? It is miraculous that no one was hurt, but how will these seniors, dependent on a government rent subsidy, replace their precious belongings and find suitable housing? Concern about these consequences prompts the media to pursue this story.

Human interest

Taken literally, *human interest* should refer to all things that interest humans. But in news parlance it involves what is unusual, humorous, sad or ironic. News in this category certainly is timely, but it rarely deals with urgency or prominence. The local angle—proximity—also is not important, as this kind of news tells a more universal story that touches all of us in one way or another. Here are some typical human interest ideas:

— *Humor.* A Chicago woman, angry that her purse has been snatched from her twice in the past year, just after she had cashed her social security check, loses another purse yesterday.

But this time she is smiling. She had filled an old purse with an unusual currency—neighborhood "dog doo." Now she wonders, with great relish, what the snatcher said when he opened the purse. . . .

— *Irony and tragedy.* A Cleveland woman, who lost a leg to cancer as a teenager and who received an artificial one on a national TV show so that she could remain on the cheerleading squad, marries her high school sweetheart.

Two years later, she thinks she is pregnant. Instead, she discovers that her cancer has spread. She dies five months later and is eulogized for her tenacity and courage.

— *The unusual.* The United States Senate pressures the U.S. Department of Transportation to cease a bizarre testing procedure: using corpses to test the reliability of air bags during auto crashes.

The department complies but argues that cadavers were more reliable than dummies.

Although stories of this type encourage colorful writing, they don't occupy much space. Their style is more open, and that makes them more difficult to write than so-called straight news. But they are so interesting and compelling that the content holds the audience. Here is a wire service story, "Man Shoots Wrong Woman":

ROCHESTER, N.Y.—A retired Army sergeant fatally shot a 70-year-old woman as she left Mother's Day church services, then admitted he mistook her for his estranged wife.

"I'm sorry about the other woman. I meant to kill my wife," Percy C. Washington told police Sunday after he surrendered and learned of his mistake. "But I forgot my glasses," he told investigators.

Yes, truth *is* stranger than fiction. That's why human interest stories will always have broad appeal.

Understanding your community and its people will bring you closer to what they consider news. Observing what media professionals choose as news will show you the industry standard of what's news. Following your own instincts also may teach you a few things about news.

With this information in hand, it's time to turn to how and why we emphasize certain newsworthy elements as we organize our story. It is the first important step in a series of critical decisions.

Finding your focus

Greek mythology tells us that before Theseus became king of Athens, he went into a labyrinth and slew the Minotaur, a bullheaded guy with a monstrous appetite for kids.

That was the easy part for Theseus.

The really tough part was getting out of the maze. He did, of course, and went on to a royal future.

Modern writers face labyrinths in their media work. They must sort out a maze of facts, opinions and hype, find the central points and avoid the confusion of false twists and turns.

Focusing on where you want to go in a story is the best way to get through it; that emphasis creates a structure, or path, for the entire story. *Everything follows it.*

Choosing your focus will also suggest how you will organize your lead. Your lead then suggests the rest of your story organization.

Let's consider focus as we review a reporter's notes about an attempted robbery. Keep asking "What happened?"—and when you can, answer that question in one short sentence:

— A man (later identified as Carl Johansen, a transient) straps himself to a device he claims is connected to 10 sticks of dynamite.

— He walks into the downtown branch of the Thomasville Bank at 10 a.m. He says he will blow up the bank unless tellers give him $50,000 in small bills.

— A police tactical unit arrives and tries to talk Johansen into leaving the bank. At about 10:30, he agrees to let everyone out of the bank (about 35 customers and employees), except the manager, Carla Redding.

— Shortly after 11, manager Redding knocks down Johansen, runs out of the bank and yells to officers that the man doesn't have a bomb. Police rush in and arrest the man, who is 27.

— Redding, 37, said: "I yelled that the guy's bomb was a fake. I finally got a good look and saw that all he had were some safety flares."

— Johansen's wrist was broken when he was knocked down. He is now in the Thomasville City-County Jail and is charged with attempted bank robbery and second-degree assault. Charges of kidnapping are pending.

So—what happened? Let's examine some possibilities:

Police arrested a transient who tried to rob a Thomasville bank this morning.

(Ho-hum. . . . There's got to be more to the story than that.)

A transient who claimed to have a bomb took hostages in a Thomasville bank, released them and then was arrested after it was discovered that all he had were safety flares.

(More detail here—too much, in fact. This broadens the focus too much and still misses a central point.)

The Thomasville Bank manager foiled a robbery this morning when she knocked down a man who claimed he was a "human bomb."

(This is a better focus. The person who ended the standoff must be mentioned. The story can be built around her, the human bomb, the hostages and the police. But selection of manager Redding creates a common pathway for the entire story.)

Focusing calls for narrowing your view about where to begin your story. It calls for the cutting of details that can wait or be eliminated. It's not an easy process, but it helps you begin your story with confidence. As an example of this, let's move on to lead writing and see how our focus translates into a relatively easy arrangement of words.

Writing that lead

*Like all good journalists, we shall present our facts
in an order that will satisfy the famous five W's:
wow, whoopee, wahoo, why-not and whew.*

—Tom Robbins
Even Cowgirls Get the Blues

You've sorted through your news values. You've focused. You have some idea about your direction. Now's the time to write.

In basic newswriting this rule is paramount: *Be complete, but keep it simple.* Focus on the simple first, and then examine how completely you've done your job.

The *lead* is the drum major of your story. It struts out, ahead of the rest, calling attention to the rest of the parade. But the lead can't be all flash. It must inform as directly and as concisely as possible.

Let's look again at the Thomasville Bank robbery attempt. In looking for a story focus, we fixed our attention on the manager's "disarming" of the human bomb. It was a potentially serious story that ended with no harm. To develop this and other leads, we suggest a four-step process:

1. *Hey!!! Guess what happened?* Get this first breathless burst out of the way, so you can really focus. You're at the scene of the Thomasville Bank robbery attempt, and someone rushes up to you and asks, "What happened?"

   Application: Chances are you'll repeat a chronology. "Some guy came into the bank and threatened to blow it up. But the bank manager knocked him down and ran out. The police got him, and he didn't have a bomb, only safety flares!" You've just provided a reasonable capsule for conversation. However, people want specifics, so you'll have to do a more detailed summary for media use.

2. *The headline approach.* Written correctly, the headline is a skeleton of the story. It should be direct and informative. "Challenger explodes; 7 die" doesn't tell the entire story, but it is a significant start. Writing a sample headline for your story will suggest what might be contained in the all-important lead. Examine your local daily newspaper and see how a headline often relates directly to the core of a story. Just for fun (and also to help you focus), try to create a headline of not more than five words.

Application: For the bank story, here are some suggestions:

BANK MANAGER FOILS ROBBERY ATTEMPT

BANK MANAGER "DISARMS" HUMAN BOMB

BANK MANAGER DEFUSES ROBBERY TRY

In writing the lead, you take this skeleton and add just a bit of flesh. Let's put more meat on in two stages; in step three, write a simple sentence that picks up where the headline stops.

3. *The simple sentence.* Now write a simple sentence (one subject, one verb, with a supplementary phrase or two) that captures the essence of the event. You want to base this sentence on your headline. It is possible to pack *who, what, where, when, why* and *how* into this sentence.

Application:

The bank manager (who) knocks down a robbery suspect (what) today (when) in the Thomasville Bank's downtown branch (where) after seeing safety flares, not a bomb, attached to the man (why).

Although this is a simple sentence (only one subject, one verb), it's too complicated. Media writers are selective; in a lead they use information that focuses rather than complicates. Here's a more economical option:

The manager of the Thomasville Bank's downtown branch halted a robbery this morning by knocking down the suspect and escaping from him.

Note that the writing is in the past tense because the event has already happened; headlines retain what is called the "historical present." The who, what, when and how are included here. But we haven't learned the why—and it's not clear from the sentence that the robbery actually took place in the bank. One more try:

The manager of Thomasville Bank's downtown branch foiled a robbery there this morning by knocking down the suspect, a 27-year-old transient.

Note that this version closely follows our first headline (BANK MAN-AGER FOILS ROBBERY ATTEMPT). Now you can work with this "raw material" in the final step.

4. *The more-detailed sentence.* A traditional news lead tries to summarize without being wordy. For this reason, most lead paragraphs usually have fewer than 30 words. This is not that difficult to do. Include one main thought, build around it and avoid repetition.

Application: The previous lead attempts do a pretty fair job, but they leave out an important detail: The man claimed to have a bomb and on the strength of that took hostages and held police at bay. Can you insert something about the bomb/safety flare issue in the lead?

The manager of Thomasville Bank's downtown branch foiled a robbery attempt there this morning when she knocked down a man claiming to have a bomb.

This lead sets the scene for the rest of the story. Now is the time to examine the fourth part of a writer's basic task: organizing the rest of the story.

Organizing the body

A good lead will suggest story structure and flow. Using the Thomasville Bank story, consider what facts were *not* used in the opening paragraph and what questions naturally arise from the information offered there.

The facts not used that deserve some emphasis include the taking and releasing of hostages, the arrival of police, the bank manager's discovery that the robbery suspect's "bomb" was really safety flares, and the arrest of the suspect.

Questions the audience might ask include: Was anyone hurt? What are the names of the manager and the suspect? What did the man want?

Following the lead of your opening paragraph, make a list of these details in the order you will use them in the body of your story. Here's our suggested order for the Thomasville story:

1. *Lead:* Bank manager knocks down robbery suspect claiming to have bomb.

2. Name and age of manager; why she acted; length of "siege."

3. Name and age of robbery suspect; charges.

4. How situation began; taking and releasing of hostages.

5. Injuries?

This is not a long list because this is a basic news story. (We'll get to more complicated ones in the next chapter.) Just to see how this process works, let's write five paragraphs that correspond with the five areas we've outlined. These paragraphs present information in a *declining order of importance*—what journalists long have called the "inverted pyramid":

The manager of Thomasville Bank's downtown branch foiled a robbery attempt there this morning when she knocked down a man claiming to have a bomb.

Carla Redding, 37, made her move when she noticed the man was carrying only safety flares. The suspect had walked into the bank an hour earlier, claiming he had 10 sticks of dynamite strapped to himself.

Police arrested Carl Johansen, a 27-year-old transient, when Redding fled the bank shortly after 11. He is being held in the Thomasville City-County Jail, charged with attempted bank robbery and second-degree assault.

Redding was the only hostage left in the bank after Johansen had released about 35 employees and customers. Johansen reportedly said he would blow up the bank unless he received $50,000 in small bills.

The incident resulted in only one injury—to Johansen. He suffered a broken wrist when Redding knocked him to the ground.

This organization allows the audience to stop reading or listening to a story after the first few paragraphs without losing the most important information. The less important details are buried deeper in the body of the story. The inverted pyramid structure is tied to the tradition of Civil War reporters who squeezed in their important information for fear that the telegraph might fail during their story transmission. It also reflects the concern that picky, hurried readers might not take the time to read an entire story.

To recap the writing process:

— Summarize the story in your lead paragraph.

— Present related information in subsequent paragraphs, in order of descending importance. Add detail that builds on the core of the story.

— Your story ends when further information becomes repetitive or unnecessary. This is also influenced by space and time allocations for the story.

Organizing the story for broadcast

Broadcast writers preparing a story about the Thomasville Bank incident would need to consider a few style and format concerns not applicable to print. Broadcast veterans usually cite these differences:

— The language is more conversational and informal.

— The story is briefer because of time constraints.

— The format must allow placement of audio and video information.

Keeping these differences in mind, let's review the print version of the bank story and see what, if anything, should be changed. (Remember that style differences are not indicative of differences in news values.)

1. *The story may need a more informal lead-in.* Broadcast reporters often use a "throwaway lead"—usually a sentence fragment designed to attract the audience. Here are two examples, with a full sentence following each throwaway:

IN MARION, UTAH, A VIOLENT END TO A
13-DAY STANDOFF.
   A SHOOTOUT BETWEEN POLICE AND A
VIOLENT POLYGAMIST CLAN HAS LEFT ONE

POLICE OFFICER DEAD AND THE FAMILY'S
LEADER CRITICALLY WOUNDED.

MORE TROUBLE FOR OLIVER NORTH
TODAY.
   HIS ASSOCIATE GLENN ROBINETTE
TOLD INVESTIGATORS AT TODAY'S IRAN-
CONTRA HEARINGS THAT NORTH USED
MONEY FROM THE IRAN ARMS SALES TO
PURCHASE A SECURITY SYSTEM AT
NORTH'S HOME.

As you can see, the throwaway is a headline of sorts. Perhaps it's more of a label, but it does announce what's coming up. Some broadcast writers suggest that such an announcement helps the brain catch up with the ear. Would such an approach work for the Thomasville Bank story? Perhaps—let's try one.

ROBBERY ATTEMPT AT THE THOMASVILLE
BANK.
   THE MANAGER OF THE BANK'S
DOWNTOWN BRANCH FOILED THE TRY
WHEN SHE KNOCKED DOWN A MAN WHO
SAID HE HAD A BOMB.

This throwaway seems bland. It needs more power to attract the audience. It needs a better *sound:*

A ROBBER CAME UP EMPTY TODAY AT THE
THOMASVILLE BANK.

Sometimes broadcast writers prefer an opening sentence that is light and informal:

A THOMASVILLE BANK MANAGER IS ALSO
THE BANK'S HERO TODAY AFTER STOPPING
A ROBBERY ATTEMPT AT THE DOWNTOWN
BRANCH.

Or, for a lighter approach:

A ROBBERY TRY THIS MORNING AT THE
THOMASVILLE BANK TURNED OUT TO BE A
DUD.

The second example is similar to the print media's feature approach to newswriting. It uses informality and imagery.

2. *The bank story is brief enough.* The print version is only five paragraphs—a studio announcer could easily read it in less than one minute. Obviously, some broadcast stories are longer than others, but it's not unusual to have as many as 40 stories or "packages" in a one-hour newscast.

3. *Several audio and video opportunities exist for the bank story.* In a radio newscast, some tape "actualities" of the bank manager and a police official commenting on the incident would add more color and personality to the story. Similarly, the video "bite" possibilities are great: the bank interior, an on-camera interview with the manager, the arrest of the suspect. This information—sound and action—is not possible in print, although the still photograph and the story with liberal quotations add greater dimension to that medium's presentation. Let's consider television's approach to the story and add visual bites to the information. In this format you will see directions in the script specifying who is to read the information and what tape is to be added.

STUDIO ANNOUNCER: A ROBBERY THIS MORNING AT THE THOMASVILLE BANK TURNED OUT TO BE A DUD. HERE IS STANTON LONG WITH THE REPORT.

LONG WITH BANK EXTERIOR TAPE: THIRTY-SIX PEOPLE WERE IN THE THOMASVILLE DOWNTOWN BRANCH AROUND 10 WHEN A 27-YEAR-OLD MAN REPORTEDLY THREATENED TO BLOW UP THE BANK.

HE DEMANDED $50,000, SAYING HE WOULD DETONATE 10 STICKS OF DYNAMITE HE CLAIMED WERE STRAPPED TO HIS BODY.

THAT NEVER HAPPENED, THANKS TO THE SHARP EYES OF BANK MANAGER CARLA REDDING.

REDDING TAPE: WE TALKED THE MAN INTO RELEASING EVERYONE BUT ME. HE WAS GETTING NERVOUS AND SCRATCHING HIMSELF. THAT'S WHEN I NOTICED THAT ALL HE HAD ON HIMSELF WERE SAFETY FLARES.

LONG VOICE-OVER ARREST TAPE: REDDING KNOCKED DOWN THE MAN, WHO WAS LATER IDENTIFIED AS CARL JOHANSEN, A

TRANSIENT. SHE RAN OUT OF THE BANK,
AND POLICE RUSHED IN.
JOHANSEN WAS ARRESTED AND
CHARGED WITH ATTEMPTED BANK
ROBBERY AND SECOND DEGREE ASSAULT.

LONG AT BANK EXTERIOR: ONLY ONE INJURY
WAS REPORTED IN THE HOUR-LONG
INCIDENT. THAT WAS THE BROKEN WRIST
JOHANSEN SUFFERED WHEN THE 37-
YEAR-OLD REDDING KNOCKED HIM DOWN.
THIS IS STANTON LONG REPORTING.

This story is not much longer than the print version, but it definitely is more of a "package." The writer and producer had to coordinate copy and tape, providing essentially the same copy as the print version with the added benefit of videos of the bank, the hero and the suspect. In addition, an announcer introduced the story, and the on-scene reporter ended it.

If this seems like a bit of show biz to you, you're partially correct. There is pressure to use what the medium can provide; in the case of television good video competes with copy for the spotlight. Television can't be all "talking heads." As a visual medium, television must deliver compelling images. In the Thomasville Bank story the tape of the arrest, showing the suspect with the police, enhances the copy. However, the use of strong visuals doesn't diminish the need for effective copy connections and transitions.

Broadcast writing is not easy. It requires the same focusing and organizing skills as print. And the severe time constraints and technological considerations may make good writing for broadcast even harder. We'll examine this subject more in Chapter 9.

The public relations format

The successful public relations writer considers not only the audience and the medium, but also a third force: the client. An important function of public relations is to supply information to the public to benefit a client. Such information must be disseminated through the media to a properly targeted audience. Therefore, the traditional view of news isn't always upheld in the PR function—the publicity needs of the client generally are paramount. News professionals in both print and broadcast recognize the PR goals and try to reconcile any differences in favor of the broader audience.

Let's look at what the public relations department of KeyThrift, the corporation that owns the Thomasville Bank, would do with the story on their manager's heroism.

Several factors are important in understanding why KeyThrift's handling of this information will not be exactly the same as the media's immediate handling of the news:

1. The PR department's information on this story will not be as timely as the media's. Therefore, a new angle is important.

2. It is important to the company to downplay any negative information (like the hostages) and to put the firm in a favorable light.

3. The PR writer must consider both print and broadcast formats in any information release.

With those needs in mind, let's examine how KeyThrift announces that the company has awarded manager Redding a distinguished service award, as well as a two-week paid vacation to Jamaica, for her heroism. The news now is that she has been rewarded. The news release gives some background on the robbery attempt, but the danger to customers is not emphasized. In addition, the release gives some attention to the parent organization, KeyThrift.

FOR IMMEDIATE RELEASE

Carla Redding, manager of the downtown branch of the Thomasville Bank, has been honored for her heroism during last week's robbery attempt at the bank.

KeyThrift Corp., parent firm of a four-state banking chain that includes Thomasville, has given Redding its distinguished service award and a two-week paid vacation in Jamaica.

(The PR department gives its version of the latest news as well as citing information about KeyThrift.)

Redding, a 10-year KeyThrift employee, was held hostage last Thursday when a man claiming to have a bomb demanded $50,000 from the bank.

After persuading the man to release 35 other people held in the bank, the 37-year-old mother of three knocked the man down when she noticed that his "bomb" was nothing but safety flares.

The man has been charged with attempted bank robbery and is awaiting trial. Only the suspect was injured in the robbery try. He broke his wrist when Redding knocked him down.

(Appropriate background is given here. The bank's image is well-served by pointing out that its heroic manager is also the mother of three children and that only the robbery suspect was injured.)

"I am justifiably proud of Carla Redding," said C. Grant Stanfield, KeyThrift president. "Not only did she ensure the safety of her customers and fellow workers, but she used good judgment in bringing this incident to an end."

(Note that the president's quotation doesn't dwell on the negative aspects of a bank robbery. The incident had a happy, safe ending, and that's the chosen focus.)

Redding was a teller and loan officer at the Thomasville Bank's Riverfront branch before taking over as manager of the downtown branch last year.

The three Thomasville banks are part of a 38-bank KeyThrift operation, which held more than $600 million in savings and checking accounts during the last fiscal year.

(A little background on Redding is followed by a corporate statement of health.)

Most PR writers understand that the media are not going to eagerly use everything that is sent their way. Some rewriting is to be expected; the important goal is to receive notice and mention for a positive story.

Although this release has a print orientation, it also is a signal to broadcast outlets for a possible package. To facilitate broadcast use, the PR writer may alert radio and TV stations to the availability of Redding and the KeyThrift president for an interview or may even supply some tape. The story as written is acceptable for the company newsletter or magazine.

Summing up

The beginning media writer would be wise to learn the basics of writing news from the print perspective and then become familiar with techniques of broadcast preparation and style. Such knowledge obviously is vital to the writer who desires to work in public relations.

To review the formats we've discussed so far, examine these story beginnings. Start with the PR writer's version, and then compare how print and broadcast journalists handled the story:

The PR news release

The State Board of Higher Education today voted to stop university investments in companies doing business in South Africa.

"This is a great blow against the tyranny of apartheid," said Chancellor Jim Clark after the board's vote. "We can hold our heads high."

The print media version

After rejecting student protests and faculty overtures for 10 years, a divided State Board of Higher Education today agreed to stop investing in companies that do business in South Africa.

By a 5–3 vote, the board set a Jan. 1 date for divestiture of all stocks, bonds and notes of firms operating in a country widely condemned for its apartheid policies.

The broadcast media version

A LONG-AWAITED TRIUMPH FOR ANTI-APARTHEID FORCES:

THE STATE BOARD OF HIGHER EDUCATION SAYS IT WILL NO LONGER INVEST IN COMPANIES THAT DO BUSINESS IN SOUTH AFRICA.

THE BOARD'S VOTE TODAY WAS 5–3. BUT IT WAS SWEET NONETHELESS FOR THE UNIVERSITY COALITION FOR MORALITY. KIMBERLY ROGERS REPORTS. . . .

Mastering basic newswriting takes time and experience. Print and broadcast writers working on the Mount Hood climbing tragedy combined basic skills with their speed and experience to handle this fast-paced, complicated story. These skills are also needed for public relations writers; their handling of the news burst needs the same speedy but precise approach.

In Chapter 9 we'll continue our examination of the organization and presentation of news. We'll focus on other approaches to leads, handling of quotations and methods of transitions. Let's call it Take 2.

Writing the News Burst

Take 2

Mastering basic newswriting is a lot like building a simple shelter. Your refuge from wind, rain and cold may be a canvas lean-to or four plywood walls with a tin roof; however, your Spartan creation is for survival only. You don't worry about where to put the gourmet kitchen or marble washroom; you're happy enough to have protection from the elements.

A basic news story provides enough information to answer fundamental questions. It's not rich in detail; it is simple in layout and function. Whereas many people can build survival shelters, only a true artisan can create an elegant home. So it is with newswriting. A beginning news writer can fashion a summary lead and several explanatory paragraphs, but going successfully beyond that stage requires an apprenticeship that exposes the writer to other techniques—and to other tools.

Moving past basic newswriting is not simply a matter of length. It is a matter of depth of both information and understanding. Without skills honed by experience and criticism, a long story is nothing more than an oversized lean-to. Whether your story is three or 30 paragraphs, the steps in basic newswriting are the same. However, three more advanced newswriting elements can help you move to a higher level of writing: understanding different types of leads, handling attribution and quotations, and creating effective transitions. These elements will assist you in improving your organization, detail and style of presentation. After discussing these elements, we will examine several stories to see how the newswriting has moved to a higher level.

Lead variations

Most of the leads we have shown thus far have been direct constructions that summarize an event. But leads also can begin with a question, quotation, narrative, direct address or description to draw the audience into the story. You have already seen how broadcasting media sometimes use a sentence fragment called the throwaway to introduce a story (Chapter 8).

The question lead

An opening question is intended to be provocative. It encourages interest while somewhat delaying the key point:

Will Clinton finally get its civic center?

Organizers of the $12 million project feel confident that voters will approve the East Broadway complex after three previous defeats at the polls.

Opponents, however, say the center bond issue will suffer its worst defeat ever in Tuesday's balloting.

The question lead must be used selectively. The readers of this story obviously are knowledgeable about an issue they have dealt with three times. A question about the center's fate seems appropriate—

and central to the story. It also has a good sound—this question would work well in broadcast. But remember: If you ask a question in a lead, be prepared to answer it in the next paragraph. However, be aware that many editors dislike the question lead when the construction merely delays important facts. For example, you could use a declarative sentence to inject some human interest into the civic center story:

A patient Hal Pfeifer thinks the fourth time will be the charm for Clinton's proposed civic center.

On the other hand, you could argue persuasively that the "fourth time" angle works well in question form:

Will the fourth time be the charm for the Clinton Civic Center?

Remember that question leads should be used sparingly and that you can't often go wrong with a well-crafted summary lead.

The quotation lead

Sometimes a key figure in the story makes a statement that sets an important tone. No amount of paraphrasing or summarizing would match its effectiveness:

"You deserve to die—and I wish it were in my power to make sure you do."
  With those words, a shaken, angry Circuit Court Judge Thomas Greenfield sentenced 19-year-old Benny Lansdowne to a 15-year prison term for the rape and torture of a 70-year-old Midville woman.

Again, the audience is already familiar with this story. A crime had been committed, the arrest made, the trial conducted. The power of the judge's words helps create a compelling lead.

The narrative lead

The opening for this story sets a scene and creates some suspense:

It didn't take Albany police officer William Craig long to find his man.

It was just a matter of following loud screams and curses.

In the sharp, twisted bramble of blackberry bushes on Huntington Avenue, there was Craig's quarry—wearing only his socks and clutching a can of beer.

This style works well with the human interest story, which is sometimes humorous, sometimes sad. It requires an intriguing opening to capture interest and then a fast-paced chronology to keep audience attention.

The direct-address lead

Taking the personal approach by speaking directly to your audience can be an effective way to begin the story—if the subject is appropriate:

As of today, you're working for yourself, not the government.

That's the assessment of the National Taxpayers' Union, which has calculated that you spend more than 40 percent of your working year making money to pay your federal, state and local taxes.

Obviously, the audience must have a keen interest in the story material to make the lead effective. The tone should be informal to avoid any hint of lecturing.

The descriptive lead

This approach, which sets the scene with vivid images, reveals the news while examining the environment of the event. It is particularly characteristic of sportswriting, as in Richard Hoffer's opening paragraphs about a heavyweight boxing match between Gerry Cooney and Michael Spinks:

ATLANTIC CITY, N.J.—It ended as it had once before, Gerry Cooney's eyes focused in a distant stare, his long, slightly knock-kneed legs

about to fold like a carpenter's rule. He wasn't
down, but he was out and, as far as the cruel
world of boxing is concerned, finally gone
as well.

This *Los Angeles Times* story, 23 paragraphs in all, was not created at
the writer's leisure. It was done on deadline—as a news burst—but it
was done with color and style. Somehow, for a story with a circuslike
atmosphere and macho posturing, it isn't enough to say:

Michael Spinks knocked down Gerry Cooney
twice in Round 5 of their Atlantic City bout
before referee Frank Cappuccino awarded
Spinks the victory on a technical knockout.

No, this story demands description. Descriptive newswriting requires
the ability to write creatively without fattening the prose. It must be
colorful, lean and fast.

Choosing a lead form is but another in a series of decisions all
media writers make in crafting their messages. The novice writer
should summarize the event and organize a possible presentation before deciding whether to vary the opening paragraph. An understanding of the story and of the audience, as well as the confidence to
handle a different opening, are important factors in this decision.

Attribution and quotations

When we connect a statement to its author or source, we *attribute* that
information. This adds to a story's value and credibility; the audience
realizes we have searched for information and sources. Attribution is
important when the audience would naturally wonder about the
source. Here's a sentence that needs attribution:

Property taxes will climb by 15 percent if
voters approve the Clinton Civic Center.

Who says so? This claim (which may be a fact) needs an author. Attribution helps the audience judge the truthfulness and context of
a statement. The following sentence, with attribution that identifies

the author and her position, gives the audience more complete information:

Property taxes will climb by 15 percent if voters approve the Clinton Civic Complex, charges Mavis Mates, head of Clinton Citizens for Fair Taxation.

Although the writer has attributed the claim of higher taxes, the audience may want additional information. For example, where did Mavis get her information? This is a predictable question. It is part of the natural flow or sequence of a story; the elements that make up this sequence require good transitions to make them clear. (More about this in the next section.)

Quotations bring both credibility and variety to a story. They are the mark of more advanced writing because the use of others' words reflects greater research and a desire to resolve some conflicting information in a story. However, they must be placed in the correct context in news stories. This means quotations must be introduced at an appropriate point in a story. Here is an example, using the first three paragraphs of a story:

Striking workers at Gale Products will vote tonight on a tentative agreement reached between management and the Amalgamated Machinists of America Local 1410.

However, there will be at least one "no" vote on the contract, which would settle the two-month walkout. It comes from the president of the local, Howard Butkus.

"This contract sells our workers down the river," Butkus angrily charged this morning. "I can't approve a settlement that won't guarantee future work for most of my members."

Other ways to handle a source's words are the partial quotation and the paraphrase. Here's an example of the partial quotation:

Charging that a tentative contract settlement with Gale Products "sells our workers down the

river," Howard Butkus, president of Amalgamated Machinists of America Local 1410, today urged rejection of the pact.

Writers looking for a more compact opening might choose the partial
quotation because it retains the "meat" of the statement while allowing
the paragraph to be less wordy than the statement. But excessive use
of partial quotations scatters pieces of statements all over a story,
destroying its rhythm.

Here's the paraphrase:

A proposed contract settlement that would
end a two-month strike at Gale Products aban-
dons the workers and their future employment
prospects, their union chief charged today.

Writers must ensure that the summarizing and restatement of another's words are accurate. A paraphrase is called for when the quotation
is long-winded and murky or when the writer has failed to record the
exact words of a source.

Attribution and quotations not only add credibility to a story, but
they also enhance story rhythm. They also aid in story transitions.

Effective transitions

A well-written news story is not a long series of unrelated, disjointed
paragraphs. It focuses on a main topic. Its subtopics are related, and
they are connected to the main thought by devices that serve as
bridges or pathways. These devices are called *transitions*.

Transitional words, phrases and clauses serve many functions.
Here are sentences that illustrate some of these functions:

Linking thoughts
In addition to his 5-year-term for robbery,
Thompson also received a two years' suspended sentence and a $10,000 fine for crim-
inal fraud.

*(The introductory phrase in this sentence obviously
is connected to the main focus, a prison sentence,
mentioned earlier in the story.)*

***Showing sequence
or time***

Earlier in the meeting the council approved purchase of three police cars from Jumping Al's Auto Mart.

(The opening phrase shows that this sentence refers to an earlier action of the council, whose most important activities were reported first.)

Contrasting ideas

However, the lack of a stock dividend this year does not mean that AgriCorp. will be a bad investment, according to president Ellen Gifford.

(Although earlier paragraphs indicated a bad financial condition for the company, one word—however—is an effective transition for an idea that counters this impression.)

Other transitional words serve important functions: cause/effect (*because, consequently*); emphasis (*certainly, indeed*); and comparison (*as well as, likewise*).

Consider the transitional device as a story signpost that guides the audience when the natural direction of a story changes. Without effective transition, story rhythm can falter. In the first three paragraphs of this *New York Times* story, the word *but* creates a contrast with the first paragraph and sets up the quotation that makes up the third:

He was willing to take the hit. He was ready to be dropped like a hot rock. He would play the "fall guy," as he put it in his tough-guy lingo, allowing his superiors to finger him on a scheme that was going down the tubes.

But Lieut. Col. Oliver North would not play the patsy.

"When I heard the words criminal investigation," he told the Iran committee today, "my mindset changed considerably."

As a story becomes more complex, transitions increase in importance. In tying together a complex organization, a transition can be a sentence or even an entire paragraph. However, when a writer has to search too hard to create an effective transition, it may be that the story organization is unnatural or lacks logic.

Putting it all together

Let's look at several stories whose organization illustrates what we have been discussing thus far. We'll examine a fast-breaking news story for print, a colorfully written analysis for a non-profit organization's magazine and a broadcast version of an obituary.

ALL "TWILIGHT ZONE" FIGURES ACQUITTED

(Los Angeles Times)

A Los Angeles Superior Court jury, taking only one round of balloting after a stormy 10-month trial, found film director John Landis and four associates not guilty Friday of involuntary manslaughter charges stemming from the 1982 deaths of Vic Morrow and two children on the set of the "Twilight Zone."

(This 50-word lead, not excessive by Times *standards, illustrates a classic summary approach. The who, what, when, where and how are treated. The why follows in the second paragraph. This lead focuses on the result of a 10-month trial and the charges that led to it.* Everything *in this story will relate to this.)*

"We believe this was all an unforeseeable accident—you don't prosecute people for unforeseeable accidents," jury foreman Lois Rogers, a North Hollywood homemaker, told a courtroom press conference as the beaming defendants looked on.

(The lead quickly mentions the jury and its decision. It is natural, then, to follow that with a statement from the jury foreman. In this case, the juror's own words are direct and unmistakable. A partial quotation or a paraphrase would weaken the statement. Note how this paragraph ends with the defendants, a key to the next paragraph.)

Minutes earlier, as the court clerk intoned the 15 identical verdicts to a packed, silent courtroom, Landis dabbed his eyes with a handkerchief. The 36-year-old director then turned toward the jurors and grinned. Judge Roger W. Boren declared, "The defendants are discharged," and several of Landis' family members and supporters, led by director Michael Ritchie, broke into loud applause.

(Note the use of a transitional word—earlier—to reflect the correct time sequence but to indicate that this information is of lesser importance. This transition allows the writer to focus now on the most newsworthy (the most prominent) defendant. Note also how writer Paul Feldman uses contrasts: First the courtroom is silent, then it breaks into cheers; first Landis dabs his eyes, then he grins. Colorful detail [discussed in Chapter 6] makes this much more than a basic story that answers common questions. This paragraph leads us to some commentary from Landis.)

"A truly terrible, tragic accident happened on the set of the 'Twilight Zone.' I'm very relieved, but I feel very sorry for the families of the children," Landis said, speaking haltingly to reporters. "I feel extremely grateful to the jury for their common sense and patience."

(Again, a paraphrase here would not work unless Landis' words were rambling and disjointed. The audience expects a direct statement at the end of such a draining trial. This quotation continues the natural, expected sequence of the story.)

Landis and his wife, Deborah, hugged each of the jurors before they departed.

(Obviously, we're not going to hear anything more from Landis. And we've already heard from the head of the jury. What's left? A comment from the prosecutor and some background on the charges are obvious choices.)

The prosecutor in the closely watched Hollywood case, Deputy District Attorney Lea Purwin D'Agostino, left the courtroom without waiting to speak to the mostly blue-collar jury. D'Agostino, who looked ashen-faced as the verdicts were read, said later she was "shocked" at the verdict and added that she

still believed that the evidence of criminal negligence "was overwhelming."

*(This is an ideal place to introduce another actor in
the story, the prosecutor. She is identified here, and
the writer uses the opportunity to describe the jury.
Looking at the second sentence in this paragraph,
however, one wonders why the writer chose to use
such small partial quotations—"shocked" and "was
overwhelming"—when a paraphrase would have
been sufficient, especially considering the next
paragraph.)*

"If nothing else," D'Agostino said, "hopefully
this prosecution has made other directors
more cautious."

*(This is the prosecutor's only post-trial comment,
although she will be cited in story background. Her
reference to the case gives the writer an opportunity
to give some background on the trial.)*

The five defendants were accused of acting
with criminal negligence in the July 1982
deaths of the three actors, who were struck
and killed by a combat-style Huey UH-1B helicopter during the late-night filming of a mock
Vietnam battle scene at rustic Indian Dunes
Park near Saugus.

*(This begins the case background, and a brief
chronological account follows. Note that "five defendants" and "three actors" are direct references to
material in the lead paragraph.)*

According to D'Agostino, the accident was the
first ever in which young children were killed
on a Hollywood film set. And Landis is the only
Hollywood director ever to have been crim-
inally charged for deaths on a set, authorities said.

*(Important historical perspective is provided here.
Note the attribution to D'Agostino and to "authorities." However, "blind" attributions, such as "authorities said" or "according to an informed
source," are unfortunately too common in newswriting today. The audience is better-served by more
specific attribution.)*

Yet the trial seemed to produce as much histrionics as history, with the team of seven defense attorneys incessantly swapping insults
with the prosecutor, and with D'Agostino herself labeling Landis a "master puppeteer" and
a "tyrannical dictator."

(The word yet *provides a transition of contrast,
pitting histrionics [melodramatic overacting]
against history. Note the excellent use of the partial
quotations at the end of the paragraph. Terms like
"master puppeteer" don't need a paraphrase.)*

The 12 jurors, who deliberated for nine days,
arrived at their decision after their very first
round of balloting Friday morning. A day earlier, they had viewed videotaped footage of the
accident on a television monitor installed in the
jury room. About half of their 32 hours of delib-
erations was spent listening to a rereading of
testimony from four witnesses.

*(The move from prosecutor to jurors is natural. This
paragraph summarizes activity hinted at in the
lead. The last sentence is a perfect setup for the
quotation that will follow.)*

"We wanted to be absolutely sure [before bal-
loting]," Rogers said at the unusual courtroom press conference, in which the jurors sat
in their usual seats in the jury box. "We were
going to stick to the facts and evidence. . . .
We didn't want personalities [to intrude]."

*(Although the transition to the quotation is smooth,
the writer must have encountered some difficulty
with the length and clarity of the juror's words. Note
the bracketed information, which is the writer's attempt to clarify. The writer used only a portion of
the quotation, as you can see from the ellipsis.)*

As the jurors explained their verdicts, the defendants and their lawyers, looking on from
their own customary seats at the defense table, smiled and cheered.

*(This smooth transition shows a parallel activity
during the conference. It leads us naturally to a
warm conclusion for the story.)*

"When I'm back in Tennessee," concluded Landis' Nashville-based attorney James Neal, a former Watergate prosecutor, "whenever anybody talks to me about Southern hospitality, I will think of Southern California. Thank you."

(This story can conclude nicely after 14 fact- and description-filled paragraphs. Actually, it continues with a great deal more background on the case, but this is a good ending point for our example.)

Greenpeace, an international environmental organization, has a high media profile. It depends on publicity to heighten public awareness about the environmental causes it champions. It also produces its own magazine to promote its own agenda. The success of its activism and of its fund-raising to support its causes depend on public acceptance of those causes and of Greenpeace's methods of bringing about change.

Thus, Greenpeace is much like any corporation that depends on good public relations. Greenpeace, for example, might expose what it considers to be dangerous practices by the U.S. chemical industry; a chemical company, through its quarterly magazine, might respond and put forth its point of view. This hybrid of news and persuasion is the thrust of public relations.

Let's examine a portion of a Greenpeace article to see how it approaches a "depth" story with both facts and emotion:

THE TANGLED WEB: DRIFTNETS AND THE DECLINE OF THE NORTH PACIFIC

(*Greenpeace* magazine, adapted from article in *Defenders* magazine)

The sea is calm, but a heavy fog closes in as crew members slowly let out the nine miles of driftnet off the stern of the 130-foot catcher boat. Part of a Japanese fleet operating in the North Pacific, this boat drifts 150 miles south of Attu Island, Alaska, westernmost link in the Aleutian chain.

While the crew sleeps, the net fishes the top 26 feet of the ocean. Detached and unattended until dawn, it is capable of snaring everything larger than its two-inch mesh. When the sun is barely visible through the early morning mist, the captain steers toward the radio signal from a buoy attached to the net, now four miles away. It takes three hours for the winches to pull the great nylon curtain over the side of the vessel and onto the work deck. Experienced Japanese fishermen deftly flip thousands of salmon, the prized catch, out of the net and onto the deck.

(Although this is not a "straight news" approach, this writing style nonetheless presents the news with precise detail: We are on a 130-foot-long fishing boat that casts nine miles of nylon net that drifts, unattended until dawn—when the Japanese crew harvests a treasure of salmon. The writer, using reporting based on first-person observation, sets up the reader for a startling transition.)

It takes only a little longer for the men to extract the occasional dead bird. A short-tailed shearwater, still alive, is removed carefully by a crew member and thrown back into the sea. Stunned, it rests motionless for several moments before paddling off.

Another crew member quickly shuts down the winches as two larger forms emerge from the water about 10 feet apart, bagged in several layers of mesh. Hauled on deck, they turn out, as expected, to be Dall's porpoises—a lactating female and her young calf, both drowned in the net sometime during the night. Their bodies will be taken to the fleet's mother ship, where researchers will examine and dissect them. The findings will be incorporated in a research program being conducted jointly by the governments of Japan and the United States.

(Note the juxtaposition of "the occasional dead bird" and "two larger forms." Such contrast adds to the surprise in the fourth paragraph, which informs the reader of this story's theme. At this point the story does not lash out at these fishing practices. It rather objectively relates what is done with both bird and porpoises.)

"Dall's porpoises tend to struggle a lot when they collide with a driftnet," says Tom Jefferson of Santa Cruz, California. As an observer for the U.S. National Marine Fisheries Service (NMFS), Jefferson spent several days with the Japanese driftnet fleet during their 1984 salmon-fishing season. "We found very few alive during net retrieval," he adds. "They would hit the net and start to spin, wrapping themselves in layers of net. Even those that were alive when we unraveled them from the net likely died later from all the cuts and abrasions."

(By the fifth paragraph, we get some attribution— an authoritative source—for the story. By using Jefferson's words here instead of observation and paraphrase, the writer brings another voice into the story.)

Scientists have been unable to explain why the vast majority of Dall's porpoises killed in the nets are females. Because the fishing season coincides with the calving period, most are pregnant or lactating. This suggests, as one observer said, "there must be a lot of orphan porpoises in the Bering Sea each July." Orphan porpoises, according to many cetologists, usually starve or fall prey to predators.

(The fourth paragraph mentioned the dead female and her calf. The sixth addresses this fact and provides some explanation. Unfortunately, the use of an unidentified source, who offers a comment that fits in nicely with the paragraph, somewhat diminishes the strength of this presentation.)

Tom Jefferson believes this type of research provides vital information and should continue. Others say benefits from the research program are irrelevant. The North Pacific driftnet fleets, they insist, are exacting a devastating toll on marine creatures, both the targeted animals and the varieties of sea life that chance upon their nets. They say the use of driftnets should be sharply curtailed, and in some cases, eliminated.

(We'll end our excerpt at this point. The writer goes on to analyze the fishing practices of countries fishing in the North Pacific. He mentions a change in government policy, which seems to be more restrictive against driftnetting. Although both Greenpeace and Defenders of Wildlife are activist groups, the tenor of their article is calm, rational and well-paced. It is a good example of how a special-interest publication can handle news well, give it dimension and still have influence over an audience.)

Beginning writers often are assigned obituary stories (obits) to hone their organizational skills under time pressure. Senior writers write them, too; ABC's Judd Rose, a former reporter with Associated Press, was able to weave color, detail and emotion in the following story because obits of the famous often are done in advance. Although some of this story was ready to go at a moment's notice, Rose had to quickly pull together recent facts to make the story timely. Let's review this script by beginning with the program opening.

FRED ASTAIRE DEAD AT 88
(ABC World News Tonight)

ANNOUNCER: From ABC, this is World News Tonight with Peter Jennings. Reporting tonight is 20/20 correspondent Tom Jarriel.

TOM JARRIEL: Good evening.
And tonight's headline . . . Syria is demanding the release of American journalist Charles Glass from his kidnappers in Lebanon, and the head of Syrian intelligence has gone there on that mission. In South Korea amid talks of compromise, violent anti-government demonstrations continued for the 14th day. We'll have full reports. But we begin tonight with the passing of an American legend. Fred Astaire, who captivated audiences for more than half a century, has died of pneumonia at the age of 88. For a story of his life and his amazing career, here's ABC's Judd Rose.

JUDD ROSE: (*"Top Hat" scene*) Take away the top hat, white tie and tails, and he was just a skinny guy with big ears who came from Omaha. The last man you'd choose as the last word in sophistication. Fred Astaire himself once said, "I'm just a dancer," but oh, how he danced. (*"Blue Skies" scene*) He was, of course, the very definition of debonair. But within the Astaire dance was more—pain and passion, tenderness and strength, sometimes in a small gesture, sometimes in a miracle of motion.

GENE KELLY: (*1980 interview tape*) I think the history of dance begins with Astaire.

JUDD ROSE: The history of Astaire begins with dance. Frederick Austerlitz was just 4 when he began dancing with his sister Adele. (*old photos*) Soon, they were a popular vaudeville act. Then came a series of hits on Broadway and by 1923 they were the toast of the town in London, too. Both got Hollywood screen tests and as an oft-told tale goes, the verdict on Fred was, "can't act, can't sing, balding, can dance a little."

FRED ASTAIRE: (*1980 interview tape*) It was something like that. It made me laugh because the thing really didn't come out until I'd made good in the movies years later.

JUDD ROSE: He failed his first screen test. Soon, Adele had left the act and Hollywood beckoned again. Astaire's debut was with Joan Crawford in "Dancing Lady," but his second film, with another dancing lady, made a movie star out of a dancing man. (*Fred–Ginger scene*) They would make 10 movies together, different titles, forgettable plots, but who cared about plots? When Fred and Ginger were together there was magic in the movie. It was said, "She gave him sex, he gave her class" and theirs was an elegant mating dance, one never quite consummated.

FRED ASTAIRE: We avoided purposely sloppy love scenes between us and I think one of the reasons for success that we had is that they'd wish we'd grab each other.

JUDD ROSE: (*montage of Fred with dancing partners*) But eventually Astaire changed partners and danced. He was so graceful he made all his partners graceful too, human or otherwise. It looked effortless, but in fact Astaire rehearsed relentlessly.

MIKHAIL BARYSHNIKOV: I have been invited to say something about how dancers feel about Fred Astaire. It's no secret we hate him.

BOB FOSSE: (*1980 interview tape*) Everybody who's ever put on a pair of dancing shoes or gone out to a ballroom on a Friday night or Saturday night and went social dancing owes a debt to Fred Astaire.

JUDD ROSE: (*dance scenes*) His medium was film, so the art of Astaire will survive on the screen. And somewhere in the dark a clumsy man will see himself in top hat and tails, a plain woman will dream of being swept up in graceful arms, and Fred Astaire will be still alive. The dance is done now, but some things they can't take away. Judd Rose, ABC News, Hollywood.

Good broadcast writing has all the elements of dance: rhythm, flexibility, style. Judd Rose's package shows how broadcast goes beyond print. The audience receives both sound and image; mindful of this, the broadcast writer must provide transitions for the eye as well as the ear. Let's point out elements that guide the audience through the story:

1. Judd Rose doesn't begin with a conventional lead because the news anchor has already announced that Astaire has died. This allows Rose to interpose scenes from a 1935 movie, with a voice-over setting a "take away" theme. He begins with "Take away" and ends the story with a play on the Gershwin song "They Can't Take That Away from Me," an Astaire trademark.

2. It is important that the broadcast writer set up interview bites (taped quotations) properly. In this story, Rose uses the "history" comment of Gene Kelly to lead into the early life of Astaire. He ends one section of his voice-over with the famous "can dance a little" comment so that a tape of Astaire commenting on that

remark can be used. He does it again with the Ginger Rogers "mating dance" observation, so Astaire can also comment on that.

3. As you can see from this production script, the writer must address the visual. A print writer may be aware of an accompanying picture for a story, but that doesn't place any demands to speak directly about the picture in the copy. Not so with television. A partnership exists between words and images here; to destroy their rhythm would spoil the dance.

Just for comparison's sake, how did the print media approach this story? Let's look at several paragraphs from *USA Today*:

Fred Astaire never really needed a dance partner.

A hat rack would do just fine.

Once dismissed by a studio executive with the words, "Can't act . . . can't sing . . . balding . . . can dance a little," Astaire went on to become the most acclaimed dancer in movie history, dancing with hat racks, pianos, and, yes, Ginger Rogers.

"He was the best partner anyone could ever have," Rogers said after learning of Astaire's death Monday.

Astaire died of pneumonia in the arms of his wife of seven years, Robyn Smith, 41. He was 88. . . .

Because many morning papers missed the Astaire death in their Monday editions, the Tuesday story couldn't burst forth with startling news that a cinema legend had died. Anyone listening to a radio or watching television would have heard that news already. Understanding the already-shared information of the audience, the print writers focused more on description and color to organize their stories.

The news never ends— but your story has to

In purely physical terms, you know that your story has a certain length or air time. "Give me 15 column inches," the editor says. "We can do a 90-second package on this," the producer announces. It is the rare media boss who says, "Write till you drop! Gimme all you got." The prospect of unlimited space and time can, in fact, seem more frightening than the miserly allocations of a media gatekeeper.

However, translating that space into meaningful, logical story organization is cause enough for anxiety.

If you are told to "write short," you naturally are going to compress information and withhold detail. But a simple story still requires a logical opening and some transition to a reasonable conclusion. Virtually every story, however, leaves the audience asking some questions about it. That's because the news is never complete—it really is just a series of information bursts.

Remember that all stories start off as a seed of information:

EIGHT CLIMBERS DIE IN SNOWSTORM

DIRECTOR LANDIS FOUND NOT GUILTY

FRED ASTAIRE DIES

These are, of course, just beginnings. How these stories grow depends on your ability to organize under the space and time constraints of your medium. You may be surprised to discover that it's more difficult to write briefly, with clarity, than it is to fill a 30-room palace with your prose.

The News Burst

**Recognizing the similarities,
remembering the differences**

Whether a writer is preparing a news story for print or broadcast or as part of the public relations function, these characteristics generally will be part of that work:

— The story will be timely, if not urgent.

— The story will summarize an event, although a story of greater inportance may have greater detail.

— The story usually will be organized according to the importance of the information, rather than by its chronological sequence.

— The story may try to attract an audience by going beyond the summary approach.

— The story will always be incomplete.

The news burst is a fast, timely, "quick fix" for a busy, distracted audience. In the rush to produce these timely stories that probably won't receive undivided attention, writers can't put in all the detail they may have or want to obtain. The burst is merely a piece of the story.

Regardless of the medium used, a basic news story most often focuses on the *what, who, when* and *where*. That information is easiest to obtain and works well with a summary approach. However, more detailed stories generally treat the *process* as well as the event; writers will focus on the *why* and *how* to produce the detail typical of a more advanced news story.

Differences in approach and style

Print

The form of newswriting we have described appears most often in newspapers, although many magazines today use a summary approach for their news briefs. The print approach is broad, reflecting the medium's audience. Print usually can provide greater detail and even some context in newswriting because it has more space than broadcast has time. However, print writers cannot use the audiovisual stimuli of broadcast, so their words must convey both picture and sound. Because the audience makes a conscious decision to read a particular story (unlike broadcast, which may be a companion during morning drive time or at the dinner table), the writer should be comfortable about conveying more detail in this medium. Because of their greater dependence on language to convey ideas, the print media usually maintain a higher level of formality than is used in broadcast, in which all writing is eventually heard.

Broadcast

Because it appeals to the senses more than any other medium, broadcast uses a packaging approach to writing. The taped interview of a striker on radio, the video of a fire on the evening news—these set the tone for the writing and also accomplish what would have taken several paragraphs to do in print. When appropriate to the story, broadcast adopts a less formal tone than print. Bernard Goldberg, national correspondent for CBS News, has told us that he believes a good broadcast story should "tell itself" by letting the audience see and hear the characters. He is concerned, he says, about words getting in the way of a good broadcast story. Because of time constraints on broadcast, the audience does not usually expect much detail in these stories, but it does want immediacy and impact.

Public relations

In some ways the PR format may be the most difficult of all media writing. The public relations writer must serve two often-contradictory masters: the client, who wants to direct the content of the message, and the publication editor, who may not see the news value or propriety of the news release. This is why the *subject* and the *targeted audience* of a PR news release may be more important than the actual writing. In fact, it is likely that the news release may be rewritten or at least edited at the publication. All of this places great pressure on the writer. Producing good content while being urged to "sell" the client's story is a challenge indeed. The trick is to write more news than persuasion and to write it in an acceptable form for print and broadcast.

But the similarities between writing techniques for various media far outweigh the differences. Good writing is good writing, regardless of the medium or its format. In the news burst approach, the writing is good because it presents accurate information with clarity, immediacy and impact. It helps draw the audience through the story rather than shoving or dragging it. It doesn't get in the way of the story because content is always superior to form.

Whether you write the news under time pressure for a wire service, write a 3,000-word news analysis for a magazine or write a news release for a corporate president to deliver on television, you must understand the message before you can deliver it. That takes a lot of listening. And it requires an understanding of the audience and the medium.

Time may appear to be your enemy in this type of writing. It's not, of course. It's just a constant, pressing reminder that some messages are urgent and they need to burst forth. Many writers enjoy this writing form because they enjoy the challenge of producing clear, concise prose under time pressure. They have learned what you must learn: The news may be breathless, but it shouldn't leave you so.

Breathlessness can leave you speechless; that's not good for a storyteller. Stay calm, stay focused, and write the news.

Good luck!

Depth-and-Context Writing

The news burst satisfies our initial curiosity about an event, issue or person. But many people hunger for something more. They want to know *why* something happened, what it *means* and what *effect* it will have. They want journalism that helps them make sense of their world by connecting separate fragments of reality. They are looking for longer stories that analyze, explore and promote a deeper level of understanding.

We call this variety of journalism *depth-and-context writing*. It appears in all media, from newspaper features and magazine articles to radio and television reports and documentaries.

The depth-and-context or in-depth approach presents writers with a new set of challenges, from generating story ideas to organizing and writing. Chapters 11–14 detail these challenges and offer numerous examples of good in-depth writing. You will learn what makes this form of writing unique and who practices it. You will be taken step by step through the process of creating a story. In these chapters we focus on the techniques and concerns common to all in-depth writing, whether for newspapers, magazines, radio or television. But we recognize and analyze the differences as well.

You will find that your experience and understanding of the news burst help you tackle the depth-and-context style. Let's move on to this next set of challenges.

What Is Depth-and-Context Writing?

At 7:30 on a gray spring morning, 28-year-old police beat reporter Tom Hallman Jr. was making his usual round of calls to local police agencies. The call to the county sheriff's office turned up something: A deputy read Hallman a short press release about a car accident the night before. A young woman was dead. A young man was being accused of manslaughter. Hallman scribbled notes as the deputy talked. Then he did what any police beat reporter would do with this information: He quickly banged out a 100-word story in standard news burst style.

Peter Cavellero, 21, of Portland was accused of manslaughter Tuesday in connection with the death of a woman following a Monday night automobile accident, the Multnomah County Sheriff's department reported.

> Shana Marie Griffith, 23, died at Portland Adventist Medical Center Tuesday morning. Deputies said Cavellero, 2150 N.E. Multnomah St., was heading west in the eastbound lanes of Southeast Harold Street near 114th Avenue when he collided with the eastbound car driven by Thomas Griffith.

The story ran the next morning on an inside page in the B section of the paper, the Portland *Oregonian.* Hallman had written hundreds like it in his two years as police reporter, but something about this little story gnawed at him. In his free moments, he made a few phone calls. He started to see a story behind the story.

Several months and more than 50 interviews later, Hallman wrote a 3,000-word narrative reconstructing the night of the fatal accident. Published in the Sunday magazine of the *Oregonian,* it was a powerful portrait of two ordinary lives that tragically intertwined. Here is a piece of that narrative:

Tom Griffith turned on to Harold Street, his car's headlights on low beam. Usually he used the high beams when he drove the dark street. But a fuse had blown.

Shana, her eyes closed, dozed in the seat next to her husband. Tiana slept in the back seat. In the trunk was a large, sealed can of yellow paint.

The Volvo passed 116th Avenue, the passenger compartment completely quiet.

The oncoming car, like something out of a nightmare, was there so quickly that Tom didn't have time to scream.

He cranked the steering wheel hard to his left, but the reflex came too late. Shana never saw what hit them.

At impact, in the middle of the dark street, the Volvo and the Oldsmobile performed a macabre dance of horror. Their rear ends rose off the pavement together, for a moment defying gravity, before slamming violently back to the ground.

The right side of the Volvo collapsed, and the steering wheel broke. The can of paint in the trunk literally exploded, and paint gushed into the passenger compartment through stereo speaker holes.

A front tire blew, and the car hit the street with such a force that it gouged the asphalt.

The hood on the Oldsmobile flew 30 feet down Harold Street. The battery tore loose and sailed 20 feet beyond the hood. The windshield ripped out of the frame.

For a second, Tom Griffith thought he was OK. . . .

The first, quickly written news burst had answered these immediate questions: *What* happened? *Who* was involved? *When* and *where* did it happen? Hallman's second story now asked: *How* does something like this happen? What does it *mean* to those involved? What can the rest of us *learn* from it?

By approaching the accident in a different way, by asking different questions and using different techniques to get answers, Hallman crossed over from news burst reporter to depth-and-context writer. It's a transition many writers make, sometimes just for a single story, sometimes as a permanent career move. Haunted by unanswered questions and often frustrated by the limits of the news burst form, these writers feel a strong need to see a story through. They want to understand and communicate the meaning behind the facts. An audience who craves this completeness is ready to read the long newspaper features and magazine stories, listen to the radio documentaries and watch the in-depth television reports.

In the news burst, life exists as a series of separate events: A man robs a bank; Congress passes a bill; a union calls a strike. These fragments of reality perform the vital function of signaling the occurrence of events for readers and viewers who want to keep tabs on their world. But people also need to make sense of the world. They need to know how events are connected. This is the function of depth-and-context writing.

Purposes of depth-and-context writing

Found in newspapers, magazines, radio and television, depth-and-context writing naturally follows the news burst. "This is what happened," announces the news burst. "This is why it happened and what it means," explains the longer, more detailed story. But it isn't just length and detail that separate these two approaches. A news burst can be long and rich with information, as the story about film director John Landis' trial illustrates (Chapter 9). The depth-and-context story, in whatever medium it appears, is a separate form because its purposes are different:

— Depth-and-context stories are written to promote a sophisticated *understanding* of an issue, event or person. Hallman's news burst story of the car accident offered readers one level of understanding: The accident happened because Cavellero's car was traveling the wrong way down a city street. That's the superficial answer to *how* the accident happened. But how *could* it have happened? That's the deeper question. Why were those two cars traveling on that street that night? Why was Cavellero in the wrong lane? And, on yet a deeper level, how can "good" people do "bad" things? What effect can one mistake have on many people's lives?

— Depth-and-context stories are written to *connect* separate fragments of reality. These fragments may be a series of separate news bursts brought together and woven into a cohesive whole. For example, the (Denver) *Rocky Mountain News* offered its readers an eight-part series on "dying in the age of miracles" that connected and made larger sense out of many distinct stories: euthanasia, organ transplants, high-tech heroics to sustain life, AIDS, cancer, handicapped newborns. Readers learned of important ethical and religious concerns underlying all these stories. Connected, these fragments of reality made more sense than they did separately.

— Depth-and-context stories can also connect events over time, creating an ongoing context in which to understand what is happening or has happened. The multipart PBS documentary on the history of U.S. involvement in Vietnam is a good example. Led through decades of history, viewers came to realize how decisions made in the 1950s affected actions taken in the 1970s. What was once a meaningless parade of names, dates and places became a meaningful story.

— Depth-and-context stories are written to *analyze,* not merely to present, an issue, event or person to an audience. The focus of the depth-and-context story is most often *why.* The story methodically examines the reasons behind the event, the decisions behind the action, the motivation behind the behavior. Unlike the news burst, the depth-and-context story often analyzes *consequences,* delving into what did happen or could happen as a result of the event or events being reported. The *Philadelphia Inquirer*'s multi-part report on land speculation in Atlantic City is a good example. Seven years after the first casino opened, a staff reporter set out to discover how the people and businesses of Atlantic City had been affected by the frenzy of buying, selling and building. News burst stories had reported on individual land deals. This depth-and-context series analyzed the economic and emotional impact of these deals on the community.

— Depth-and-context stories are often written for the purpose of *revealing* and *exploring* a subject either unknown to or not well understood by most people. The subject can be a person, event, idea, issue or entire "world." When the magazine *Mother Jones* invited a General Motors worker to write about life on the assembly line, it gave its readers a chance to experience a world few knew about. When WETA-TV and Louisiana Public Broadcasting produced a 90-minute documentary on renowned Louisiana politician Huey Long, they offered viewers a richly textured portrait of a man few people understood.

— Depth-and-context stories often *sensitize* an audience to a problem or issue, in addition to explaining and analyzing it. CBS's Bernard Goldberg did this masterfully in a 4½-minute story on conditions at the Rosebud Sioux Reservation on the anniversary of the Battle of Little Big Horn. As the story unfolded through brief interviews with people on the reservation, the problems of unemployment, alcoholism and suicide became real to viewers. No longer simply statistics, they were human problems with human victims.

Characteristics of depth-and-context writing

Be they newspaper series or features, magazine articles, television documentaries, or radio features, depth-and-context stories share common characteristics:

— The story may be about a *timely* subject, but it *lacks the immediacy* of the news burst. It is not an instant announcement but rather a considered report that offers detail, context and understanding. A depth-and-context writer may be reacting to a "hot" story like the court battle between a surrogate mother and adoptive parents, but the writer doesn't cover the here-and-now of the trial. Instead, the writer takes a longer view, exploring the issue of surrogacy by examining its psychological, ethical, legal and medical implications.

— The story may also be about a *timeless* subject. As news burst writers scurry to keep up with the daily chaos of plane disasters, presidential pronouncements and drug busts, depth-and-context writers have the opportunity to consider issues and ideas of lasting importance. Consider the difference between covering a war as news, announcing battles, casualties and troop movements as they occur, and exploring war as one of the central institutions of human civilization, as Canadian journalist Gwynne Dyer did. His series, produced for the Canadian Broadcasting Corporation and shown on PBS in this country, asked timeless questions: Why do human beings make war? How do societies create soldiers? Will there always be war?

— Depth-and-context stories may be about subjects not classic enough to be timeless but important enough to be of *enduring human interest*. Human interest news burst stories are often quirky, "gee-whiz" snippets—the man who drowns at a party of lifeguards, the 85-year-old store clerk who foils a robbery. These stories have immediate but not necessarily lasting appeal. Depth-and-context stories tackle larger issues of human interest that will be important to people for some time to come. While the 85-year-old store clerk will be forgotten tomorrow, a story on older Americans as crime victims will endure.

— Depth-and-context stories often deal with subjects that have *widespread effects*. Whereas the closeness of a story to home (proximity) may be a major criterion for a news burst, the opposite is frequently true for the depth-and-context story. Problems that affect large numbers of people—divorce, teenage pregnancy—issues that touch all of us—high-tech medicine, nuclear war—are the stuff of depth-and-context writing.

— Depth-and-context stories are likely to have a *point of view*. This does not mean they are biased; it means they take a particular approach to a subject. It means that, unlike the news burst, the depth-and-context story undoubtedly has a thesis. Its information and analysis are often structured around a central point. When a National Public Radio economics reporter put together a story on how America's top executives are paid, the story had a central, unifying point: The current system of bonuses works against good, long-range business planning. This wasn't the journalist's opinion. It was a point brought up by all his sources. The story was organized around that thesis.

— *Mood* and *emotion* often have a place in depth-and-context writing. To help an audience understand an issue, problem, event or person on a deep level, writers frequently establish an emotional context for the story. They explore the atmosphere in which the story took place, communicating sensory details and personal sensibilities of their sources. The story takes on an emotional life that makes it compelling.

What questions does it answer?

The news burst is defined by the traditional "five Ws and H." *Who* did *what, when, where* and *how? Why*, the final W, is generally dealt with superficially because of time and space constraints. The depth-and-context story attempts to answer a different set of questions:

— *Why*, on a deep level, did this happen?

— What does it *mean?*

— What *effect* or *consequences* might it have?

— What can we *learn* from it that will help us *understand* something about our world?

Who writes depth-and-context stories?

Most depth-and-context writers are experienced journalists who first learned the basics by writing news bursts or simple feature stories. Because depth-and-context writing involves sophisticated information-gathering, organizing and writing skills, few come to this craft straight from school. Of course, there are exceptions. A particularly talented young writer who has had the opportunity to develop superior skills through classwork, internships and summer employment may find a place as a depth-and-context writer soon after graduation. But it is far more likely that someone with three or more years of solid newswriting experience decides that he or she wants to try a new form of journalism.

Newspapers

At newspapers, depth-and-context writers may be "crossovers," like the *Oregonian*'s police reporter who wrote the long narrative of the automobile accident. If they can find time and persuade their editors, news burst writers often take the plunge. Read the blurbs (the sentences identifying the author of a story) that accompany most depth-and-context stories published in the special sections or magazine supplements of newspapers. You will discover that many of the writers are regular news burst reporters following through on complex stories.

Newspapers also employ depth-and-context specialists. Some are called feature writers. Working independently of news reporters under their own feature or special-section editor, they tackle only the longer, more detailed stories found in the paper. Especially at larger newspapers, these writers further specialize, concentrating on major areas like the arts, economics, science and medicine.

Many large newspapers also have other depth-and-context writers who specialize in investigative journalism. These seasoned reporters—sometimes working alone, sometimes working in teams—use their considerable information-gathering skills to uncover corruption, dishonesty, deception, misconduct and wrongdoing in society's institutions.

Magazines

Like newspapers, magazines also employ staff writers who normally write brief, news burst stories but sometimes cross over to try their hand at depth-and-context stories. Staff writers may also be depth-

and-context specialists who work exclusively on longer pieces and, as in newspapers, have their own specialties.

But many of the meatier articles published by magazines are not written by staff writers. They are the products of freelancers, self-employed journalists who sell stories to different magazines. Some freelancers are generalists, but many specialize. Because this country's tens of thousands of magazines represent a wider diversity of interests than our 1,600+ daily newspapers, freelance specialists may carve niches for themselves that newspaper reporters can't: wilderness adventure, food technology, landscape architecture. Other freelancers specialize in fields such as agriculture, computers, health and fashion.

When a magazine editor uses and learns to trust a particular freelancer, the freelancer may become a correspondent, contributing writer or contributing editor. Listed on the masthead as an official member of the staff, the freelancer continues to work at home but enjoys easier access to editors, special assignments and higher pay.

Television

At most television stations outside the country's largest cities, reporting staffs are so small that there is usually little division of labor. Anchors go out in the field to report. Reporters who cover a teacher's strike one day report on toxic waste the next. News burst reporters double as depth-and-context writers when the station can afford to make such assignments. But most small stations do not allocate their limited resources with an eye to much depth-and-context reporting. A community issue of major concern may generate a three- or four-minute report (considered long by broadcast standards) or even, occasionally, a multipart series. But between crises most small stations do little in-depth reporting.

At larger stations and at the national networks, the picture is different. Anchors, although occasionally placed in the field, are primarily anchors. Specialists cover their own areas of expertise: crime, business, government, education, the arts. Network reporters' assignments are even more specialized: the White House, Congress, the Supreme Court, Wall Street. These are news burst reporters who, like their newspaper counterparts, occasionally cross over to write depth-and-context stories.

Other reporters may work only on longer, analytical stories. In the Public Broadcasting System most reporters concentrate on in-depth writing because this is their station's approach to covering the news. Taking their cue from the "MacNeil/Lehrer Newshour" with its detailed, analytical coverage of a few stories, local PBS stations that can afford to produce their own programs often do only in-depth reporting. Some of these stations regularly produce what they call "minidocumentaries."

The networks also employ depth-and-context specialists who write the scripts for documentaries and special reports. These are seasoned writers who have come up through the ranks. But at PBS, documentaries are often produced and written by freelancers, who create a package and sell it to the station. Like their magazine counterparts, they may write documentaries for different stations at different times or may establish a regular relationship with a particular station.

Radio

Depth-and-context writers are least plentiful in the radio industry. Most of the country's more than 9,000 radio stations concentrate on music, not news. When they offer news to their listeners, it's typically a five-minute condensation of the day's top stories rewritten from the Associated Press news wire or that morning's local newspaper. Other stations may carry only network-produced material and employ no reporters of their own. At the growing number of all-talk radio stations, the emphasis is on casual conversation and impromptu responses to listeners' questions and comments. Virtually none of the material is written beforehand.

Where depth-and-context writing shines is at National Public Radio and at many of the more than 1,000 public stations. During NPR's daily "Morning Edition" and "All Things Considered," the emphasis is on longer, analytical stories. Although each program contains quick news burst updates, the majority of the time—and the station's reporting resources—is devoted to stories that dig beneath the surface to explore the complex whys and hows of depth-and-context writing. In addition to these regular segments in the daily newscasts, NPR produces special reports and documentaries on a variety of subjects.

Many public stations, from large, listener-supported operations in major cities to tiny, struggling, university-related stations, also concentrate their efforts on depth-and-context reporting. Leaving the news burst form to commercial radio and television and the local newspaper, they take the interpretive, analytical approach to community issues. At the smaller stations, especially those affiliated with universities and colleges, a novice journalist can acquire useful experience.

What skills do depth-and-context writers need?

To be competent, a depth-and-context writer must master all the skills of a good news burst writer and then move on to develop higher levels of expertise. Consider these skills:

— *Recognizing a story.* A news burst generally answers a simple question: What happened? The writer must sift through information to determine the core of the story, but this is usually a simple task. In depth-and-context writing it's far more difficult to recognize just what the story is. There's more information to sift through; the topic is bigger and more complex; controversy is more likely to complicate the picture. Because the writer has no formula like the five Ws and H to fall back on, each in-depth story must be a fresh creation. In addition, many depth-and-context writers— magazine and broadcast freelancers, for example—are not assigned stories by editors. They must find the story themselves.

— *Establishing a focus.* What happened or who did what is almost always the focus of the news burst. Occasionally, one of the other elements, when, where, why or how, may be important enough to grab the spotlight. In any case the choices for a focus are explicit, and tradition provides strong guidance. But in the depth-and-context story, the focus is not limited to one of a few elements. A unique focus, based on the material gathered, emerges (or must be pulled) from each story. Sometimes the focus is *motivation,* sometimes *effects and consequences,* sometimes *meaning.* An *individual* can be the focus. A *place* can be at the story's core. An *event, idea, controversy* or *mystery* can provide the focus. Remember that the in-depth story has a thesis, a major unifying idea at the heart of the story.

— *Gathering information.* Depth-and-context writers gather information more detailed and broader in scope than do news burst reporters. This means the depth-and-context writer must have superior information-gathering skills, from knowledge of library reference tools to familiarity with public documents. Because controversy is often a part of an analytical story, the writer must develop a wide range of credible, knowledgeable sources. Even interviewing skills must be more sharply honed. Remember the car accident story and the police beat reporter at the *Oregonian?* Consider the skill needed to ask a desk sergeant basic questions about the accident. Now think about conducting lengthy, highly personal, emotionally charged interviews with family and friends of those involved. This requires a different level of expertise entirely.

— *Organizing.* The more material a writer has to work with, the more challenging the story is to organize. A news burst reporter may have a few pages of notes or one or two audio or video bites. With this limited material, choosing what to use and in what order is a relatively simple task. The depth-and-context writer may have reams of notes and hours of audio or video tape. In fact, a team of newspaper reporters working on a series analyzing the problems of a regional nuclear power facility said they contacted 400 people, conducted several hundred hours of interviews, attended dozens of meetings and waded through a 20-foot-high stack of reports. Making sense of all this takes time, patience, concentration and organizational skill learned through years of working on smaller stories.

— *Writing.* Like all forms of public communication, depth-and-context writing must be clear, precise and coherent. But depth-and-context stories are generally longer, more complex and more demanding of audience attention than other media writing. That means the writing must be particularly involving and lively. Pace, tone and point of view, concerns virtually unknown to the news burst reporter, are of great importance to the depth-and-context writer. To create a dynamic story that pulls an audience through with little effort, the depth-and-context writer becomes an expert in three techniques: exposition, narration and description (see Chapter 12).

The challenge of depth-and-context writing

With its complex intent and sophisticated style, depth-and-context writing presents long-term challenges—and rewards. Best approached from a solid base of news burst skills, this more complicated form gives journalists a chance to stretch their abilities as researchers, organizers and writers. The next chapter will introduce you to some of the techniques basic to in-depth writing for both the print and broadcast media.

Depth-and-Context Writing

Take 1

The writer was "off duty" at a small party, just about to dip a chip in the salsa, when his ears perked up.

"I can't believe it," his friend, a drug rehabilitation nurse, was telling someone. "I've been at this job for five years, and I've never seen as many amphetamine abusers as I have this past month. Something's happening out there. . . ."

Antenna up, the writer moved in to listen. "Could this be a story?" he asked himself as the nurse continued to talk.

The next day he phoned the local police, then the county's special drug task force, then the state cops. He called around to a few rehab centers. There just might be a story. It would take the writer a week of research to discover the story's focus and another week to fill in the gaps. He spent two days reading his notes, listening to tapes and puzzling over story organization and style. Then he was ready to write.

The challenge of creating good in-depth journalism begins long before the writer sits at the keyboard. It starts with *generating ideas* worthy of in-depth treatment. It continues with *finding a focus* for a worthy idea and *creating a structure* to present it. Let's consider these vital prewriting activities before discussing basic writing approaches for the depth-and-context story.

Generating ideas

A good story starts with a good idea. But where does a good idea start? It starts with a question, often unfocused and vague, that grabs a journalist and won't let go. Some in-depth writers are handed their good ideas by bright editors, but many writers generate their own story ideas. Whether an editor or a writer is the originator, the process of generating ideas is the same.

Ideas from friends and colleagues

The writer at the party who overhears a friend talking about amphetamine abuse asks himself: "Is there a big problem here (and elsewhere)?" This question starts the long process that will take the writer from a general question to a specific, researchable idea. From hints dropped in casual conversation to blatant demands of "you really ought to write about this," friends and colleagues are often excellent sources of story ideas. The trick, if it can be considered a "trick" at all, is taking an interest in those around you, drawing them out in conversation, truly listening to what they have to say and staying alert to new ideas.

Ideas from observation

A good writer's powers of observation are keen. While most people walk through life screening out stimuli—walking blindly past billboards, crossing the street to avoid crowds, listening to their own thoughts rather than the tumult around them—writers keep all senses on alert. They notice things. They pay attention. They stop while others pass by.

Consider the student writer walking across campus for the umpteenth time in four years. While other campus veterans have long ceased looking at their environment, this writer-in-training actively scans her world. She begins to notice a lot of older people rushing to classes, drinking coffee in the union and studying in the library. Who are these people? Is the campus population changing? The writer's powers of observation have started her on the path to a good story.

Ideas from reading

Writers are voracious readers, from books to bulletin board notices, from daily newspapers to junk mail. They gobble up the written word, seeking information, inspiration and ideas. Many of the in-depth writer's story ideas come from news burst stories that leave questions unanswered. In fact, the daily newspaper and nightly newscast are undoubtedly the in-depth writer's best sources of ideas.

Taking off where a news burst story ends is a classic approach. A local broadcast spends 20 seconds highlighting a civil suit just won by a man suffering from the dire health effects of working with asbestos 30 years ago. A depth-and-context writer picks up the story, studies court cases and corporate documents, talks to lawyers, physicians, researchers, public health officials and other asbestos victims. The story that emerges deals with an important, national problem. It started with a news burst about one man.

Specifically, in-depth writers use news bursts as a basis for either *nationalizing the local* or *localizing the national*. The writer who pursued the asbestos story took a local story and found its national context. Another writer might take the opposite tack. Suppose, for example, that a writer has read dozens of national stories about the crisis in American education. Various magazine and newspaper articles suggest that there's a growing home education movement instigated by parents fed up with the public school system. Has this movement touched the local community? The writer works on localizing a national story.

Writers also get ideas from other in-depth reports. While these stories, if they're good, don't leave important questions unanswered, they represent only one approach to what is undoubtedly a complex issue. Consider the case of the tragic Challenger accident. When the NASA space shuttle blew up, killing all astronauts aboard, the media covered the accident first as a news story, then with greater and greater depth as technological, political and human stories. Writer

Scott Spencer read all the stories and watched all the TV specials. He then went on to write an "investigative obituary" of Judith Resnick, one of the astronauts. The story delved deep into her psyche, attempting to answer—without the benefit of access to its main character—what kind of a person Resnick was and why she chose to be an astronaut. Published in *Esquire* months after the media blitz of Challenger stories, it offered new insights and a broader human context.

Ideas discovered while doing other stories

Writers need to be focused on the story they're doing. But they should also be alert and flexible enough to recognize new story ideas when they unexpectedly appear. A writer searching through reports and documents for certain information must be single-minded enough to concentrate on the search yet be open-minded enough to scribble down interesting tidbits of information not relevant to that particular story. The writer interviewing a source should keep the conversation focused but at the same time be alert to interesting tangents.

Many good ideas come to writers in the course of researching unrelated stories. For example, National Public Radio's Robert Krowitch was interviewing an assistant commissioner at the Treasury Department on an economics story. During the interview Krowitch noticed some odd-looking paperweights on the shelves above the commissioner's desk. When the formal interview was over, Krowitch asked about the paperweights. They were filled with shredded old currency, the commissioner explained, going on to regale Krowitch with stories about businesses that specialize in producing souvenirs stuffed with money confetti. The NPR reporter was immediately off and running on a new story.

Ideas from personal interest and curiosity

Writers are, by nature, curious people, and often their best story ideas come from their own nosiness. Shopping at a supermarket one day, writer David Owen grabbed a Fresh 'N Frosty milkshake from the frozen food case. When he ate it, right from the freezer, it was soft and liquid, not frozen solid. How odd, he thought. His curiosity about this strange product led him to write a lengthy, light-hearted article on modern food technology, "The Soul of a New Dessert," for *Harper's* magazine.

Finding a focus

Writers are never at a loss for interesting story ideas. But an interesting idea does not necessarily make a good story. A good story emerges from a *well-focused, sharply honed* idea. Before writers can approach the writing process, they must transform their vague ideas and general questions into the central, specific concern that lies at the core of the story. It is the main idea or unifying concept that will hold the story together and give it a sense of direction.

As we mentioned in the previous chapter, the choices of focus for an in-depth story are unlimited. While news burst writers know that what happened or who did what will almost certainly be the focus of their stories, in-depth writers have no such guidelines. A new focus emerges from each story they write. Finding this focus is one of the major challenges of depth-and-context writing. How is it done?

Brainstorming

The first step, strangely enough, is to expand the story idea rather than immediately trying to limit it. Starting from your original idea, ask as many related questions as come to mind, but don't worry about how they relate. Don't try to put them in any order. Don't be concerned with where you might find the answers. The idea is to let yourself think freely and creatively about the story.

Consider the writer who overhears the conversation about increased amphetamine addiction. He thinks there might be a story. But what is it? What will be its focus? First he brainstorms:

— Is there really a *documented rise* in amphetamine use?

— Is this a *new* problem in the area?

— Is it an *old* problem that's suddenly *worsened*?

— In either case, *why?*

— Are users getting the drug *locally?*

— How are law enforcement agencies *responding?*

— What are the *physical and psychological effects* on users?

— What's the *societal effect?*

— How do *rehab programs* deal with amphetamine addicts?

The questions may be all over the map. In fact, that's the idea. A wide scope of questions encourages the writer to think in new ways about the story. One of these ways may very well emerge as the focus of the story. Some questions the writer poses may be discarded because they stray too far from the main focus. Some may already have been answered adequately by the media. Other questions will emerge as having primary importance. The writer studies the list of brainstormed questions and puzzles this through.

Our writer on the amphetamine story looks at his list of questions. He quickly realizes that the primary question is: Does a problem exist? If one does, he might have a story. If it's a new or suddenly worsening problem, he'll definitely have a story. But what will the story be?

Pre-research research

Writers spend a great deal of time gathering information before they write. They also gather information before they know whether they have something to write about. This is pre-research, a vital part of the process of finding a focus.

Our writer has a small set of preliminary questions that emerged as important from his brainstormed list. Now he needs answers. In the pre-research phase, he won't be looking for deep or complete answers. That's the full-scale job he will tackle later after the amphetamine story has a clear direction. For the moment, he needs to quickly explore his top questions to see what lies beneath the surface.

Our writer calls various law enforcement agencies and discovers that there is a local problem with amphetamine abuse. It's not a new problem, but it's much worse now than anyone can remember. The cops have a theory about this. He calls a few rehab centers. Yes, there are more people in treatment. Counselors have their own theories about why.

Closing in on the thesis

Pre-researching your primary questions may lead nowhere. Perhaps there is no story. Perhaps the story is elsewhere, hidden in the answers to other discarded questions on your brainstormed list. But if you have brainstormed well and thought hard about your list, the chances are that pre-research will lead you to—or at least within shouting distance of—the main idea around which the story will revolve. This is called the thesis, and every in-depth story has one. In depth-and-context writing, the thesis is often why something happened or the consequences of something happening. Meaning and motivation are also sometimes at the core of the story.

For our writer the major question is why the amphetamine problem has suddenly worsened. This will be the focus of the story. The thesis, he knows, will relate to the theories he is hearing about the worsening problem. Perhaps the thesis will be that cocaine prices have shot up, leaving amphetamines as the new drug of choice. That's what the counselors think. Perhaps the thesis will be that a newly discovered hole in the state law makes possession of chemicals needed to produce amphetamines legal. That's what the cops think. More research will clarify the thesis.

And that's the next big step in the prewriting process: research. Just as a sensible strategy can guide you in finding a focus, so a search strategy can make information-gathering time productive and efficient (see Chapter 3).

Creating a structure

You've finished researching a story. Now it's time to decide how the information you've gathered can best be presented to your audience. Where will the story begin? In what order will ideas, events and facts be presented? Creating a basic structure for the story is the next step in the prewriting process.

Unlike news burst writers who are guided by tradition and formula, in-depth writers must create a new organizational pattern for each story they tackle. The material itself, as well as the length of the story, the intended audience and the medium, will determine what that structure will be. That means the variations are almost limitless, and the challenge to create structure is never-ending.

Each story suggests its own organization, but all successful story structures have certain qualities in common:

— *They are logical.* The organizational pattern makes sense internally (within the unfolding story itself) and externally (with the audience). It is rational, consistent and easy to follow.

— *They are orderly.* The audience learns, at the correct time, what it needs to know to understand the story as it unravels.

— *They are smooth.* Pieces of the story fit together snugly. Transitions don't show like sloppily sewn seams.

— *They are designed to aid audience comprehension.* The first goal of a media message is to be understood. Story structure, no matter what else it does, must help clarify information and guide the audience through the story.

— *They are designed to enhance audience involvement.* Good structure does more than make material comprehensible. It grabs the audience's attention and promotes involvement. The carefully chosen pattern helps maintain interest as it pulls the audience through the story.

The importance of outlining

All in-depth writers outline before they write. The mass of material they must coordinate, the complexities of the structure they must create and the length of the piece they must produce make this step vital. Most students know what a formal outline looks like:

    I. Writing depth-and-context stories
       A. Generating ideas
          1. Ideas from friends and colleagues
          2. Ideas from observation
          3. Ideas from reading
             a. Magazines
             b. Newspapers
       B. Finding a focus
       C. Creating a structure
          1. The importance of outlining

Journalists, an informal bunch in many ways, are also casual in their outlining style. Few, if any, would construct a classic outline like the one shown here. Instead, most scribble key words and concepts, accompanied by some personally comprehensible system of dashes, asterisks, brackets, underlinings or circles. Form is unimportant for the moment. Content is everything.

How can you create an outline that will guide you in the writing process? First, review all the information you have gathered. Study the clippings and reports; reread your notes; listen or look at tapes. Know exactly what you have. As you read, scribble down a very brief summary of the main ideas you encounter. A single interview may contain four major ideas. Articulate each in a phrase or two and note where the idea comes from.

Let's use the amphetamine story as an example. While reviewing the research, our writer scribbles the following:

30 percent increase in arrests—city police stats

westside has most arrests—police chief interview

loophole in state law blamed for increased drug use—police chief interview

increased arrests due to new drug task force not bigger problem—*Daily Journal* editorial

22 percent increase in teen treatment—interview with hospital director

cocaine prices soaring locally—interview with hospital director

loophole in state law accounts for increase—interview, drug task force rep

state law—state revised statutes

loophole explained—interview with attorney

After stating every major idea that emerges from the research, the writer then begins to group items with common themes, choosing the strongest among repetitious items and discarding obviously tangential ideas. Reviewing the amended list, the writer can create major subject headings based on the grouped items. For example, the writer might group the items this way:

Increase in drug arrests

Increase in drug treatment

Theories about causes of increase in use

Remember: The unit of organization is the *idea,* not its source. Many different sources may contribute to one idea. Local police, the special drug task force, hospital representatives, drug rehabilitation workers and lawyers may all discuss a single idea at different times.

At this point in the outlining process, you will be pleasantly surprised to see that a sensible order is becoming evident. When you look at your amended list, you see that some ideas or subject areas must be presented before others if the audience is to follow the story. It's often clear at this point which areas naturally flow into or from others, which are truly main ideas and which are subcategories. If the thesis of the piece has not emerged during the research process, it will emerge now. (If it doesn't, you don't have a story. Additional research and thinking are needed.)

Based on the thesis and the logical order of the amended subject headings, you recast your list. You've now created a working outline that will help guide you as you write. Of course, you may change the outline, even drastically, as you go along. But the process of creating it has familiarized you with the material and helped you link related ideas. This intense mental exercise has primed you for the even more intense mental exercise of writing.

Recurring story patterns

Each in-depth story demands its own structure. But that doesn't mean every story you write will have a unique structure. There is no standard formula, but there are at least a few common story patterns. Let's consider them.

CHRONOLOGY.   Some stories are best told in the order in which they occur. When a story has a strong narrative line, it's often best to let it unfold as it happened. This step-by-step chronological telling can string readers and viewers along, keeping them waiting for the "big moment," the climax of the action. The story itself must have natural drama. This treatment merely enhances it.

The magazine article about the fatal car crash discussed in Chapter 11 is a good example. The writer carefully detailed the hourly activities of the drunk driver and his victims. Each hour brought the two parties closer to the moment of the crash. Organizing the material chronologically was both the most sensible and the most powerful approach.

MODIFIED CHRONOLOGY. Often a story has a strong narrative line, but some vital material won't fit into a strict chronological structure. Perhaps important background needs to be included. Maybe the story requires flashbacks or flash-forwards. Using modified chronology, a writer establishes a strong, "as it happened" framework. Within that framework, from time to time, the writer departs from chronology to introduce material that stands outside time.

Consider, for example, a story of the first heart transplant operation done at a nearby hospital. A dramatic, minute-by-minute story needs to be told: A man is hospitalized. His heart fails. He's hooked into machines. The hospital searches for a donor. A donor is found, and so on. But there is also information about the background of the heart recipient and donor, as well as the surgeons who perform the operation. There is information about the technology of such an operation and the history of the find-a-donor program. The writer incorporates this information as it is relevant but always returns to the chronological main story.

PERSONALIZING AN ISSUE. Many in-depth stories are issue-centered. To humanize them, writers often include the personal stories of people involved in or affected by the issue. The writer, then, has two stories to tell simultaneously: the unfolding of the issue itself and the tale of the people involved. Weaving these two stories creates a rich, textured story pattern. With graceful transitions, the writer moves from one "subplot" to another, using the personal tale to punctuate the larger-issue story.

This would be one way of approaching the amphetamine story. The issue segment of the story would include relevant statistics, information from law enforcement and rehabilitation experts on the scope and nature of the problem, theories about its cause, suggestions for its cure and so forth. Interwoven with these facts, figures and opinions would be the real story of someone addicted to amphetamines. This personal story would unfold, piece by piece, with each piece integrated into the main body of the story as called for. A writer could take the opposite approach, depending on the material. The main body of the story might be the personal tale with the issue used as an integrated subplot.

BUILDING A CASE.   Some stories are structured the way a lawyer might organize a legal argument. The writer proposes a thesis and then, bit by bit, introduces evidence to support it. Each segment of the story presents new information that bolsters the story's main contention. That thesis is not the personal opinion of the writer, of course. If it were, the writer would be producing an editorial, a column or a piece of advocacy journalism. The thesis is the overwhelming judgment of experts or the inescapable conclusion the writer draws from various credible studies and reports.

Consider a story on the overcrowding in state penitentiaries. The story contends that overcrowding is a major problem. The latest studies say so, and the penal experts concur. The writer bases the story on this contention and then goes on to introduce specific evidence to support it: sanitary conditions, spread of disease, prison violence, personal anecdotes. The evidence mounts as the story progresses.

CONFLICTING INFORMATION.   Many in-depth stories involve conflict and controversy. The structure of such a story must help clarify the issue itself while presenting the scope of opinions and evidence. Here the writer is ruled by logic: What does the audience need to know to understand this piece of evidence or that argument? Which argument logically follows another? When must background be introduced so the audience can judge the credibility of sources? The writer pieces together the story carefully, first introducing the issue, then summarizing the scope of opinions, then presenting each argument in logical order while integrating material about its source.

Consider a controversial story about conditions in area nursing homes. Nursing home operators believe they are doing a good job. The state regulatory committee, somewhat dismayed about the quality of care, has issued a few citations. Meanwhile, some nursing home occupants and their families are filing suits over what they allege to be inadequate nursing care in three area homes. The writer carefully introduces and backgrounds the issue, answering such questions as: How many nursing homes are operating with how many occupants? How long have they operated? What is the scope of care offered? How are they regulated? Have there been problems in the past? Next the controversy itself must be clarified: Who believes what and why. Then, piece by piece, the writer presents the arguments, opinions and evidence from all those involved.

PIECES OF A PUZZLE. Some stories unfold like good detective novels and should be told that way. A reporter discovers a piece of information, then another seemingly unrelated piece, then another. At some point pieces begin to interlock; slowly a pattern begins to emerge. This pattern merges with another to create a clear picture. When well executed, this structure can keep an audience interested and curious. The writer must be careful not to confuse the audience by introducing too many separate pieces of the puzzle before making some connections between them. The emerging patterns must be clearly linked as the story progresses. Without explicit guideposts, the audience will be lost.

You might think this puzzle structure would be suitable for only the occasional investigative story involving political or corporate intrigue. The reporter uncovers a slush fund, an airplane ticket, a tape of a phone call, a leaked document, a missing file. But the puzzle structure also works for a far more common kind of story: the personality profile. The writer presents bits and pieces of a person's life—scenes, conversations, anecdotes, background—that slowly interlock to form a complex portrait of the person being profiled.

These patterns can't and shouldn't be applied to all stories. A writer must let the material itself suggest structure. An organizational pattern is not imposed from above but emerges from within.

Choosing a prose form

News burst writers, constrained by time, space and formula, almost always use only one prose style, exposition, to communicate their messages. But in-depth writers are free to use three different prose forms: exposition, description and narration. Each has its advantages and disadvantages; each is useful for certain kinds of material. The in-depth writer matches prose form to material, changing forms within a single story to suit different material, create mood and change pace. Let's examine the prose forms.

Exposition

Exposition informs, defines, explains, clarifies or makes a point. It is straightforward prose that, if written well, communicates maximum ideas in minimum words. That's why it's the preferred style of news reporters, speech writers, lecturers and others who need to make their points clearly and succinctly. Most textbooks are written as exposition. This paragraph explaining exposition *is* exposition.

An economical, no-nonsense form, exposition is well-suited to the communication of complex concepts. The in-depth writer might choose this form to introduce an idea or issue, offer a summary, present background or explain the nature of conflict and controversy. Print writers often use exposition to create a bridge between materials presented in other prose forms. Broadcast writers use it to make transitions between video or audio bites. Because relatively brief expository passages can present much material, they can move the story rapidly ahead. When a writer needs the story's pace to quicken, exposition can do the job.

But for all its advantages, expository writing distances the audience from the subject being written about. The author clearly stands between the material and the audience, explaining and telling rather than allowing the material to explain itself. Because of this, exposition can be monotonous and tedious, especially in big chunks. It is best used when the material warrants the treatment.

Consider the purposeful use of exposition in these introductory paragraphs to a 4½-minute CBS story. First, Dan Rather explains; then reporter Bernard Goldberg summarizes:

DAN RATHER: TODAY IS THE ANNIVERSARY OF THE BATTLE OF LITTLE BIG HORN, WHEN PERHAPS THE LARGEST GATHERING OF INDIAN WARRIORS IN WESTERN HISTORY ROUTED THE U.S. ARMY TROOPS OF GEORGE ARMSTRONG CUSTER. THERE ARE ABOUT 1,400,000 INDIANS IN THE UNITED STATES TODAY; AND IF THIS IS A TIME FOR THEM TO LOOK BACK WITH PRIDE, IT IS ALSO A TIME WHEN MANY AMERICAN INDIANS CAN ONLY LOOK AHEAD WITH DESPAIR. BERNARD GOLDBERG REPORTS.

BERNARD GOLDBERG: THEIR ANCESTORS FOUGHT AT THE LITTLE BIG HORN, BUT

CUSTER'S LAST STAND MAY ALSO HAVE
BEEN THEIRS. THIS IS THE ROSEBUD
SIOUX RESERVATION ON THE PRAIRIE OF
SOUTH DAKOTA, TODAY ONE OF THE
POOREST PLACES IN AMERICA. IT'S 10:30
IN THE MORNING, AND A BOTTLE OF
MUSCATEL IS WELL ON ITS WAY TO
BECOMING A MEMORY.

Note how much information is packed into those two paragraphs. The audience very quickly gets a sense of time, place and history. Important background facts are economically presented, leaving the audience ready to experience the story. Exposition has done its job. Goldberg now moves to videotaped interviews.

In this next passage, a *Washington Post* reporter uses exposition to summarize and offer background. Note how quickly the years pass in these two short paragraphs. The story is an in-depth profile of Alice Roosevelt Longworth, President Theodore Roosevelt's daughter, who was celebrating her 90th birthday at the time this piece was published.

Alice Longworth has lived in Washington since William McKinley was assassinated and her father became president in 1901. She was 17 years old. She has known every president since Benjamin Harrison, who was in office from 1889 to 1893. Some she liked and some she didn't; over the years she has never hesitated to reveal her exact sentiments about them, or anyone else for that matter.

She has been a favorite of Harry Truman, John Kennedy, Lyndon Johnson and Richard Nixon, but there was no love lost between her and Warren Harding, and Woodrow Wilson. President Eisenhower bored her.

As you can see, exposition can be spirited and lively. It can also be dramatic, as in this opening paragraph of a magazine story by science writer Tom Hager:

The war on drugs cost Richard Anderson his job. The young millworker didn't get hooked on heroin or crazed on crack. He didn't sell dope to co-workers or get high on the job. All he did was refuse to take a drug test.

Description

Description captures the texture of person or event by presenting sensory details. It paints a picture of something seen or experienced and, in at least a limited sense, allows the audience to experience it. Unlike exposition, which tends to distance the audience from the subject, description brings them closer together as the audience glimpses a moment. That moment can be spent scanning a landscape or examining an interior, scrutinizing a face or observing an action.

But well-chosen descriptive passages do more than paint a particular picture. They also reveal the larger meaning of the story. When the face of a person or the sweep of a landscape symbolizes something crucial to the story, the skilled in-depth writer stops the action of the piece and describes. Not everyone in a story is described. Everyone who is described is not described fully. The writer chooses the details that carry meaning and enhance the story as a whole.

Writers for all media use description, but print journalists are more likely than their broadcast colleagues to write descriptive passages. Print writers must make their words do all the work; broadcasters have audio and video tape to help them. A camera can pan a landscape or focus on a face; a microphone can pick up the clang of a factory or the din of a crowd. Carefully produced and selected audio and video bites can act as descriptive passages within a story, with a minimum of introduction by the journalist.

But that doesn't mean broadcast writers never write description. In fact, radio writers must provide description of all visual elements themselves. They work hard to make their medium (sound) carry the most meaning and greatest impact, but only their words can make certain aspects of the story visible. TV writers must depend on their own descriptive words when cameras are not allowed or when they piece together details from various sources.

Descriptive passages can be vital to a story, but too much description or heavy-handed description can bog down a piece. Description moves slower than exposition and thus noticeably slows the pace of a story. Used judiciously, this is a boon to a writer looking to vary the pace of a longer story. Overused, it deadens. Also, novice writers have a tendency to equate description with overblown, flowery language. They think the sensory content of a passage is dependent on the number of adjectives, adverbs and elaborate similes they use. Overwritten description stops a story cold.

Let's look at how a few skilled writers use well-crafted description. A National Public Radio reporter quickly captures the essence of his story through description. The story concerns presidential campaign volunteers who fly around the country just ahead of their candidate to set up appearances. In the campaign Scott Simon writes about, the media have dubbed these so-called advance men and women "advance children" because of their extreme youth. Note how the writer captures their youthful spirit with this short passage:

The aisle of the airplane by now is strung up with rubber snakes and lizards. Pennants from various places are taped onto the overhead racks. There is a gallery of Polaroid pictures with the candidate in Mickey Mouse ears and the chief of the Secret Service detail sitting on the candidate's wife's lap.

In another NPR story about the emergency room of a New York City animal hospital, the same writer incorporates the following simply yet beautifully written descriptive passage:

In the examination room to the right of Dr. Cabe, a rust-colored dog is lying very still on the mirror steel table, its four legs splaying out at odd angles over the counter, as the couple who owns him hold one another, their faces colorless and almost round from crying.

Descriptive passages are commonly used to paint portraits of individuals. Here is magazine and book writer Gay Talese describing a *New York Times* obituary writer. The piece appeared in *Esquire* magazine.

He has a plain, somewhat round face that is almost always serious, if not dour, and it is topped by a full head of brown hair which, although he is fifty-two, is without a trace of grey. Behind his horn-rimmed glasses are small, very small, blue eyes that he douses with drops of pilocarpine every three hours for his case of controlled glaucoma, and he has a thick, reddish moustache beneath which protrudes, most of the day, a pipe held tightly between a full bridge of false teeth.

Talese uses elements of this description—the small eyes, the false teeth—to delve into the character of the obituary writer. This is what good description does: It offers insight and layers of meaning to a story.

Narration

Narrative passages relate a story. Liberally laced with verbs, they detail a sequence of actions or events either directly experienced or pieced together later from credible evidence. If the writer has observed the action, the writer narrates. If someone else is the witness, the writer quotes that person or incorporates audio or video tape of that person telling the story.

Narrative passages can be involving, immediate and dramatic. They can give the audience a "you are there" feeling that brings the action closer then any other kind of writing. They can boldly *show* what exposition quietly *tells*. But they must be well-crafted and well-chosen to work.

A well-crafted narrative presents precise, meaningful detail in logical order. The sequence of events is clear; the story has a beginning, middle and end. A well-chosen narrative subject is not just a story but a story worth telling. It means something more than itself. It enhances audience understanding of the larger story by indirectly offering insights.

Although an occasional in-depth story may be constructed as one continuous narrative, most stories contain distinct narrative passages sandwiched between exposition and description. A writer introduces a story through exposition and then lets it unfold through narration, or relates a story through narration and explains it via exposition. When a sequence of events unfolds in front of a camera or microphone, the edited video or audio tape can become the narrative passage. This means that broadcast writers construct narratives from their own words less frequently than print writers. But when tape doesn't exist or witnesses refuse to be taped (or are too inarticulate on tape), broadcast writers must depend on their own words.

All writers must use narration (or narrative tape segments) judiciously. Although the passage itself may be fast-paced, narration slows the movement of a story. It takes longer for action to reveal itself than for a writer to summarize the action. This means too much narration, albeit vividly written, can deaden a story. Like the other prose forms, it must be chosen only if it meshes with the material and adds to the feeling and pace of the story. Let's see how some masters do it.

Here is newspaper journalist Sally Quinn narrating a horrific incident. In these first two paragraphs of her *Washington Post* story, note the clinical precision of detail:

Christine Chubbuck flicked her long dark hair back away from her face, swallowed, twitched her lips only slightly and reached with her left hand to turn the next page of her script. Looking down on the anchor desk she began to read: "In keeping with Channel 40's policy of bringing you the latest in"—she looked up from the script, directly into the camera and smiled a tentative smile. Her voice took on a sarcastic tone as she emphasized "blood and guts . . . and in living color." She looked back down at her script, her left hand shook almost unnoticeably.

Her right arm stiffened. "We bring you another first." Her voice was steady. She looked up again into the camera. Her eyes were dark, direct and challenging. "An attempted suicide." Her right hand came up from under the anchor desk. In it was a .38-caliber revolver. She pointed it at the lower back of her head and pulled the trigger.

It would have been far more economical—but much less powerful—if Quinn had presented this material as exposition: "TV anchorwoman Christine Chubbuck shot herself in the head while reading the evening news." The narration sets a tone vital to the story. Quinn uses understated language and terse construction to communicate a wealth of detail.

In the following narrative passage, the writer takes the opposite approach. Where Quinn painstakingly recorded every movement, this writer breezily summarizes. The tone fits the material beautifully. The anecdote concerns a wrestling match between Haystacks Calhoun, the subject of the writer's in-depth profile, and Calhoun's archrival, Killer Kowalski.

Killer growled. Killer snarled. Killer picked up Haystacks' horseshoe chain from the ropes and began to swing it at his face. The unavoidable fact that the horseshoe never made contact did not prevent Calhoun from groaning with pain or the crowd from angry invective or the referee from going bananas. . . .

A gong rang. An announcer in snappy attire raised Haystacks Calhoun's broad arm and pronounced him the winner by default.

Finally, here's an oddity: a 3½-minute broadcast story written as a narrative poem. As you read, note how the scene and the controversy unfold. The author is veteran CBS news broadcaster Charles Osgood. Here, in part, is the poem:

'Twas the week before Christmas, and much
like a fairyland
Was the mallfull of stores that they call Halfway
merryland.
The shoppers were busily shopping away.
It was clear they were thinking about Christ-
mas day.
The stores were all done up in Christmassy
scenes,
With angels and tinsel, with reds and with
greens.
There were trees full of glitter and stockings to
fill,
And carolers were singing of peace and good
will.
And inside that center in front of a store,
The Salvation Army was there by the door
With the kettle they use to collect Christmas
cheer
For those who are needy this time of the year.
And the bell that they ring is a way to remind
us:
"Here we are folks, it's real easy to find us.
Merry Christmas and thank you, the world's in
a mess,
But Christmas is coming, good cheer and God
bless."
You know the sound well 'cause you've heard
it before,
And the sound of those bells you could hear in
the store.

So suddenly, like an Iranian mullah,
Comes the Halfway Mall manager named Wil-
   liam Bulla.
And what manager Bulla reportedly said,
Was it's okay to stay with their kettle of red,
But the bells could be heard everywhere in the
   mall
And the merchants, he said, might not like that
   at all.
The bells we don't want, said this Bulla, and so
The kettle can stay, but the bells have to go.
The Salvation Army has done this for years,
And Debbie Thron, one of the good volunteers,
Couldn't believe what she heard Bulla tell.
"What a shame," Debbie says, "that I can't ring
   a bell.
Bells go with Christmas, it's Christmas they
   bring."

Osgood communicates the irony of this story—the decidedly un-Christmaslike spirit of the mall manager set against the holiday environment of the mall—through a clever parody. The form, a takeoff on "'Twas the Night before Christmas,'" is well-suited to the content. Meshing form with content, as Osgood does, is the major challenge to all writers in choosing between exposition, description and narration.

The basics of in-depth writing

An in-depth story begins as a general area of interest or concern in the mind of a writer or an editor. It becomes the seed of a story only after it is transformed into a focused idea. The focus then guides the writer's information-gathering efforts. From the information emerges the core or thesis of the story. This, in turn, guides the writer in organizing the material. Finally, the writer presents the information, choosing the prose form that best suits each chunk of material.

These are the basics of the in-depth writing process. In the next chapter we'll concentrate on some special elements of depth-and-context style: extended leads, establishing sections and transitions.

Depth-and-Context Writing

Take 2

We won't lie to you.

As a novice writer who has just read two chapters on depth-and-context writing, you're not likely to be able to sit down today and actually write a solid in-depth piece. Mastering this kind of writing takes years.

But you can take some initial steps. You can begin to plug into the long and challenging process of learning to write in-depth stories by tackling individual elements of the story. You can practice writing extended leads. You can try your hand at writing establishing sections. You can see how in-depth writers link story elements by creating transitions. Let's concentrate on these three building blocks of the in-depth story.

Extended leads

All writers, regardless of the medium or form they use, know the importance of the lead. The first words an audience is exposed to carry a heavy burden. In traditional newswriting the lead must support the weight of the entire story, summarizing it and capturing its essence. Good news burst leads are thus simple, direct expository statements, sturdy sentences that get the job done quickly and with little fuss.

But the leads of depth-and-context stories are quite different: They need not summarize. They need not be expository. They need not be as efficient. Unlike the news lead, their form and presentation can vary widely, emerging naturally from the material itself. That means the in-depth writer has no formula to fall back on. Each lead must be created anew.

Because they introduce stories of greater complexity and length than the news burst, in-depth leads tend to be longer and more complex. While a typical news burst lead is a sentence or two, an in-depth lead may run several paragraphs or several hundred words. These longer leads give more to—and demand more from—the audience than the traditional summary lead. They invite the audience into the story rather than spelling out exactly what the story is. The in-depth writer has the time and space to do this. Furthermore, the audience expects it.

Specifically, in-depth leads tend to serve four sometimes overlapping purposes:

— They introduce an idea, issue or person.

— They set a tone or establish a theme.

— They pique audience interest.

— They grab audience attention.

How a lead accomplishes these purposes is up to the careful, creative writer. Free to use exposition, description or narration, in-depth writers look to their material and allow it to suggest the best approach. Although the variety is theoretically limitless, most in-depth leads follow a few specific approaches. Let's examine them closely.

The scene-setting lead

Certain stories lend themselves to descriptive leads. These opening passages are designed to give the audience the flavor of the piece by concentrating on one concrete scene. Like good description anywhere in a story, the scene-setting lead must offer concrete details that make the scene come alive in the audience's mind. The writer must choose a scene that captures a vital element in the story. The re-created image must not only stand alone as a clear picture but must also be meaningful in the context of the larger story.

Here is such a lead written for radio. It introduces an in-depth profile of Chicago's City News Bureau, a kind of boot camp for urban newspaper reporters. Read it aloud and listen as the scene comes alive.

(sound of typewriters) THE CITY NEWS BUREAU OCCUPIES THE CORNER OFFICE ON A FLOOR 15 STORIES UP FROM THE STREET. IT HANGS LIKE AN OPERA BOX OVER THE TRACKS OF THE WEST LOOP ELEVATED TRAIN, AND IN THIS CONFUSING PERIOD OF CHICAGO'S SPRING, AS THE AFTERNOON WARMS, WINDOWS ARE WRENCHED OPEN TO THE CLATTER OF THE TRAINS SPRINTING PAST.

THERE ARE NO VIDEO DISPLAYS IN THIS NEWSROOM. THE DESKS ARE GLAZED IN GRIME, AND REPORTERS SOMETIMES TYPE LISTING TO ONE SIDE SO AS NOT TO SIT ON THE BARED INNER COIL OF A DESK CHAIR. THERE ARE ACTUAL IRON LINOTYPE MACHINES IN HERE THAT SLUG, SWIPE AND SLAM OUT WORDS, NOT SQUIRT THEM QUIETLY IN INKY WHISPERS AS ON MORE CONTEMPORARY UNITS. THE SOUND, THE SWELTER, THE CRUNCH OF SOOT, CIGAR ASH AND COFFEE GROUNDS AREN'T INTENDED TO MAKE THE EMPLOYEES OF THIS ORGANIZATION ENTERTAIN EVEN THE IDEA OF SPENDING A COMFORTABLE CAREER HERE.

The lead effectively envelops the listener in the world of the News Bureau. The listener *smells* the cigar smoke, *feels* the jagged point of the chair coil, *hears* the metallic clang of the linotype machines and *sees* reporters hunched over grimy desks. By itself, the lead stands as a graceful descriptive passage. But it also sets the tone for the story and communicates a larger meaning: Here is a gritty, noisy, defiantly out-of-date place that breeds tough, gritty journalists.

In the following lead, introducing a magazine profile of a successful first-time novelist, the descriptive passage acts like a camera, first panning the scene, then moving inside for a closer look before the action begins.

> The house, all 450 square feet of it, sits on a rutted dirt alley on the city's downwardly mobile west side. It's a squat, mud brown shack stuck in the weedy backyard of a larger, equally seedy house. In a muddy triangle that passes for a driveway sits a faded blue '56 Ford flatbed truck.
>
> Inside, Michael McCool relaxes on a battered wooden rocker that moans in protest each time he rocks. The chair and a few other tired pieces of furniture sit on the threadbare braided rug that covers the floor of the tiny living room. The ceilings are low, the walls thickly plastered. The air is warm and close, like the inside of an incubator.

The author offers description, but the reader picks up something more: lifestyle. The house, the truck, the furniture say much about how McCool lives and what his values are. The reader has some insight into the subject of the profile without yet having met him.

Scene-setting leads can establish mood and tone while they pique audience interest. Common in both print and broadcast journalism, they can exist as words written by the writer, images captured by the camera or sounds picked up by the microphone. In television, the medium that can provide both visual and aural detail without the writer's words, scene-setting passages are mostly tape with the writer's words used sparingly, like a condiment.

The anecdotal lead

An anecdotal lead is a narrative passage that tells a small story. It includes description but differs from the scene-setting lead because something happens, some action takes place that has importance to the story as a whole. A good anecdotal lead is rich in precise detail. Vibrant and immediate, it sets a tone and establishes a theme as it effortlessly pulls the audience into the larger story.

The anecdote must be interesting and involving by itself. But that is not enough. It must also have a point. And, because it is the lead, the point it makes must be a vital one. The audience must learn something. Although writers are careful to choose small, contained anecdotes, they often find themselves writing quite lengthy leads. It's difficult to tell a complete story in crisp detail without spending a few paragraphs. The anecdotal lead is among the longest a journalist writes.

As proof, here is a 10-paragraph anecdotal lead. It dramatically introduces a magazine story about a would-be cult leader from Los Angeles, who runs group counseling sessions at his remote headquarters in southern Oregon.

He is small and gaunt with huge, dark eyes behind thick glasses. He hates his mother, resents his father, despises his job and fears he might be gay. He is slouching on one of the wooden benches that ring the large gazebo. Around him stretches 373 acres of some of the sweetest land in Oregon, heavily forested, hilly country dotted with rolling meadows and ponds. The afternoon air is warm and still. It smells like the first day of Eden.

Suddenly, his body convulses. He jerks upright. His knees and elbows lock. His fists clench. He throws back his head and shrieks. Of the 50 people seated in the gazebo, only one looks at the man.

"Yes?" says the leader of the group, a small, paunchy mid-50ish man with a full head of salt-and-pepper hair. "What's happening over there?"

The man twitches and sobs. Then he leans forward and says in a thin, high voice: "When you look at me, you burn something inside me. You . . ." he hesitates, then cries a hacking cry, "you remind me of Jesus Christ."

The leader looks at him unperturbed and says nothing.

"I want to be you," says the small, gaunt man. "I think I am you. Yes, I am you . . ." His voice trails off into sobs.

"Do you resent me because I'm blessed and you're not? Because I'm right and you're not?" the leader asks calmly. "You're a wimp, a psychotic wimp," he says without raising his voice. "Your mother made a wimp out of your father and your father made a wimp out of you."

The small, gaunt man stares at him and says nothing.

The leader swivels his head and looks without compassion at the 50 people gathered in the gazebo. They have come from Boston, Philadelphia, Chicago, Minneapolis, Houston, Los Angeles, Seattle, Honolulu—even Australia—and paid $1,200 to sit in this gazebo and listen to this man.

"You are the walking wounded," he says, as if pronouncing a sentence.

It takes a while to tell this story, but when readers finish, they know something about the "therapy" sessions, the kind of people who come to them and the nature of the man who leads them. The dialogue provides insight into the leader's character. The anecdote establishes an unsettling tone that the larger story carries through.

Of course, it's possible to capture an anecdote in far fewer words. The following one introduces a *Wall Street Journal* story about women ranchers:

Out on an open range, a 1,500-pound bull with ropes looped around his middle stands drooling in the dust. He is stubbornly resisting efforts to load him into a stock trailer so he can be taken to the corral for medical care.

Jane Glennie gets out of her truck. She spits in her hand and grinds a glowing cigarette butt into her palm. While two mounted cowboys hold the ropes tight, she plants her boot on the bull's horn and shoves. The beast just jerks his head, drools some more, and digs his hoofs deeper into the dirt. Mrs. Glennie grabs a shovel. A couple of hefty whacks later, the bull plods into a livestock trailer.

This simple anecdote, quickly and colorfully told, provides great insight into Jane Glennie's character. Paragraphs of exposition or long passages of quotations couldn't show the readers as much as the single sentence that recounts her stubbing the cigarette out in her palm. Both the anecdotal and scene-setting leads derive their power from precise, well-chosen details like these.

The teaser lead

A teaser lead piques the curiosity of the audience by presenting a mystery. While offering some information about the story, it purposely withholds other important information. The audience is left with a puzzle that awaits explanation. If the lead is well-constructed, the audience is curious about the explanation and wants to solve the mystery by continuing the story.

Teaser leads should stimulate the audience, not confuse it. The writer must be surefooted, presenting just enough information to whet the intellectual appetite of the audience. Too little information confounds the audience; too much takes the mystery out of the story. Sophisticated, clever and often but not always playful, teaser leads can introduce both serious and light-hearted stories.

News burst writers sometimes begin lighter stories with one-sentence teaser leads. In-depth writers can create a deeper sense of mystery with their longer leads. Here is one that introduces a *Harper's* magazine story:

For breakfast this morning, I started out with a carton of Fresh 'N Frosty. Fresh 'N Frosty is sort of a cross between a ball park frosty malt and a McDonald's milkshake. The one I had was chocolate flavored. Then, after coffee, I had three strawberries, a couple of blueberries, a boysenberry, a peach slice, and some loganberry puree. Then I had a piece of devil's food cream cake. Then about four bites each from brand-new cartons of chocolate, vanilla, and strawberry Fresh 'N Frosty.

I was getting a little thirsty now, so I had a glass of water and a vanilla milkshake. Then I had a spoonful of tartar sauce. There was no fish to go with the tartar sauce, but, to tell you the truth, I've never been a big fan of fish for breakfast. Then half a Bavarian cream-filled eclair. Then all of a chocolate cream puff. A glass of apple juice. A slice of strawberry shortcake. And finally, a little pie-in-a-plastic-cup concoction that had a layer of cookie crumbs, a layer of minty filling, and a layer of creamy topping. I could have eaten more, but it was almost time for lunch.

What in the world is this story about? Binge eating? Sugar blues? Fast-food mania? If the lead has succeeded, readers will be compelled to read on to satisfy their curiosity. The author creates this mystery by withholding a vital piece of information: He is sitting in the tasting kitchen of Rich's Products Corporation while he eats. The story is actually about modern food technology and a high-tech freezing process that creates soft, frozen food. But if readers knew they would be reading about food technology, how many would begin the story?

The next teaser lead introduces a much more serious story about a land battle between developers and an Arizona Indian tribe. One of a Pulitzer Prize-winning series, the story appeared in the *Wall Street Journal*.

The 360 Yavapai Indians on this small reservation, the shrunken remnant of thousands who once lived on 10 million Arizona acres, have won their first great victory over the white man. He wanted to stuff some $33 million into their pockets. They told him to get lost.

How could refusing $33 million be a victory? the readers wonder. The enigmatic lead forces them to read on to find out. In another article in the same series, the author created this one-paragraph teaser:

Let us say that you work in an office building with 1,000 people and that every day at least two are hurt on the job. Some suffer such ghastly wounds—multiple compound fractures, deep cuts severing muscle, sinew and nerve, shattered pelvises—that they may never return to their old posts. And every six months or so, a body is taken to the morgue.

This story is about the life of Pacific Northwest loggers. By placing ordinary office-going readers into the loggers' world—but not telling readers what world they are in—the author creates an unsettling mystery. Teaser leads can't be forced. The material must naturally suggest this treatment, and the story itself must deliver what the lead promises: The mystery must be solved; the question must be answered.

The "this-is-it" lead

A cousin to the traditional news summary lead, this no-nonsense, expository lead tells the audience what to expect. But unlike the summary lead, it doesn't give away the conclusion of the story; it merely sketches the outlines. For example, a summary lead might state:

A four-alarm fire ripped through three city blocks last night, killing seven people and causing more than $1 million in property damage.

A this-is-it lead for the same story would introduce the idea of the story without presenting a synopsis or summarizing the important details. For example:

This is the story of what happens when a 3-year-old finds a book of matches behind the living room couch.

Here is CBS correspondent Bernard Goldberg's this-is-it lead introducing a Thanksgiving Day report on the poverty of American migrant workers:

THIS IS A STORY ABOUT THE PEOPLE WHO BRING US OUR FOOD. THEY ARE AMERICA'S MIGRANTS, MEN AND WOMEN WHO FOLLOW THE SUN ON THE HARD SEATS OF OLD BUSES. THESE ARE THE PEOPLE WHO WORK IN THE SWEATSHOPS OF THE SOIL. THAT'S HOW EDWARD R. MURROW PUT IT IN 1960, THE YEAR THEY BROUGHT IN A HARVEST OF SHAME.

Viewers know that Goldberg's story, filed on the 25th anniversary of Murrow's famous "Harvest of Shame" documentary, will detail the lives of American migrants. His introductory paragraph clearly states that without summing up what his investigation has found. Viewers must stay tuned for the details.

The following lead takes a similar approach. The story it introduces was part of a three-day series on Atlantic City land speculation published in the *Philadelphia Inquirer*.

The most important game in this town is not
craps, or blackjack, or roulette.
   It is real estate, and nobody plays it better
than Resorts International.

Again, the audience knows what the story will be *about* but not what the story *is*. Note that this-is-it leads are brief, straightforward and powerfully written. Obviously, only certain kinds of stories lend themselves to this treatment.

Of course, these four lead approaches—scene-setting, anecdotal, teaser and this-is-it—don't cover all the possible ways of beginning an in-depth story. Countless unique and unclassifiable leads emerge from the material a writer gathers or reflect the sensibilities of that particular writer. But these four are a starting point for novice writers ready to move from standard summary leads to more challenging beginnings.

Establishing sections

An establishing section does what its name implies: It establishes the foundation of the story. Immediately following the extended lead, it is a straightforward, expository statement that sketches the outlines of the story to come. It tells the audience what to expect from the piece and often sets up its structure. Acting as a link or transition between the lead and the body of the story, the establishing section gives audience members the information they need to evaluate whether the story is worth their time.

Establishing sections may be a single sentence or several meaty paragraphs and may contain any or all of the following elements:

— *The thesis.* This is the one essential in the establishing section. If the section does nothing else, it explains to the audience what the core issue or concern of the story will be. If controversy is at the heart of the piece, the establishing section quickly sketches the battleground and introduces the combatants. If the piece is about an individual, the section establishes the central theme that the profile will explore.

— *The peg.* Many establishing sections answer the question: Why is this subject being written about now? The question may also be framed: Why should the audience care about this subject enough right now to read or listen to the story? The answer to this question is the "peg" on which the story is hung. The peg may be a recent event, change or breakthrough. It may also be the accumulation of a series of happenings. Perhaps nothing in particular touched off the story, but it is a subject of enduring concern. There is almost always some particular reason the writer is writing the story at this moment. Sometimes the reason should be spelled out in the establishing section; other times it is implied. In some instances, the author may choose to let the reason evolve slowly as the story unfolds.

— *Background.* What does the audience need to know, in the briefest terms, before being able to appreciate the story to come? Sometimes the answer is nothing, and background information can be introduced elsewhere as needed. Other times, it may be vital for the audience to know, for example, that the controversy has been raging for four years or that the legislature has vetoed a similar bill twice.

— *Context.* Certain leads deal with one example of a larger phenomenon. For example, the lead introducing ranch owner Jane Glennie (page 212), would be followed by an establishing section that puts Glennie in the context of the story as a whole. The audience needs to know that Glennie is one of a certain number of female ranch owners, and that the story will be about the phenomenon of female ranch owners, not merely about one individual. Writers who use the personalizing-an-issue pattern of organization (see Chapter 12) almost always include contextual information in the establishing section. This information helps link the lead with the body of the story.

— *Direction.* The direction the piece will take—the issues and ideas it will cover, the point of view it will present—may or may not be implicit in the thesis statement. If it is not, the author may choose to explain it briefly in the establishing section. More than any other element, a statement concerning direction will set up the organizational pattern of the story.

A cliché about effective communication goes like this:

Tell them what you're going to tell them.
Then tell them.
Then tell them that you've told them.

A good establishing section "tells them what you're going to tell them." Let's examine several.

Consider the following two-paragraph establishing section, part of a story about psychosomatic allergies published in *American Health* magazine. In fewer than 75 words, the author presents thesis, direction, peg, context and background. The lead introduced "Linda," a woman whose allergy to strawberries mysteriously transforms into allergies to tap water, plastic dishes and Formica table tops.

She's not alone. Thousands like her suffer from this mystery affliction that gives harmless substances the power to ruin lives. Explanations range from hysteria to "clinical ecology"—the belief that our million-year-old species is simply reacting against the modern deluge of synthetic chemicals. Some victims seem to be "allergic to the 20th century."

But recent research points out that "allergies of the mind" are very real and have a measurable physical basis. Help is now in sight.

What is the *thesis* of the piece? "Allergies of the mind" are real, not imaginary. This also presents the *direction* or point of view the story will take (based on the best medical evidence, not the author's opinion, of course). What is the *peg*? There have been recent, important research findings. More important, "help is now in sight." What about *context*? This is neatly provided by the first two sentences, which place "Linda" in the company of thousands of other allergy sufferers. Where is the *background*? The establishing section makes clear that a controversy has surrounded psychosomatic allergies and introduces two conflicting theories.

The next establishing section, written by TV reporter and documentarian Bill Moyers, sets up a 90-minute PBS report on the invisible power of the CIA entitled "The Secret Government—The

Constitution in Crisis." The lead, a series of tightly edited videotape bites, presents one-sentence comments from 12 people, ranging from Ronald Reagan to a woman on the street, about secret government dealings during the Iran-Contra affair. Note how the establishing section provides background and direction.

BILL MOYERS: DURING THIS 200TH ANNIVERSARY OF OUR CONSTITUTION, AMERICANS ARE DEBATING THE DOCUMENT'S MEANING. IT'S A DEBATE ABOUT WAR AND PEACE, FREEDOM AND JUSTICE, AND IT'S HEARD FROM THE CAPITOL DOWN TO MAIN STREET . . .
NEXT WEEK, CONGRESS WILL PUBLISH A REPORT ON THE IRAN-CONTRA SCANDAL. MY COLLEAGUES AND I HAVE BEEN INVESTIGATING IT OURSELVES. IN THIS BROADCAST WE'LL LOOK AT WHAT WE LEARNED ABOUT THE SECRET GOVERNMENT IN THE HEARINGS THIS SUMMER, THE WARS AND TRAGEDIES THAT HAVE BEEN A PART OF IT FOR 40 YEARS, AND WHERE IT WILL TAKE US IF WE, THE PEOPLE, LET IT.

The following is a brief establishing section that appeared seven paragraphs into a story on the politics of urban garbage collection. The story's anecdotal lead begins with a 30-garbage-truck convoy headed for city hall and ends with garbage haulers lobbying city councilors at a recent meeting. The piece was published in the Portland, Oregon, newsweekly *Willamette Week*.

The decision facing the city council last week was more than a simple choice between two recycling plans, one that the haulers oppose and the other that they support. It was also a decision that would [affect] the multimillion-dollar industry that handles this region's garbage. And haulers are only one part of that industry. The situation is so complicated, in fact, that it is impossible to tell the players and their agendas apart without a score card. What follows is a brief description of the game that garbage has become in this region, and the players who hope to make the cut.

Note that this paragraph quickly establishes the importance of the story to come, offers a hint of context and tells readers what they will learn if they keep reading.

Let's look at one final establishing section, a lengthy passage in a magazine story about Nobel Prize-winning scientist Linus Pauling. The story begins anecdotally with an incident from Pauling's past: an afternoon in 1914 when 13-year-old Pauling had his first encounter with a chemistry set. The establishing section provides a wealth of background information that will help the reader appreciate the man and his accomplishments.

That single afternoon would trigger the transformation of a withdrawn high school freshman into this century's greatest American scientist. Pauling would, during the next half-century: drop out of high school; redefine the chemical bond; win a Nobel Prize; father four children; uncover the basis of sickle-cell anemia; undergo investigation as a Communist; map the structure of large proteins; lead a crusade against nuclear testing; write more than 500 articles and numerous books; make vital discoveries in immunology, crystal structure, molecular psychiatry and quantum mechanics—and then become the first person in history to win singlehandedly a second Nobel, the Peace Prize.

He would become one of America's most outspoken—some say arrogant—scientists, a man unafraid to defend what he believes is right, whether in research or in politics. And, as even his severe critics would admit eventually, he almost always would be right. Pauling's insights into the structure of matter would revolutionize chemistry, giving it a new coherence, from the makeup of individual atoms to the way they join into the huge molecules that underlie life.

In the past 20 years, Pauling has fanned his notoriety by becoming an outspoken supporter of vitamin therapy—especially of high doses of vitamin C—in treating everything from the common cold to cancer. His running battle with the federal government over funding for his vitamin studies has become the stuff of scientific legend.

With this minibiography in mind, the reader is now ready to be introduced to the man himself. The thesis of the profile—Pauling is one of this century's most brilliant and most outspoken scientists—is clear.

The establishing section is vital to both audience and writer. To the audience, it provides a direct signal early on, explaining what the story is about and where it's headed. To the writer, it helps crystallize thoughts about the story. It is here the writer must come face to face with the thesis of the story. It is here the structure of the story is established. In creating an establishing section, the writer gains control of the material.

Transitions

Transitions are both the glue and the grease of writing: They fasten the story elements by connecting ideas and establishing relationships. And they keep a story moving—and an audience involved—by creating flow and direction. Single words, whole sentences, entire paragraphs or audio or video bites can help link ideas and create connections. Transitions, in whatever form, bring coherence and grace to a piece of writing.

Good transitions are a reflection of solid information gathering. When a writer has all the necessary pieces of a story, transitions don't have to plug a hole or bridge a gap. Instead, they can make small, tight connections between self-contained story elements. Good transitions are also a reflection of a good outline—which is, in itself, a reflection of clear, logical thinking. To create a sensible outline, a writer orders pieces of the story so that they follow one another in a sensible, logical progression. Transitions that link these logically ordered ideas have a good chance of being smooth and subtle. Transitions attempting to make connections between ideas that don't naturally belong near each other are likely to be clumsy and obvious.

All good writing demands good transitions, but in-depth journalism is perhaps the most demanding of all. Long, complex stories mean many ideas to introduce and many connections to make. The writer presents a variety of characters or sources. The story often moves back and forth through time or across space. The prose style changes. Each shift of idea, character, time, space and style demands a transition to smooth the way.

Within a sentence or between sentences, a single transitional word or brief phrase can spell out the relationship between ideas. Here are a few examples:

Transition	*Relationship*
and, further, next	link thoughts
also, similarly, as well as	compare like ideas
but, yet, although, however	contrast ideas
after, before, later, next, first, second	show sequence
because, due to, therefore, consequently	express cause and effect
clearly, certainly, undoubtedly	emphasize
finally, in conclusion, in short	summarize

Transitions linking paragraphs or sections of a story may be single words or brief phrases, but these more complex connectors are more likely to be full sentences or even paragraphs.

But all transitions aren't words. In magazine journalism, writers or their editors sometimes establish relationships between sections of the story by using typographical devices like these:

* * *

— — — —

These symbols can create a break between past and present or help shift from scene to scene, but they shouldn't be used to mask the writer's inability to write a transition. If the writer is stuck and can't find a way to move from one passage to another, using a typographical device is not the answer. However, if a writer wants to create a deliberately abrupt scene change, a line of asterisks may do the trick.

In broadcast journalism, transitions may be words written by the writer, words spoken by others on tape or wordless visual images or audio signals captured on tape. Carefully selected and edited video and audio passages can create smooth links between material. But the broadcast writer cannot always depend on tape to do the job.

Let's look at some transitions that work. Of course, the varieties of connections writers find themselves making as they write are practically limitless. But the following five kinds of transitions seem to be most common to in-depth writing.

Transitions between ideas

Writers present many related ideas in the complex stories that characterize in-depth journalism. Expressing the relationship between these ideas is absolutely essential to story coherence. Here is a section of the CBS story on the conditions at the Rosebud Sioux Indian Reservation in South Dakota. This excerpt begins with a taped interview between reporter Bernard Goldberg and an Indian woman, moves to an on-screen graphic and then to a voice-over of Goldberg's comments. Watch for the transitions.

GOLDBERG: HOW MANY PEOPLE LIVE IN THIS HOUSE?

INDIAN WOMAN: ELEVEN.

GOLDBERG: ELEVEN PEOPLE LIVE IN THIS HOUSE?

INDIAN WOMAN: YES.

GOLDBERG *(entering house):* I JUST WANT TO SEE WHAT—HOW 11 PEOPLE LIVE IN THIS HOUSE. WHERE DO THE BOYS SLEEP?

INDIAN WOMAN: I'M GOING TO TELL YOU THEN. I GOT—MY DAUGHTER IS A VETERAN, AND I GOT THREE BOYS VETERAN. ONE'S A . . .

GOLDBERG: HOW MANY OF THEM ARE WORKING?

INDIAN WOMAN: NONE OF 'EM. THEY CAN'T GET NO JOB. MY KIDS NEVER CAN GET NO JOB.

(graphic of unemployment statistics)

GOLDBERG *(voice-over):* IF LIVING HERE IS HARD, DYING HERE IS EASY.

(video of tomb markers for infants)

The interview starts by focusing on housing conditions. Goldberg makes the obvious link between the poverty he (and the audience) sees and unemployment by asking a question. "How many of them are working?" makes a transition between the first idea and the second. The graphic of unemployment statistics carries through on the second idea. Then Goldberg comes in with a simple, beautifully written transition sentence that changes the idea again, from how the Indians live to why they die. Within less than a minute, the writer has created two graceful transitions linking three related ideas.

Transitions between opinions

So much of journalism is about controversy that writers often find themselves presenting conflicting opinions. To make coherent transitions between conflicting opinions, the writer must provide the audience with some context. Writing "X believes this, but on the other hand Y believes that" is not terribly helpful to the audience. A good transition should clarify the connection between differing views. Here is an excerpt from a *Psychology Today* story reporting on the work of two psychologists who believe people with "hardy personalities" are resistant to stress and disease. The transitions between differing views are underlined.

The two psychologists found that the presence or absence of the hardy personality would actually predict whether the managers got sick. Hardiness was unrelated to health habits, so it could not simply be a result of the glow of physical exercise, nor was it related to a family history of health or illness. Further studies done with bus drivers, printers and lawyers confirmed these findings. They also indicated that the healthy effects cut across a variety of economic and educational boundaries. <u>What the mind actually does to the body to enhance health is still being debated; Maddi, however, is sure that hardiness works.</u>

<u>Other stress researchers are not quite convinced.</u> Psychologist Richard Lazarus of the University of California, Berkeley, has argued

that Kobassa and Maddi had no actual measure of hardiness in these studies. . . .

Maddi pleads guilty to this charge but with
an explanation and a rebuttal. . . .

Transitions between prose styles

One of the hallmarks of in-depth writing is its combining of narrative, descriptive and expository passages. As the writer moves from one prose style to another, transitions are often necessary. These transitions may be obvious, like typographical symbols that divide a scene from an expository passage, or subtle, like the following example from the master of transitions, John McPhee. The story, published in the *New Yorker,* is about wild bears in Pennsylvania. It opens with a wildlife biologist (Alt) investigating a den of black bears.

With a hypodermic jab stick, Alt now drugged the mother, putting her to sleep for the duration of the visit. From deeps of shining fur, he fished out the cubs. One. Two. A third. A fourth. Five! The fifth was a foster daughter brought earlier in the winter from two hundred miles away. Three of the four others were male—a ratio consistent with the heavy preponderance of males that Alt's studies have shown through the years. To various onlookers he handed the cubs for safekeeping while he and several assistants carried the mother into the open and weighed her with a block and tackle. To protect her eyes, Alt had blindfolded her with a red bandana. They carried her upside down, being extremely careful lest they scrape or damage her nipples. She weighed two hundred and nineteen pounds. In the den, she had lost ninety pounds. When she was four years old, she had had four cubs; two years later, four more cubs; and now after two more years, four cubs. He knew all that about her, he had caught her so many times. He referred to her as Daisy. Daisy was nothing compared to Vanessa, who was sleeping off the winter someplace else. In ten seasons, Vanessa had given birth to twenty-three cubs and had lost none. The growth and reproductive rates of

bears in Pennsylvania are greater than anywhere else. Black bears in Pennsylvania grow
more rapidly than grizzlies in Montana. Eastern
black bears are generally much larger than
western ones. A seven-hundred-pound bear is
unusual but not rare in Pennsylvania. Alt once
caught a big boar like that who had a thirty-
seven inch neck and was a hair under seven
feet long.

This bear, nose to tail, measured five feet
five. Alt said, "That's a nice long sow."

What McPhee does here is so skillful that most readers will be
unaware of the transitions. While he tells an anecdote (Alt measuring
the bear), he moves freely between narration and exposition. As readers see the cubs removed from the den (narration), they learn about
the male-female bear ratio (exposition). As readers watch Daisy being
weighed (narration), they learn about Vanessa and the seven-foot boar
(exposition). The passage begins and ends with Daisy. All of the explanatory material—and there is plenty—is neatly sandwiched in between. McPhee uses images and memories to link ideas, not particular
transitional words. It looks effortless. But it's the result of long hours
spent methodically organizing notes.

Transitions across space

Writers often have to get their audience from one place to another. A
story may begin in Baltimore but end in Biloxi. An interview may
move from office to restaurant to home. These directional transitions
are relatively easy to make. The writer needs to direct traffic, making
sure that when it's necessary for audience members to know where
they are, they do. Consider the directional transitions incorporated in
an NPR story on the emergency room of an animal hospital. To give
the audience a sense of spatial relationships, the writer uses the following cues:

In the waiting room off the second floor
ramp . . .

In the examination room on the right . . .

In the room on the left . . .

Back in the central operating arena . . .

With these directions, the radio audience can picture the emergency room and follow the action as it moves from one space to another.

Transitions across time

In-depth stories commonly integrate the past with the present. To interweave background passages (often narrative or descriptive prose) with information from the present (often exposition), the writer must create transitions that quickly move the audience from one period to another. The audience must be alerted to the time change without being jolted. Here are the first four paragraphs from a magazine story about a Japanese-American woman who was a university student at the time of Pearl Harbor:

She was being watched. The housemother peered in her dorm room every night and kept tabs on her during the day. The students cast sidelong glances—some suspicious, wary and hostile; others just confused and awkward. She thought the FBI might be watching her too. Sometimes she wondered whether the next knock on the door would be an agent come to take her away.

She was an A student, a member of the speech honorary, junior women's honorary, women's symposium team and YWCA cabinet. She wore the campus uniform of the day: saddle shoes, a pleated skirt and a cardigan sweater. But, unlike the other 2,800 students on campus that spring, she had to be in her room by 8 p.m. every night. She couldn't travel more than five miles from campus. She couldn't own a radio or a camera.

She kept to herself. In her dorm room, she studied hard and counted the days until the end of spring quarter, her last term at the university. It was late May of 1942, five long months after Pearl Harbor, and 22-year-old Michi Yasui was the only student of Japanese descent on campus—and the only member of her large, closely knit family still "at large" in Oregon.

"Of course I was lonely and afraid," she says, remembering that unhappy spring 45

years ago. "But I had to stick it out. I had to be
sure I was going to graduate."

Note that the first three paragraphs are a narrative of the woman's life on campus in 1942. To bridge the gap between past and present, the author uses a quotation taken from a recent interview. The attribution—"she says, remembering that unhappy spring 45 years ago"—quickly establishes the time change. Readers know they are hearing the woman as she speaks today and are set to receive current information. In-depth writers often use well-chosen quotations to make the transition between past and present.

Of course there is more to depth-and-context writing than crafting a good extended lead, writing a solid establishing section and creating smooth transitions. But these three skills are central, and they will take you a long way in this challenging process. An extended lead sets the tone; an establishing section spells out the story's central concern and lays the organizational groundwork; transitions move the story from idea to idea. If you combine these skills with information-gathering and organizing techniques, you are on the road to producing in-depth journalism.

Depth-and-Context Writing

**Recognizing the similarities,
remembering the differences**

Depth-and-context writing takes many forms: the newspaper feature, the magazine article, the radio report, the TV documentary. Media consumers naturally notice and appreciate the differences in these forms. Media writers, on the other hand, appreciate the similarities. A print story and a broadcast story will *look* sharply different to the casual media consumer, but—as the past three chapters have shown—they have much in common.

That's good news for media writers, many of whom begin careers in one medium and cross over to another. And it's good news for students of media writing, many of whom would like to leave their career options open while acquiring important skills. Let's recap some of the underlying similarities between all forms of in-depth writing, regardless of medium. Then, let's take special note of the few but important differences.

The similarities

From the concept of what an in-depth story is through the writing process itself, depth-and-context stories written for various media have these similarities: aim, characteristics, authorship, prewriting skills and writing techniques.

Aim

"This is what happened," says the news burst story. "This is *why* it happened and what it *means,* explains the depth-and-context piece. All in-depth writing, from four-minute broadcast reports to 4,000-word magazine articles, go beneath the surface of events, issues and people to promote understanding and make important connections. In-depth reports provide context as they analyze and explore. Often, they attempt to sensitize an audience. Always, they strive to bring insight to their subjects.

Characteristics

Common objectives naturally lead to common characteristics. Regardless of medium, depth-and-context writing

— lacks the immediacy of the news burst but may nonetheless deal with timely subjects

— may, on the other hand, deal with timeless concerns of enduring human interest

— usually concentrates on issues with widespread effects

— almost always has a point of view, a thesis (not the author's but one that emerges from the author's research)

— generally communicates mood and establishes an emotional context

Authorship

They may be called by different names—public affairs reporters, staff writers, contributing editors, documentarians—but they have one thing in common: All in-depth writers are experienced journalists. In-depth writing is not where someone *begins;* it is what someone *works toward.* Commonly, in-depth writers begin as traditional news writers. After they have honed their skills and proved their abilities as researchers and writers, they cross over to this more challenging form.

Prewriting skills

All in-depth writers go through the same process before actually sitting down to write. The specifics may vary according to the nature of the story, but they don't vary according to medium.

— All in-depth writers know how to generate story ideas. The sharp edge of their curiosity undulled, they walk through life alert to new ideas. Wherever they go, whatever they read or hear, they can recognize a good story.

— All in-depth writers work hard establishing a sharp focus for their stories before they do most of their research and before they write a word. They have a strong sense of what is at the core of the story; they know the main questions they must answer.

— All in-depth writers are careful, creative researchers who understand the process of information gathering. They know libraries. They feel at home among documents. They have honed their interviewing skills.

— All in-depth writers take time to create organizational structures for their stories before they begin to write. Regardless of medium, the organization of material must be smooth and logical. It must promote both audience comprehension and audience involvement. The story patterns used by in-depth writers vary according to the material rather than the medium. Patterns like chronology or building a case, for example, work equally well in the print and broadcast media but are suited to different kinds of stories.

Writing techniques

When it comes time to write, depth-and-context journalists for all media have three prose forms at their disposal: exposition, narration and description. They match material to prose form, changing forms within a single story to suit different material, create moods and change pace.

Regardless of medium, all in-depth writers begin their stories with extended introductions that, unlike news burst leads, need not summarize or offer a story synopsis. In-depth leads introduce an idea, issue or person; set the tone or establish the theme; or pique audience curiosity. Scene-setting, anecdotal, teaser and this-is-it leads are common approaches for both print and broadcast stories.

In the in-depth story, the lead is almost always followed by an establishing section, a straightforward expository statement that tells the audience what to expect from the piece. It always states the core issue or concern of the story and often includes background and contextual material.

All in-depth writers share another concern: transitions. These vital story elements link ideas, opinions and prose styles, and create bridges across space and time. Transitions reflect the solid information gathering and careful organizing that all good in-depth writers practice.

The differences

Considering all the similarities, it's hard to imagine any significant differences in in-depth writing among the different media. In fact, the differences are few; some are superficial, others important.

Newspaper vs. magazine writing

The few differences between newspaper and magazine writing are not earthshaking. For example, newspaper writers tend to be regular staffers, while magazine writers are more often self-employed freelancers. That means magazine writers are more likely to generate their own stories, while newspaper writers are often given assignments by their editors. Newspaper writers (and their editors) often conceive of a complex story as a multipart series, keeping each part to perhaps 2,000 words. Magazine writers are able to produce a single story as long as 5,000 or 6,000 words (or, in the special case of the *New Yorker*, as long as 15,000 words). This means story organization may differ somewhat.

Print vs. broadcast writing

The major difference comes down to this: In a broadcast story, written words do not have to do the whole job; in a print story, written words are everything. Broadcasters can use tape, instead of their own words, to create descriptive or narrative passages. They also can use tape to create transitions. Switching from their own written words to a tape segment creates an immediate change of pace that print writers must achieve by changing prose forms.

Because of this technological difference, broadcasters generally write far less than their print colleagues. Quite often, selecting and editing tape is a bigger part of the documentarian's responsibilities than writing new material. The ability to think visually takes on great importance. The technology of video and audio tape also means that broadcast journalists are joined in their efforts by specialists: camera operators, lighting and sound technicians, editors and producers. The radio or television in-depth report is a collaborative venture. Print journalists may work with photographers and, after the fact, with editors, but virtually all of their creative work is done solo.

Of course, the product of a broadcast writer's work—the script—looks different from the print journalist's manuscript. A script is presented as dialogue (as you've seen in examples in the last two chapters) with cues for various segments such as studio-produced graphics and edited tape. The script includes everything that will go on during the report, not just the writer's own words.

Radio vs. television writing

Technology imposes the only differences between radio and television writing. Television writers have both sight and sound to work with; radio writers have only sound. Thus, radio writers must create visually descriptive passages with words, whereas television journalists can use tape. Good radio writers take advantage of their medium by creating stories rich in aural images.

Writers for all media are faced with the formidable task of making complex subjects both understandable and interesting to large audiences. While writers need to appreciate and exploit the special opportunities of their particular medium, they must also understand that *good writing is good writing.*

Persuasive Writing

"**N**ow this is the section I've been waiting for! News writing is too bland, and in-depth writing is just too complicated. But persuasion? Hey, I can do that!"

Ah, the optimism of the uninitiated.

When we organized this book, we purposely placed persuasion last because it draws on many organizational and stylistic techniques that are rooted in the news and depth-and-context formats. Persuasion depends on solid information, concisely explained. It needs logical organization, the hallmark of a good news story. And it must get audience attention, a challenge that all media writers must meet.

In this section, we examine and discuss what makes persuasion a specialized form of media writing. We will look at the editorial, the advertisement, the public service announcement and the speech; in addition, we'll make some observations about the writing components of special public relations projects. As in other sections, we also will discuss broadcast applications of this form. In Chapter 15 we take a general look at persuasion as it is commonly presented in the media. In Chapter 16 we examine persuasion through a newsworthy and controversial topic: the pros and cons of a ban on all tobacco advertising in the United States. In Chapter 17 we look deeper into the editorial and the advertisement, with an emphasis on various writing styles. And in Chapter 18, as we have done with the news burst and with in-depth writing, we review similarities and differences in the persuasive form for various media.

You soon will discover that persuasion is not the starting point in media writing. You will find that it demands polished organization and style. And although you will understand that persuasive writing is difficult and challenging, you'll soon realize that this form, too, can be mastered.

CHAPTER

What Is Persuasive Writing?

*Marshalling arguments that ranged from the
flimsy to the preposterous, President Reagan
has refused to recommend the imposition of
additional economic sanctions against racist
South Africa. Given Reagan's failure to provide leadership—or even common sense—on
this urgent moral and political issue, it will be
up to Congress to force the enactment of
different sanctions.*

—From an editorial in the
Milwaukee Journal

*Someone whose opinion I respect has been advis-
ing me to use condoms. He's the Surgeon General of the United States.*

—From an advertisement in *Sports
Illustrated* for Trojan condoms

Many of our media messages deal with more than the raw commodity
of information. They are, in fact, carefully manufactured sales
pitches. In their most subtle form, they may simply raise an issue with
the public, as a first step in opinion formation. More frequently, however, these messages ask the audience to adopt a line of reasoning; to
consider a change in opinion; to make a change or to preserve tradition; and, of course, to buy a product or service.

Whether the message deals with an economic and political concept like solving the nation's trade imbalance or with a consumer decision to own a Chevrolet rather than a Toyota, its purpose is to *sell* something.

Some information presented as news also can compel us to immediate or eventual action. For example, when a community learns that three children have been killed at the same unguarded intersection in the past year, that fact alone is persuasive. A newspaper editorial, a television ad campaign, a public service announcement on radio and a grass-roots distribution of leaflets may not be necessary to stimulate people to action about the hazard.

However, an audience often requires more prompting and stimulation to react in a hoped-for manner. This is where persuasive writing plays important roles: to alert the public to something new or in transition, to mobilize opinion and to prompt action. These functions make this writing form perhaps the most challenging of all. To help us understand how persuasive writing performs these functions, let's examine its special characteristics:

— *To be successful in its persuasion or sales pitch, the message must reflect an understanding of the needs, desires and motivations of the audience.* News and depth-and-context writers do not usually analyze such needs; the information that they research and present usually does not seek action. That information becomes part of a body of facts that may or may not be influential. (Of course, many news and in-depth writers hope that their work will "make a difference.") On the other hand, a speechwriter preparing an address for a political client wants to know audience composition and attitudes in order to gain acceptance for the message. An account executive for an advertising agency wants as much market research as possible to identify typical buyers for a product and to properly target the client's messages. A politically liberal magazine is more comfortable in presenting advocacy journalism (a form of news and in-depth writing that includes a writer's political and social points of view) if the audience has been shown to be clearly sympathetic to the magazine's view.

— *Because some of these messages involve argumentation, they must have a strong foundation in logic.* Print and broadcast editorials (sometimes called opinion pieces) require a reasonable premise on which to base a point as well as orderly, sensible deductions that lead to a conclusion and a call for action. Editorials containing bold assertions without facts and reasoning to support them are hollow bellowings that usually fall on deaf ears. Similarly, an advertisement that claims its breakfast cereal is better than its competitor's must have a provable fact or acceptable premise on which to base such a claim. That claim may be reinforced, for example, when the cereal maker tells you its plump, juicy raisins are "naturally sweeter" than the other brand, which coats its raisins with sugar.

— *Some persuasive messages are overt, with a focus on attention getting.* "Zero interest and no monthly payments for six months!" "How long can this community suffer the tyranny of its school board?" "Yes, the issue before us *is* one of livability—of economic survival, not of the comfort of a spotted woodpecker!" Be it advertisement, editorial or speech, some media messages use a loud voice and attention-getting claims to reach their audience. Subtlety and understatement may work at times, but raising the semantic decibel level at the right time and with the right audience has its rewards.

— *Persuasive writing may use humor and satire not only to entertain, but to gain acceptance and make a point.* The editorial writer who presents research that shows dairy cows prefer classical music may appear to be looking for a chuckle, but that opening leads to an effective attack on U.S. dairy surpluses when the writer suggests that hard rock music in the dairy might lessen production and eliminate the surplus. The automaker Isuzu pokes fun at itself by having its commercial announcer tell lies in its ads. The announcer, for example, claims the little sedan has set a speed record of more than 900 mph. But as the audience is laughing over these outrageous claims, the commercial ends its hyperbole and makes a low-key, factual pitch. Humor is commonly heard in speeches, too. Humor can put an audience at ease and make it receptive to the message, but such an approach requires an effective, savvy speaker.

— *Not all persuasive writing is aimed at immediate action or opinion formation.* Institutional advertising and public relations campaigns often use a patient, long-term strategy for influence over an audience. Consider the forest products company that routinely advertises its commitment to ecologically safe logging practices. This message may not directly produce greater lumber sales, but it may be influential against proposed legislation that threatens the way the firm conducts forest operations. Consider also the aluminum manufacturer that depends on large amounts of low-cost electric power to operate its smelters. To maintain its operations and keep its overhead low, the company, through its public relations writing, maintains a "high profile," reminding the public of its support of recycling efforts and its impact on employment in the region. Writing for these goals requires a low-key approach over a long period of time.

Whether the method used is loud pleading or understated argumentation, the effects of persuasive writing are different from those of news and in-depth writing. Let's briefly examine the forms of persuasive writing and discuss their intended effects.

Types of persuasive writing

The six main types of persuasive writing are the editorial, the advertisement, the public service announcement, the speech, the specialized public relations project and advocacy journalism. We'll examine them briefly in this chapter and deal with their techniques in Chapters 16 and 17.

The editorial

Everybody has an opinion, and many people are not shy about expressing theirs. The large volume of letters that arrive daily at this nation's newspapers, magazines and broadcast outlets are testimony to a grass-roots dialogue that has been going on long before the mass media took hold in our society. Letters frequently comment on the editor's stand on a particular issue. Such stands are most frequently expressed in newspaper editorials; the editorial is not as frequently used in the magazine or broadcast industries.

An editorial is supposed to be a well-reasoned piece of opinion writing that raises an issue of importance to the community. It could be a global issue, such as the need to invoke the War Powers Act in a Middle East conflict. It could be local, as editors wage war over a controversial jaywalking ordinance. Whatever its target, the editorial reveals a medium's position on an issue and usually urges action. Jean Otto, editorial page editor of Denver's *Rocky Mountain News* and former president of the Society of Professional Journalists, has this view of the editorial:

> *It should stir readers to do their own decision making, giving them a view that is well-researched, for starters. The primary audience is the public, and through them, those who hold power. We may sometimes try to spur action, other times try to inform or enlarge the debate.**

Otto's view supports a commonly perceived media function: *the correlation and analysis of information.* Consider the volume of information that the media audience plows through daily. After surviving an avalanche of well-attributed information that appears to balance views, the audience may need another perspective: What does the newspaper think about this? Why hasn't our television station taken an editorial position about this issue? Whether the question is national or local, the media audience may need help in forming answers. Guidance from the medium that routinely supplies "objective" information is an essential community service. This does not mean that news and in-depth writing do not provide correlation and guidance. In editorial writing, however, information and argumentation come together to provide that guidance, to help people consider sides of issues and to reach some opinion.

An editorial position is formed in different ways. At some newspapers a committee of editors (often called the editorial board) analyzes issues and then reaches consensus on the publication's point of view. At a broadcast station the station manager, in consultation with the news director, may formulate a position. (In newspapers and magazines editorials are rarely bylined, but radio and television station managers themselves often deliver the editorials.)

Media writers do not begin their careers by writing editorials. The opinion function is viewed as the "province of the wise," so experience in gathering, writing and analyzing the news is seen as an important prerequisite.

THE COLUMN AND BROADCAST COMMENTARY. All newspapers and many magazines feature the work of columnists, writers who offer

---

*Comments of Jean Otto in the Associated Press Managing Editors' Annual Report of the Commentary Committee, Sept. 1987.

opinions on the state of the community and the world and whose work is given a place of honor on the editorial page or in the newscast. While many columnists and commentators have national exposure and distribution (for example, Ellen Goodman of the *Boston Globe* and John Chancellor of NBC News), local publications and stations often feature their own opinion leaders. These writers not only carry the influence of the medium for which they work, but they have a strong following of their own.

The advertisement

The persuasive pulling power of advertising is mighty indeed, for it drives our giant media machinery daily—at great financial profit. At the heart of much of the creativity and power of the advertisement is the advertising agency. More than 3,500 agencies in the United States—almost 400 of which post annual billings in excess of $25 million each—form a creative core that has turned advertising into an economic colossus. These agencies, with their research, marketing and creative staffs, have also made advertising a closely observed social and cultural phenomenon.

Most advertising is undisguised sales promotion. Such activity is natural in a land of plenty, where capitalism encourages both innovation and consumption. This drive for greater consumer choice also results in a product and service variety of such magnitude that consumers must be wooed. Consider the number of toothpaste brands available in the United States. How does a person choose one? Most have fluoride; all help freshen breath; all help fight decay. But some are white, others are green and still others are striped; some feature special flavors; many have distinctive packaging; and they all are looking for your brand loyalty. Enter the market researcher, the copywriter and the designer. Their game is *positioning*—finding and exploiting a niche in the market for that brand of toothpaste. So one toothpaste may promise a "fresher smile" and suggest that the user will be more popular and successful. Selling long-term dental health, another promises a taste children will love. And others may claim special ingredients that protect sensitive teeth or clean tea and coffee stains.

Creating an attractive image for a brand of toothpaste while pointing out its health benefits is challenging. The competition is tough; federal agencies are supposed to be on the lookout for unsubstantiated claims and blatant untruths. Businesses depend on the resourceful, creative copywriter to tell their story and to persuade consumers to buy their products and services.

Not all advertising is "hard sell," however.

Some advertising cultivates the long-term image of a business or organization. Mobil Oil, for example, regularly supports Public Broadcasting Service programs and advertises its support in a very understated way. In several national circulation magazines Mobil also sponsors opinion pieces about national issues, which have become known as "advertorials." Both types of ads try to show Mobil as an arts patron and a responsible corporate citizen.

The professionals who produce advertising messages are under great pressure to be both creative and concise. Their work must grab the attention of a media-saturated audience with fairly brief messages. Sometimes these messages entertain; other times they appeal to reason, fair play, thrift and sex appeal. Knowing how to reach a selected audience with the appropriate message is an absolute requirement for success in advertising.

The public service announcement (PSA)

The PSA is a combination of news burst, advertisement and public relations release. It is brief because, as an unpaid message (unlike an ad), broadcasters must devote costly air time to it. (The print media may pick up these PSAs and may develop stories based on them.) The copy must be attention-grabbing and direct—time is precious. An example:

THE "HYMNS AND HERS" GOSPEL SINGING TROUPE WANTS TO SING FOR YOU. THEY WANT YOU TO SING ALONG, CLAP YOUR HANDS AND THEN DIG DOWN IN YOUR WALLETS TO DONATE TO A WORTHY CAUSE—THE CHILDREN'S CANCER WARD AT BOOTH MEMORIAL HOSPITAL. THE SINGING STARTS AT 8 P.M. TUESDAY AT THE JOHNSTON CONCERT HALL AT 245 LINCOLN STEET. SEE YOU THERE!

The PSA must be well-written and within broadcasters' style and time constraints. It is a common and effective tool of the PR practitioner.

The speech

Being successful in speechwriting requires, among other things, empathy for the speaker and knowledge of the audience. A speech can be the most personal (and frightening) public performance of one's writing. The writer's words are under intense public scrutiny, with approval measured in the number and force of hands clapping. In many cases the speechwriter is a ghost writer, preparing addresses for other people, tailoring each talk to the characteristics of the person delivering it.

The speechwriter often works in a branch of public relations. Thus, the writer's work is often controlled by others in content and in some matters of style. For example, the writer must avoid expressions that would be awkward and unnatural for the speaker. The writer submits the speech to the speaker for review; the writer or the speaker may adjust the first draft to fit the speaker's delivery style. Like many advertising messages, the speech may be tested on selected audiences, usually co-workers and friends.

Despite its customized nature, the speech depends on good writing: a strong, creative and informative opening; a body with an easy-to-follow organization; and an ending that summarizes but leaves open the possibility for other messages and directions. Speeches aren't supposed to be bland recitations of fact; they are supposed to be *oratory*, an art that requires skill and eloquence. These characteristics obviously depend somewhat on the delivery, but even a stentorian voice and dancing gestures can't make the recitation of a soup can label persuasive. Form must follow function.

The public relations project

Most PR work is persuasive in nature. Through public relations, an organization tries to explain itself and to project an image consistent with its goals. The public relations writer is often drafted to help promote a course of action or to try to change attitudes. Consider this case:

A merchant's association wants to persuade the city council and the customers who shop at its downtown stores that a three-block-long mall should be reopened to traffic after being open only to pedestrians for the past 10 years. The merchants need information to support their position, and they want their position argued forcefully in the media. They turn to a public relations agency, which sets its planners and writers to work.

The agency prepares a well-researched position paper, which outlines economic benefits from increased shopper traffic. The paper points out to the city council that opening the mall will defuse a serious problem with transients, resulting in lower police patrol costs for that area. A brochure is produced and sent to voters; it reviews the history of the mall and cites current economic conditions that mandate a change back to street traffic.

This is just a small portion of what can be done in a PR project. Obviously, effective persuasion depends on more than a smooth turn of phrase and glittering press conferences. Whether they work to promote construction of a new hospital or to defeat a tax measure proposed by a legislature, public relations practitioners must carefully craft their messages if they are to gain acceptance; they must never forget the "public" in PR.

Advocacy journalism

Fifteen years ago, two journalism educators looked at advocacy journalism this way:

Advocacy journalists write with an unabashed commitment to particular points of view, casting their reporting of events along the lines of their beliefs. If the advocates could be found only among those who work for alternative papers and underground papers, they would not deserve a special category in the new journalism. But it is quite clear that advocacy journalists are threaded through the entire fabric of journalism.*

Only one change in this assessment seems apparent today: The effect of the so-called underground/alternative newspaper is minimal, if existent at all. Most of the alternative papers of the Vietnam era are more upscale, "lifestyle" publications today. Their rather shocking turnabout prompted a colleague to observe recently that "all these papers advocate today are wicker and Brie."

---

*Everette Dennis and William Rivers, *Other Voices: The New Journalism in America,* San Francisco: Canfield Press, 1974, p. 8.

However, the advocacy or activist style does exist among some magazines and special-interest newspapers. Publications focusing on single issues—anti-nuclear, feminist, gay, ecology, libertarian—have been very active in the 1980s.

More widely circulated magazines, such as *National Review, The Nation* and *Mother Jones,* openly employ a personal, analytical style that either directly or implicitly advocates a point of view. Here is an excerpt from *The Nation*'s article on the trial of Bernhard Goetz, the "subway vigilante":

It was an odd trial. The defense attorney was more like the prosecutor; the victims were more like defendants. Not only Bernhard Goetz but those four black youths were on trial. The verdict—not guilty of assault or attempted murder; guilty only of possessing an unlicensed gun—was both applauded and condemned. Had Goetz and his victims been judged by his peers—people who have been mugged and robbed, who have carried unlicensed guns and used them out of fear and in self defense? Black people who grew up in the ghetto, preyed on and now preying on innocent people? Does there exist such a jury to judge Goetz and Company, one that could understand the situation from both sides and deliberate on their fate?*

This excerpt is obviously slanted; depending on one's political views, it may be persuasive. It is not "mainstream journalism." However, this style of writing does have an audience: people who want analysis as well as bare facts, who want a point of view as well as dependable information.

The advocacy style of journalism is a controversial one. Most publications avoid it; we include it in the section on persuasion for obvious reasons. It can be an effective style, and it should not be overlooked.

---

*Robert Blecker, "A Verdict by Their Peers," *The Nation,* Oct. 3, 1987, p. 334.

Learning the persuasive style

Chapters 16 and 17 will focus on effective argumentation. Without knowing how to state and sustain a premise, a writer can be opinionated but not persuasive. Without a system of logic to carry an audience from premise to a call for action, a writer's message is mired in confusing rhetoric.

We will deal mainly with the editorial, advertising copywriting and the speech in these chapters. We also will examine broadcast applications and specialized public relations writing.

It is not accidental that the topic of persuasion comes last in this book. It can be the most difficult of all forms of media writing. We believe that prior exposure to both news and depth-and-context writing will enhance your understanding of the persuasive form.

Persuasive Writing

Take 1

Persuasion is both practice and art.

As daily personal practice, it can range from a pitiful plea to a high-toned demand.

As art, it can be a smooth, logical and emotional presentation that uses compelling appeals and believable argumentation.

In our mass media, persuasion ranges from the pedestrian to the artistic. You might think this means there are different strategies and structures for persuasion in the media. Actually, persuasive messages have a strikingly similar structure; it is their execution and style that set them apart.

Let's examine this common ground of strategy and structure by focusing on one topic, which will take us through the editorial, the advertisement, the speech and the public relations project: a ban on tobacco advertising in the United States.

Persuasion's common ground

No matter what media form your persuasive message takes, it will have one common characteristic: opinion. No one is persuasive by saying, "I feel strongly about both sides of this issue." An audience can use both opinion and direction; it doesn't need waffling or lukewarm support for an idea. In the case of a tobacco advertising ban, opinion will be central to the advertisement, the editorial, the speech and the PR project.

Most persuasive writing has these components:

— *The attention-getting announcement.* This alerts the audience to a problem, issue or concept. It can be the headline of an editorial, the title of a speech, or the "grabber" statement of an advertisement. It is a bold piece of information that generally carries an obvious slant.

Proponents of a ban on tobacco advertising argue that this is a serious public health issue; their method of getting attention may be a dramatic statement such as "Stop these merchants of death!" Opponents of the ban may point out its constitutional problems, opening with "Are you going to let smoking kill the First Amendment?" Both pronouncements will attract attention, and they will set the stage for a lively debate.

— *The clearly stated position.* This also is called a thesis statement. Creation of the thesis is a critical point in persuasive writing; it is the keystone of your argument and of your call for action.

The thesis is not always a simple pro or con statement. In the case of the tobacco advertising ban, the position must be obvious and direct:

Our government not only has the right to protect the lives of its citizens by halting the advertising of all tobacco products—it has the responsibility to do so now! *(pro)*

A tobacco advertising ban is a matter of life and death—for our Constitution and our personal rights. *(con)*

A position statement is much like a news lead: It sets the stage for the rest of the message. Everything is built on this statement.*

— *The properly researched background.* Research is strong fortification for a position. It protects an argument from assault. Carefully selected and well-placed information affects not only content but style as well. Chapter 3 has discussed various methods of information gathering; these techniques can make the difference between flimsy argument and powerful persuasion.

What kind of information will support a writer's argument that a tobacco advertising ban is necessary? Focusing on health and economic issues seems natural. Statistics and reports on deaths and disabilities related to the use of tobacco products; on costs to individuals, insurance companies and government; and on relationships between advertising and tobacco sales will support an argument that such a ban promotes the public welfare. On the other hand, what information will bolster an argument against such a ban? The main argument, the constitutional issues of free speech and free press, needs support with information that will show how these civil liberties are affected by such a ban. In addition, research that disputes a link between tobacco and disease will help dull proponents' claims in support of a ban.

— *The believable argument or "pitch."* With research firmly in hand and with a position constantly in mind, the writer now builds a case for an issue, concept or product. Most people want to see some string of logic woven through an argument; in the case of some advertisements, however, specific appeals (pitches) to one's well-being, self-esteem and image may hit home even though they lack logic and substance.

Tobacco ad ban proponents must carry the health and economic lines throughout their argument. If statistics and reports conflict, the audience may doubt both the premise (that tobacco use is harmful to health) and the conclusion (that tobacco ads should be banned). If the audience does not sense a natural, believable flow of fact and argumentation, it will not accept the conclusion. Therefore, the link between tobacco use and lung cancer,

---

*For an interesting overview of the arguments about tobacco promotion, see pp. 367–443 in the *Journal of Health Politics, Policy and Law,* Vol. 11, No. 3, Fall 1986.

heart disease, emphysema and larynx removal must be well-documented, citing authoritative and apolitical sources. In addition, statistics on ad expenditures by tobacco companies and the consumers they target will show the audience *why* banning advertising will help reduce tobacco use.

Opponents of the ban face a mighty obstacle as they combat the "merchants of death" theme. Are there weaknesses in these death and disability statistics? A U.S. Surgeon General's report has estimated that smoking was a factor in 85 percent of 130,000 lung cancer deaths annually. How much of a factor? Fighting what appears to be overwhelming statistical evidence, however, is probably not the right strategy here. That's why tobacco companies have targeted the issues of freedom of speech and freedom of the press. Would a ban violate the First Amendment of the U.S. Constitution? Would it muzzle a part of our economy that has a right to exist? Is anybody *forcing* people to use tobacco? You can see how lines will be drawn in this debate—and why strong, persuasive writing will be a key factor in the arguments.

— *The compelling wrap-up or conclusion.* If the opening statement is the "grabber" in persuasive writing, then the conclusion is the device that keeps the audience on your side. In sales this is known as "closing the deal." Whether the persuasive form is editorial or advertisement, the conclusion must prompt an audience decision: Do I agree with the position? Will I adopt this opinion? Will I buy the product or service? In the conclusion the writer summarizes the main points of the argument and tries to move the audience to action or to a state of mind. This component is a key difference between persuasive writing and news and in-depth writing; the latter forms may summarize and analyze information, but they make no overt attempt to influence or form opinion.

Continuity is the key to creating a successful and compelling conclusion. The conclusion must be logically related to the opening, the research and the argumentation. These parts all should build to the conclusion; throwing in new information or a new argument at the conclusion only serves to confuse and to lessen the impact of the earlier parts of the message.

In product advertising, for example, you wouldn't stress all the practical reasons for buying a new compact car (high mileage, low maintenance, excellent safety record) and then wrap up the ad by urging people to buy the car because it will turn them into care-free, sporty personalities. The clash between sensibility and care-free fun, between the practical and the impractical would steer the audience off your original track. In writing about the tobacco advertising ban, proponents will conclude their presentation by emphasizing public health concerns as they urge government to protect the public and urge the audience to pressure members of Congress to support the ban. Opponents cannot abandon their civil liberties theme by introducing new argumentation at the conclusion—such as the claim that there is a "liberal conspiracy" to destroy the free-enterprise system.

A note about differences

The common-ground approach is helpful in explaining the general form of persuasion, but there are obvious differences in the styles and approaches of the various media industries. For example, a product advertisement may not be as informative and analytical as an editorial; the ad may rely more on psychological appeals than on substantive information. The special public relations project may be more one-sided than an editorial, which may try to present several perspectives to show the strength of its own. Using a particular speaker's power of delivery, a speech may be more heavy-handed and aggressive than a printed editorial. We'll look at all these differences soon; for now, however, we continue to emphasize the common ground as we take an initial look at various media forms.

Media's use of the common ground

The editorial

The editorial, a persuasive form common in the newspaper but infrequently used in broadcast, influences other media forms because of its long history of successful argumentation. Before we try our hand at an editorial on the tobacco ad ban, let's quickly examine a brief

editorial from the *Milwaukee Journal*. It has a simple, direct thesis—
that Congress is evading its responsibility by failing to invoke the War
Powers Act in the Persian Gulf.

CONGRESS DUCKING WAR-POWERS DUTY

Sen. Lowell Weicker (R-Conn.) didn't get it quite right. "We all look like fools—fools that are disregarding the law," Weicker said the other day in complaining about the lawmakers' failure to force President Reagan to invoke the 1973 War Powers Act, which designates Congress as a partner in the deployment of U.S. military forces in war.

It's not only wisdom that Congress has seemed to lack on this issue; it's also guts.

(The editorial begins by citing an authoritative source who criticizes the inaction of his fellow law-makers, creating a perfect opening for the writer to forcefully state the paper's position in the second paragraph. Note how the brief second paragraph contrasts with the much-longer first; such a change in rhythm makes the editorial position obvious and direct.)

The law—of which the late Milwaukee Rep. Clement Zablocki was a key designer—requires the president to notify Congress when U.S. forces are sent "into hostilities or into situations where imminent involvement in hostilities is clearly indicated." Once that notification is given, the forces must be withdrawn within 60 days unless Congress authorizes their continued presence.

The Persian Gulf, obviously, is a hostile area today. In fact, a Pentagon spokesman came close to admitting that fact when he described Thursday's attack by Iranian gunboats on a U.S. patrol helicopter as "clearly a hostile act." U.S. forces coming to the aid of the chopper sank three of the boats. The incident was only the most recent clash between U.S. and Iranian forces in the war-plagued gulf.

(The Journal *writer gives the audience some background on the issue in order to return to more*

argumentation and to make a call for action in the next paragraph.)

Many lawmakers dispute the administration's ridiculous claim that the Persian Gulf is not a hostile area within the meaning of the law. But they aren't willing to back their talk with action. Measures in Congress to force the president's hand have failed to attract much support. "They're just afraid that something will happen out there that will make the president look right and them look like fools," Weicker says of his colleagues. In our judgment, the lawmakers have evaded their responsibility and allowed the president to have his way while the lives of thousands of U.S. military personnel are put at risk.

Mixing metaphors and scrambling logic at the same time, Sen. John Warner (R-Va.) says that invoking the law would send Congress into "a Byzantine thicket of quicksand." Warner fails to acknowledge that the situation is already a mess: a supine Congress unable or unwilling to challenge an undefined and seemingly open-ended U.S. military commitment in an increasingly dangerous part of the world.

(The editorial returns to a comment from Sen. Weicker to provide authority and to strengthen the argument. By quoting Sen. Warner, the editorial provides another viewpoint—but quickly rebuts it.)

Invoking the law would not itself end that commitment but only make Congress part of it. And that in turn might finally spark full debate over neglected questions: To what lengths is this country prepared to go in the Persian Gulf? How much longer are U.S. forces likely to be there? Are diplomatic alternatives being fully explored?

Congress had better stand up and ask these and related questions soon, before this country finds itself in an even more hostile and dangerous mess in the Persian Gulf.

(After a brief recitation of facts and arguments, the editorial moves toward a conclusion: a promise of

benefits and a warning. Readers now can answer
their own question: "What's in it for us?")

Remember that an effective editorial always does the following:

— states the problem or issue

— takes a clear position

— provides sufficient background to help the audience evaluate the issue

— is logical in its argumentation

— comes to a conclusion or calls for action

Now let's return to the tobacco ad ban and look at several ways to *begin* an editorial on the issue.

QUICK DEVELOPMENT OF POSITION.   Let's take the pro stand in this example. If you are going to start with a strong, clearly stated position, you must at least give some hint about the problem, which you de-scribe in more detail later. The pro statement on page 250 is just the beginning of a position statement that you might make in the first paragraph of the editorial:

How many deaths from lung cancer and emphysema will it take to remind our government
that it has the responsibility to protect its citizens? Congress must act now to halt the advertising of all tobacco products and finally
recognize that "free enterprise" is not a license
to kill.

This paragraph can be followed by a thorough statement of the problem, citing relevant medical statistics, sales of tobacco products and advertising expenditures for them. Some history of the congres-sional ban on broadcast advertising of smoking products also would show important precedent for the editorial's position.

DELAYED PRESENTATION OF POSITION.   Using the con side as an example, let's try a quieter tone before embracing a position:

The last time we looked, the United States was
still a free country. It still has freedom of reli-

gion, freedom of association and freedom of expression. It is a country where freedom of choice and competition in the marketplace have created a strong economy and an enviable lifestyle.

But a proposal now before Congress threatens our liberties as never before. Using misguided logic and allowing a "Big Brother" form of government to threaten civil liberties, a powerful group of lobbyists would outlaw any advertising of all tobacco products.

Such a sweeping action would vandalize our Constitution—and it must be stopped now before "regulation hysteria" overcomes our lawmakers.

This appeal to traditional values is used to prompt an audience before the statement of the specific problem. It would then utilize information described on page 251, working its way to a call for action.

These are just two examples of ways to begin an editorial. The ability to argue important issues obviously isn't valuable only in a college debating society. The debates that society follows daily are important to the formation of opinion and the spread of influence.

We'll deal with editorial styles more deeply and discuss their use in broadcast in Chapter 17.

The advertisement

From the $3 classified notice to the $100,000, four-color, double-page magazine spread, to the $1 million Super Bowl TV minute, the advertisement is the mass media's biggest workhorse and its largest financial supporter.

In a complex, competitive economy, advertisements also serve as a special sales force, reaching out to consumers and voters for support of products, institutions and ideas.

For an Advertisement to be successful, it must:

1. Attract the intended audience

2. Make its position (sales pitch) clear

3. Show the benefits of following the ad's advice (or the disadvantages of not following it)

4. "Close the deal" with an effective wrap-up

5. Leave the audience with a strong impression that will aid product or issue retention

To meet this test, an ad doesn't always require a "hard sell." A low-key advertisement can be successful if its message is meaningful and memorable. Examine the following brief message from the DuPont Company ("Better things for better living"). Note how similar in organization and rhythm this advertising copy is to a newspaper human interest or feature story. It points out a problem (blood transfusion in the age of AIDS) and tells of its solution—a highly reliable testing system created by DuPont:

THE DIFFERENCE BETWEEN SAVING A LIFE AND THREATENING IT

It started out as a trip across town. Suddenly, you're in an ambulance racing to the hospital. It's an emergency. A matter of life and death. You've lost blood. The doctors tell you that you're going to need a transfusion.

Now you're really scared.

The AIDS virus has changed the way we think about transfusions. It's made us cautious. What hasn't changed is the importance of the transfusion to our medical procedures. It's vital.

Which is why DuPont worked to create a highly accurate method of testing to help protect the nation's blood supply from the deadly AIDS virus.

Today that testing system serves more than 1,200 hospitals in more than 20 states, helping millions of people feel more secure that the blood they may one day need won't be hazardous to their health.

This achievement, the dedication of the people who created it, and the urgency with which they worked indicate DuPont's commitment to maintain confidence in our nation's blood supply.

At DuPont, we make the things that make a difference.

This is an example of an institutional advertisement. DuPont is trying to "sell" only one thing here—good will. No hard sell is needed here; the audience is already interested in the AIDS epidemic, and information about a blood-screening system is good news indeed for people worrying about the safety of blood transfusions. DuPont is not mentioned until the fourth paragraph; the company emerges from this ad as a quiet, responsible corporate citizen. The ad is part of a long-term persuasive effort by the company.

Compare the institutional approach with this novel plea from the Greenpeace organization. It asks directly for financial support, but it focuses on a young woman who is pictured with this copy:

FOR ONE DOLLAR, THIS WOMAN WILL DODGE HARPOONS, DEFY MEN WITH CLUBS, AND DIVE INTO TOXIC WASTE

Her name's Kate Karam.

And she doesn't do these things for money.

Yet she doesn't do them for nothing.

So far, Kate and hundreds of activists like her have been able to stop the slaughter of seals in Canada. Spare the whales from extinction. And obtain criminal indictments against some of the world's worst polluters.

And those are just a few of the job's benefits.

For fifteen years now, Greenpeace activists have put their life and health on the line. For the life and health of our planet.

And even though we don't do this for money, it would be extremely hard for us to accomplish anything without it.

That's why we ask for your support in helping these extraordinary people continue their extraordinary work.

Please make a donation.

You'll be surprised what some people will do for a buck.

Note the short-burst approach in this copy, which uses some license in making the "one dollar" connection. It's a novel way to ask for money. As in the DuPont ad, the lively but concise style is reminiscent of some feature writing.

Now let's return to our case study. How would you begin an advertisement that opposes a ban on tobacco advertising? Assume that you have a mixed audience of smokers and non-smokers. Let's first consider two headlines that will attract attention:

1. WILL OUR CONSTITUTION GO UP IN
SMOKE?

2. THIS AD MAY SOON BE ILLEGAL.

Both headlines should attract a broad, heterogeneous audience. Both stimulate curiosity; neither gives a real clue as to the subject matter of the ad—an important factor because the campaign does not want to focus on obvious health matters.

For the sake of example, let's choose headline 1 and assume we'll write a brief ad. That means our position statement should be made early in the message. What might our first (lead) paragraph look like?

That will happen if Congress approves a law being pushed by one of the nation's most powerful political lobbies—to ban all advertising of all tobacco products.

Already the audience can *infer* the position—which is important in the low-key, somewhat defensive presentation. This statement is brief and follows directly from the headline we've chosen. Now let's work on one version of the body of the ad, listing reasons to oppose this ban:

If the American Medical Association has its way, its prescription for eliminating tobacco products will cost you dearly.

It will cost you your freedom of choice.

And it will cost all of us our freedom of expression.

When we ban advertising—a method of expression that has built our economy—what's next?

We shudder to think about it.

We now have met the third criterion of the successful ad by showing the disadvantages of the proposed ban. To oppose the ban, then, is to benefit the public and protect the nation's governing document. This is low-key flag-waving.

To conclude this brief message, we need a closing statement that will call for action and leave a memorable impression.

It may be fashionable today to bash companies that produce tobacco products with the
help of many dedicated farm families, but it will
never be right in this country to tell people how
they can live and what they can say. That's why
the American Civil Liberties Union opposes
this ban.

We hope you will, too.

Eight brief paragraphs avoid the obvious health issues and instead focus on "heartland" appeals—to patriotism and personal rights. Does it work? That depends on the predisposition of the audience; however, it may be most effective in creating a point of view for the undecided. That's an important function of persuasion.

Before we move on to speechwriting, we should consider an important question: Are there *always* two sides to an issue? (You might be wondering about this after our copywriting exercise, especially if you're a non-smoker.) Our answer has to be no. Some propositions are so blatantly wrong and harmful that it would be impossible for any moral person to write in favor of them. Some examples: arguing that nuclear war is good for society; advocating child abuse; and urging leniency for drunk drivers. Although these examples are extremes, other ideas are tinged with enough potential harm and wrong to prompt many writers not to support them. Therefore, we must always remember that in persuasive writing, we write *opinion* and we try to reinforce it with the best selection of the most compelling *facts* we can.

We'll see this process in action in our next persuasive form, speechwriting.

The speech

A little more than 125 years ago, a weary Abraham Lincoln stood on the Civil War battlefield of Gettysburg, Pennsylvania, and gave a brief speech to dedicate a cemetery. It was less than 300 words in length, three paragraphs in all. Historians claim that the president wrote five versions of this speech; if so, it is testament to a writing process that benefits from edits and revisions. Still, it is hard to imagine a more emotional final sentence than this one, which attempted to heal the wounds of a young, war-torn country:

It is rather for us to be here dedicated to the great task remaining before us—that from these honored dead we take increased devotion to that cause for which they gave their last full measure of devotion—that we here highly resolve that these dead shall not have died in vain—that this nation, under God, shall have a new birth of freedom—and that government of the people, by the people and for the people shall not perish from the earth.

Generations of school children, required to memorize and deliver this address, would attest that great words and classic thoughts don't always *sound* wonderful. An important part of the speech is in the delivery—and that brings us to a key point affecting speechwriting: Most people won't *see* your writing. Most people won't even know *you* wrote the speech because most writers of public addresses are ghost-writers—they operate in the shadows, writing on behalf of others. Your efforts may shine in the oratory of a person who is articulate, forceful and even a bit theatrical; they may be diminished by a reticent delivery. Just as you can't write without your audience in mind, you can't ignore the capabilities and characteristics of the person who is going to give the speech.

Understanding that you write a speech with the ear, the speaker and the audience in mind, you can proceed with your organization in much the same way you would an editorial or advertisement: get attention, hold interest, develop the argument or thesis and call for action. Remember that the speech may have a more personal and conversational style.

To continue our tobacco case study, let's examine several portions of a speech entitled, "To End the Scourge of Tobacco." It is delivered by Charles LeMaistre, president of the University of Texas M. D. Anderson Hospital and Tumor Institute. After acknowledging his audience and thanking everyone for an award he has received, he announces the thrust of his talk:

This afternoon, I would like to focus upon the enormous impact of tobacco on the health of our nation by giving you my perspective on just one aspect of the problem—lung cancer.

I choose this single illness as my example because of the great ironies inherent in lung cancer. In the therapeutic battleground against cancer, we are at a stalemate with lung cancer. Despite many treatment successes with other types of cancer over the last decade, the picture remains bleak for most people diagnosed with lung cancer—90 percent will die within five years of their diagnosis. And yet, the most difficult type of cancer to <u>cure</u> is also the easiest to <u>prevent</u> in the first place—80 percent to 85 percent of all lung cancers are directly, unequivocally, linked to prolonged tobacco use. . . .

(Although LeMaistre is speaking to a group of physicians, he also has a larger audience—through the media—so he must be methodical and speak in plain terms whenever possible. In the third and fourth paragraphs of his speech, he announces his intention to show the relationship between tobacco use and lung cancer. His tone is set by the effective juxtaposition of lung cancer cure *[difficult] and lung cancer* prevention *[easy]. After providing analysis of the problem of lung cancer, he continues to hold audience interest by developing an attack on tobacco manufacturers.)*

Lung cancer, then, is an epidemic out of control. We know the cause of the epidemic. And we know our current diagnostic and therapeutic weapons cannot stem the tide.

Today, the problem of smoking and lung cancer must be viewed within the larger context of a major social, economic and moral issue that looms before this nation and the world.

Tobacco is the largest non-food cash crop grown on the face of the earth. Six major American merchants of death produce 600 billion cigarettes each year for sale. Their industry is essentially unregulated by any scientific or agricultural watchdog agency of the federal or any state government. . . .

In the United States alone, the six major tobacco companies will spend more than $2 billion this year on advertising and sales promotion. The tobacco companies will tell you that those advertising dollars are designed only to persuade smokers to switch brands—not to entice more people to smoke.

Common sense tells us differently. That advertising has, as its minimal goal, replacing with new cigarette smokers at least the 350,000 to 500,000 Americans who will die of smoking-related causes this year alone.

Historians in years to come will shake their heads and marvel over the epidemic of lung cancer, as it has occurred in the supposedly civilized world during the 20th century. The enormous increase in lung cancer during the 50 years between 1935 and 1985 will provide a lasting model of destructive human behavior that will be studied by social scientists far into the future. . . .

(LeMaistre's position is now clear: He makes a strong connection between the "epidemic" of lung cancer and the aggressive sales promotion of tobacco products. Obviously, he supports an advertising ban. Having stated both the problem and his position, LeMaistre has turned to harsher language— for example, "merchants of death," "Common sense tells us differently," and "supposedly civilized world." He is trying to gather support for his position so he can issue an important call for action. We'll jump now to the final part of his speech, where he urges political action at all levels to fight the epidemic.)

Our focus must be expanded to include an even larger target: the legal manufacture of death-dealing products continues unabated, resulting in almost 500,000 American deaths each year, or about one in four of all Americans who die from all causes, or almost as many Americans sacrificed in one year as lost their lives in all wars this century.

Is the change occurring fast enough? There can be no greater humanitarian effort than renewed and vigorous prosecution of this issue politically at local, state and national levels. There can be no greater or more worthwhile health crusade than the education of America's young to avoid the use of tobacco.

The solution is not going to come from the American tobacco companies. For over 20 years, the facts have been known, but they have taken no positive action to aid in the solution. It is wishful thinking to believe that a new sense of responsibility will arise to aid us in raising a smoke-free young America. In fact, the response of the tobacco industry has been just the opposite—seductive, deceitful and misleading advertising aimed at the aspirations and insecurities of the young, ostensibly offering them an "image maker" by which they can announce their maturity.

Our task together is but half-done. I know that the volunteers of the American Lung Association and the American Thoracic Society are committed to a future free from the ravages of tobacco-caused illness, injury and death. I share your pride in the leadership you have displayed and in the progress you have achieved.

But it is not enough. We must finish the job.

The only question that remains is whether your will—and mine—is sufficient to end the scourge of tobacco.

History will record whether or not we settle for a substantial gain or whether we have the guts to go all the way.

As we mentioned before, a speech can be much more personal and emotional than an editorial or advertisement. This speech certainly proves that. It drew immediate attention to the problem, and it carried the audience through the argumentation and call for action.

One of the most important public relations functions is speechwriting. In preparing an address for a client or a boss, the writer can reach into an inventory of humor, anecdotes, quotations, statistics and even satire to get closer to the audience and to make key points. The speech must be appropriate for the intended audience, and, for the sake of the person who must face the audience, it must be *deliverable*. Clumsy constructions, hard-to-pronounce words, inept attempts at humor and, perhaps worst of all, insufferable length will doom a speech.

We'll return to persuasive speechwriting in Chapter 17.

The public relations project

One of the most dramatic examples of a "persuasion war" to win the hearts, minds (and lungs?) of American society is the lengthy, well-financed public relations clash between health and tobacco organizations over the issue of smoking. In one battle camp sit the forces of the American Cancer Society, the American Medical Association and the U.S. Department of Health and Human Services, just to start the list; in the other sit, in addition to the "Big Three" tobacco manufacturers, such organizations as the Tobacco Institute, Tobacco Associates, Inc., and the National Association of Tobacco Distributors. All these organizations conduct long-term, highly orchestrated campaigns of persuasion—with radically different goals, of course.

These organizations deal in information that will foster and cement attitudes about the use of tobacco products. Research is a vital component in their persuasion strategy. Consider the materials the Tobacco Institute provides interested parties as a "briefing" to oppose a tobacco advertising ban:

— copies of magazine and newspaper editorials opposing the ban

— a policy statement from the American Advertising Federation, also opposing the ban

— a background paper, prepared by the Tobacco Institute, challenging "invented" data that claims 300,000 died in a single year from disease related to smoking

— constitutional analyses of laws banning tobacco advertising and disallowing tax deductions for tobacco advertising

— congressional testimony by various parties opposing the ban

On the side of health organizations, we see:

— a quarterly magazine called *Cancer News,* featuring a discussion of nicotine addiction

— a research report on lung cancer

— a booklet on reducing smoking at the work site

— media kits to promote The Great American Smokeout, a program started in 1974 to encourage people to quit smoking for 24 hours

Part of the tobacco industry's persuasive strategy in opposing an advertising ban was to get the public involved in the debate. Philip Morris, Inc., offering $80,000 in prizes (first prize: $15,000), solicited 2,500-word essays on the "ramifications of a tobacco advertising ban on the future of free expression in a free market economy." This was the company's announcement:

IS LIBERTY WORTH WRITING FOR?
Our Founders Thought So.
And We Think So Too.

Announcing the first annual Philip Morris Magazine Essay Competition:

The First Amendment, those few carefully crafted phrases appended to the Constitution of the United States, placed religion outside of government, assured uncensored speech, and protected peaceable assembly.

It guarded us from those who would impose their religious convictions; those who would muzzle town meetings; and those whose admiration for free speech ends where their prejudices begin.

The First Amendment has been a preoccupation of writers and scholars, journalists and politicians for the last 200 years. It has also drawn the grateful attention of business leaders because it promised that the flow of information about legally sold goods and services would not be infringed upon by the government.

The men and women of Philip Morris believe in the principles set forth in the First Amendment and rise to defend its long-standing application to American business. We believe that a tobacco advertising ban, currently under consideration in Congress, is a clear infringement of free expression in a free market economy.

According to *Philip Morris Magazine,* almost 4,000 people submitted essays. The winning entries (more than 50) were published in a book called *American Voices.* Having "ordinary citizens" comment on an important public issue instead of depending on expert sources can be an effective persuasive strategy.

Without the expense and flourish of a contest, the American Cancer Society has combatted these pro-tobacco activities with a low-key but widely distributed report called "Cancer Facts and Figures." It shows, for example, that in 1987 the largest number of new cases among all cancers was of lung cancer, with 150,000 new diagnoses. They add to this report this comment on prevention, which obviously is intended to be persuasive:

Cigarette smoking is responsible for 85% of lung cancer cases among men and 75% among women—about 83% overall. Smoking accounts for about 30% of all cancer deaths. Those who smoke two or more packs of cigarettes a day have lung cancer mortality rates 15 to 25 times greater than nonsmokers. . . . The heavy use of alcohol, especially when accompanied by cigarette smoking or chewing tobacco, increases risk of cancers of the mouth, larynx, throat, esophagus and liver.

This information can be nicely tailored for a public service announcement on behalf of the American Cancer Society:

THE GREAT AMERICAN SMOKEOUT BEGINS
TOMORROW, AND YOUR CHAPTER OF THE
AMERICAN CANCER SOCIETY ASKS YOU TO
HELP US ALL BREATHE MORE FREELY BY
NOT LIGHTING UP. THE SOCIETY REMINDS
US THAT CIGARETTE SMOKING IS
RESPONSIBLE FOR MORE THAN 80
PERCENT OF ALL LUNG CANCER CASES.
THINK ABOUT THAT TOMORROW—THINK
ABOUT THAT FOR THE REST OF YOUR LIFE.

The special public relations project may involve speechwriting, ad copywriting and background report writing to be sent to editorial writers. It requires long-term planning, intensive research and generally low-key presentation. In addition to the public relations practitioner, representatives of trade associations, special consultants and legislative lobbyists may be active in the administration of these projects.

Taking sides

In acknowledging that two sides of most issues *can* be argued, we must also understand that a person's political, social and religious background will profoundly affect what position he or she will argue. Successful persuasive writers believe in their position; they seek relevant research to support their thesis; they avoid demagoguery and "cheap shots"; they present both argument and evidence and hope that the public will adopt their stance. In the case of a tobacco advertising ban, writers who are non-smokers but who have strong feelings about protection of commercial speech may be comfortable in opposing an ad ban; however, they may not be willing to use their writing skills to promote the sale of tobacco products.

Successful persuasive writers must enjoy argumentation and the selling of ideas. It is more aggressive work than any other media form. This is especially true in advertising copywriting. Because the client is *paying* to have a message disseminated (and supporting news and feature distribution in the process), that message will not contain an admission of any weakness in the argument or sales pitch. For example, an ad urging you to buy car X because it costs only $9,995, gets 25 miles per gallon in city driving and has a 40,000-mile warranty is not going to admit that its nearest competitor, car Y, sells for the same price and gets equal, if not better, mileage. The ad will sell reputation, reliability and service.

Even in an editorial, argumentation relies on *selected* information, forcefully presented. In taking sides, the persuasive writer tries to win. Information may be at the heart of that presentation, but strategy and style are the soul. That's why we have the news: to bring a balance and perspective to all the forces of persuasion that society faces daily.

In Chapter 17 we'll continue our examination of strategies and styles in persuasive writing and also look at various broadcast forms.

Persuasive Writing

Take 2

Sixty seconds.

That's not much time for a phone call, a conversation or even a rushed memo.

But it's a generous allocation for a television message, especially in the age of 15- and 30-second "spot" commercials. It was more than enough time for a Houston advertising agency to mix sight, sound and words into an award-winning public service ad.

Follow us through the script to observe this mix. It may seem more effective to see and hear all these elements, but persuasive writers often don't have this advantage when they are creating an idea. The power of the idea and the strength of the words are all that's needed to send the message from planning stages to final production.

In this commercial script, material set in italics indicates placement and use of visuals. The spoken words are in regular type.

(*Announcer, voice-over [V/O], with white letters against black background being read.*)

A killer is loose.
One that stalks only children.

(*Medium camera shot on little girl rocking an infant, as V/O continues.*)

It's cystic fibrosis—the Number One genetic killer of children.

(*Close-up of the girl and infant.*)

Yet most people don't know what cystic fibrosis is.

(*Camera cuts to close-up of Dr. Ralph Rucker, who speaks.*)

"It is relentless, progressive pulmonary destruction."

(*Dr. Rucker is still heard, but camera moves closer to his hands as they point out sections of an X-ray.*)

"Small elements of the lungs get infected and then scar—and then disappear."

(*Camera cuts to small boy [Roger Johnson] in hospital bed. He breathes with the aid of oxygen fed through nasal tubes. He speaks softly and in gasps.*)

"In a sense, it's my second home."

(*Camera cuts to scene in which Roger is wheeled around hospital. V/O from Dr. Rucker.*)

"Gradually the breathing difficulties get to a point where they can't participate in exercise."

(*Cut to Roger in bed, coughing. Dr. Rucker V/O.*)

"Then it progresses to where they're short of breath even at rest."

(*Dr. Rucker, back on camera.*)

". . . and then short of breath, even on oxygen."

(*Camera returns to young Roger in bed. Roger speaks.*)

"I think about it a lot."

(*Dr. Rucker, back on camera.*)

"It's a very devastating death."

(*To Roger in bed.*)

"I just get worried."

(*To Dr. Rucker.*)

"It's a very uncomfortable death. It's suffocation."

(*To Roger.*)

"I guess when the time comes, I'll have to do it. But it seems so quick."

(*Shift to freeze frame of Roger in bed. Announcer V/O.*)

Roger Johnson died shortly after this film was made.

(*Fade to black. Bring up white type against black, with announcer reading type V/O.*)

There's no cure for cystic fibrosis.
Yet.
Blue Bell Creameries ask you to please help.
For the children.

This heart-wrenching presentation effectively used the words of both patient and doctor, with only the opening and close depending on the words of a copywriter to set the scene and make a plea. It's a persuasive technique that requires the ability to evaluate the power of the image and to intersperse sound bites with the copywriter's words. By not overpowering this message with the writer's words—by stressing both the simplicity and power of the plea—the writer and producer thrust the audience into a reality it could not possibly ignore.

Such mixing also is common in broadcast news and depth-and-context forms, as you have seen in earlier chapters. We'll examine some persuasive techniques for broadcast in this chapter, and we'll also look at some common stylistic devices in persuasive writing. But first, let's look once more at two of the most common persuasive formats, the editorial and the advertisement, and review the basic elements of their structure. Such a review is helpful not only for emphasis but to offer more examples outside of the tobacco ad ban assignment.

A second look at structure

Let's first examine an editorial by George Gladney, former managing editor of Wyoming's *Jackson Hole News*. The editorial, which opposes surrogate motherhood, won the Eric W. Allen Jr. Award in 1987 for excellence in opinion writing.

Gladney's thesis is that any benefits of surrogate motherhood are dramatically outweighed by adverse effects not only on the parties involved but also on society. His secondary position is that the world does not need more population—especially under such unnatural circumstances.

He begins his low-key presentation with a position statement and follows with a brief explanation of the surrogate process and of a nationally publicized conflict over a surrogate contract.

Unhappiness Is Inevitable
NIX SURROGATE MOTHERHOOD
By George Gladney

Surrogate motherhood is society's newest experiment to circumvent the simple truth in life that we can't always get what we want. It is an experiment that tampers with the natural order of things, and the results, predictably, are less than desirable. In the case of surrogate motherhood, nobody benefits, even if it works the way its proponents say it should.

The concept is simple enough. Taking advantage of the unnatural wonder of artificial insemination, a married couple who cannot produce a child naturally on their own (because the wife is unable to bear a child) goes to a special agency to contract with a woman who agrees to be implanted with the male's sperm, nurture the fetus through pregnancy and then hand over the infant to the couple after childbirth.

This system works well until the surrogate mother, overpowered by the maternal instinct of the child-bearing experience, wants out of the contract. This is what happened in the "Baby M" case now being argued in a New Jersey courtroom. In that case, Mary Beth Whitehead agreed, through an organization that arranges surrogacy, to bear a child for Dr. Elizabeth and William Stern, but now is contesting the pact and is seeking custody of the infant girl.

(This is a complicated topic; it's not easy to express it in thin, simple constructions. Editorials are not generally written in the short-paragraph style of newswriting. There is more context and background to explain. Such perspective helps the audience form a solid opinion.)

Gladney next explains two perspectives on the issue and then restates his position, citing a study that claims adverse effects of surrogacy.

The Baby M case has focused national debate on the legality of surrogate motherhood contracts, and the issue is divided between mothers' rights on the one hand and contractual obligations on the other. Some people argue that no prior contract can override the fact that the woman who gives birth is the legal mother and must voluntarily decide whether to give up the baby—contract or no contract; others argue that the procreative liberty of a married couple includes the right to hire a substitute mother and that a freely signed agreement can be enforced.

But all of this sidesteps the real issue: Does society want to condone surrogate motherhood and the ill effects for all parties involved, including society itself?

Although fewer than one in 100 surrogate mothers have refused to give up their babies, research by Dr. Philip Parker, a Detroit Psychiatrist, shows that three out of 30 surrogate mothers studied were so distraught after giving up their infants that they needed therapeutic counseling. Parker found that most of the 30 women felt some loss and all felt grief, ranging from a single crying spell to months of remorse. Parker contends that despite use of the most elaborate screening methods, it is impossible to predict how a surrogate mother will react when it is time to give up the child.

(In addition to stating the two sides of this issue, Gladney now uses some research that reveals some of the ill effects he is citing as a reason to oppose surrogacy.)

Gladney continues his debate format by citing an argument for surrogacy and then showing weaknesses in that argument, finally focusing on the needs of the child.

Proponents of surrogate motherhood say the experience is good for the mother because it lets her experience the joy and fulfillment of pregnancy and a sense of altruism and compassion for the married couple. However, studies show that money (usually $10,000 plus expenses) is a significant factor in nine of 10 cases and that some surrogate mothers are motivated by guilt over a past abortion, a need to re-enact their own childhood abandonment, emptiness to their life and a weak sense of self.

But what about the father? Given the availability of traditional adoption, the real motivation behind the surrogate motherhood arrangements is the father's egocentric desire that his genes be carried onto another generation. In fact, this whole mess of surrogate motherhood is brought about by the father's less-than-noble unwillingness to accept responsibly the consequences of the reality that he married a woman who cannot propagate his genes. He is unwilling to accept that marriage has its risks, that we cannot always get what we want.

Lost in most of the ethical and legal debates are the effects on the child, but these should be obvious from the Whitehead case. The infant is called Sara by Whitehead, Melissa by the Sterns and Baby M by the court. Bestowed with three identities and caught in a tug of war between parents is hardly the way to start one's life.

(With more information backing his case, Gladney becomes more forceful and direct. He calls surrogacy a "mess" and criticizes a father's selfishness for not accepting the cards that are dealt to him and his spouse. Such forcefulness helps propel the argument toward its conclusion.)

Gladney now is ready to address a solution that already has been proposed and to try to rebut it, thus setting up his wrap-up of the issue.

Some believe the answer is for state legislatures to enact laws making surrogate motherhood contracts legal, while perhaps giving the biological mother 30 days or so to change her mind about giving up the baby. That would resolve the legal uncertainties, but it would still mean society is willing to accept a situation where one of the parties is very likely to be unhappy—the surrogate mother, if the baby is forced from her; the father, if the child is raised by the surrogate mother, against his wishes; or the child, always left to ponder the meaning of being conceived by the bind of contract rather than by parental affection.

Finally, it should be underscored that in screening prospective surrogate mothers, agencies find that the candidates are women who can thoroughly detach themselves from the maternal bond. In this way, surrogate motherhood fosters a most unnatural behavior—the bearing of a child one does not want to love and keep.

Rather than devise new legal and technological means to get what we want, against the advice of nature and skirting the realities of risk and consequence in life, society should concentrate on doing better with what it has. Society would do better to expend its energy and resources trying to reduce the large incidence of children brought into the world under less than desirable circumstances, by teenage mothers, for example.

(Rather than to come out directly in favor of a law prohibiting surrogacy contracts, Gladney continues to persuade the audience, in a low-key manner, to oppose the notion of surrogacy. Presumably, a climate in which surrogacy is seen as unwise and unhealthy will itself be persuasive to legislative bodies in search of a solution to this problem.)

Somewhat sarcastically, Gladney concludes his message with an observation about overpopulation, leaving the audience to ponder all the effects of the surrogacy question.

The world is not underpopulated. Society does not need surrogate motherhood as a new means of ensuring that more infants will enter the world under undesirable circumstances.

Although this editorial is somewhat longer than most daily newspaper opinion pieces, it does an excellent job of stating the problem, taking a position, giving background, developing arguments and coming to a conclusion. Because this is not a lighthearted topic, the tone remains serious throughout, and the writer avoids pushing the audience to a premature or illogical conclusion.

Like the editorial, the advertisement also depends on persuasion; unlike an opinion piece, however, the ad often depends on strong visual treatment, entertainment and even lighthearted appeals to make its point. The pace and direction of many ads can be friskier than an editorial because what is being sold may not be as serious. As an example, let's look at some ad copy directed to a student consumer. The product: a word processor. We'll start with the grabber headline and then move to the position statement.

If only typewriters let you proofread your work before they printed it on the page.

What a mess!

You've just proofread your term paper and it's got typos, spelling errors and misplaced paragraphs.

Now, you can't turn in a paper like this. So no matter how tired you are, you've got to re-type the entire thing.

That is, unless you typed it on a Videowriter.

(Notice the light, friendly approach in this copy. The copywriter has stated a wish [If only. . . .], a problem [the mess] and a solution [the Videowriter]. The solution is the position: the Videowriter is the answer. Note that the solution is stated as a sentence fragment; this would be unacceptable in most media writing, but it can be effective in the looser style of ad copywriting. The writer now moves to a long list of reasons to support the "argument" that the student should buy this word processor. Note also that the headline is actually the lead paragraph of the message, one of the main structural differences between ad copywriting and other media writing forms.)

The Videowriter solves all your typing problems.

Take the most obvious one: typos.

On an ordinary typewriter it would mean a bottle of white-out and a frustrating interruption.

On a Videowriter it just means pressing the key marked "delete." That's all. Because you type your work out on a screen before you print it on a page.

It edits.

And how about those bigger problems like wanting to rearrange paragraphs? On an ordinary typewriter you have to "cut and paste" them.

On a Videowriter you only have to press the key marked "move" and then indicate the area you want it moved to. It's that simple.

It spells.

What happens when you're typing and you come to a word you can't spell?

On an ordinary typewriter you have to stop typing, find a dictionary and look it up.

Not so on a Videowriter. Spelling problems can be corrected simply by pressing the key marked "spell."

It counts words.

If you've ever had a teacher tell you to write a thousand word essay, you know what a pain it is trying to count your words.

On an ordinary typewriter you have to do it with your finger.

But on a Videowriter you can press a mere two buttons and it does the counting for you.

It makes multiple copies.

From time to time you want a copy of what you've typed, right?

Well, if you use a Videowriter you won't have to go to the school library to look for a copier machine.

All you'll have to look for is the button marked "print." Press it and the Videowriter will make another original.

And because your work is automatically stored on a standard 3½" floppy disk, you can make those copies whenever you want.

(Having made its pitch [The Videowriter solves all your typing problems], this advertisment breezily backs up its thesis by selling the consumer on time-saving features: It edits; it spells; it counts words; it makes multiple copies. By stating a typical typing problem and then showing how this machine solves that problem, the ad creates a rhythm and flow that make for easy reading and effective persuasion. The ad ends by restating its pitch and adding a clincher to close the sale: It's not expensive. Note the use of secondary headlines in this copy. They help with transitions in thought and also add a graphic boldness to the presentation.)

It obviously does a lot more than type.

That's because the word processing features just go on and on. What's more, we sell the Videowriter Word Processor for around the price of a good electronic typewriter.

And that's quite a bargain when you consider the amount of time it'll save you. Time you can spend doing the work for your other classes.

You would do that, wouldn't you?

(The ad closes with a conspiratorial wink that suggests that students have other things to do with their free time. And so, in 27 brief paragraphs, a sales pitch is made, promising academic success and hinting at free time for socialization. Note that this ad doesn't examine and prove its claims in any detail; its research is not as intense as that of an editorial. But then, people have different expectations from an editorial.)

These two persuasive forms reflect important similarities, but they also reveal interesting differences. We'll highlight only one difference at this point—that the argumentation (building of a case) generally has more depth and seriousness in an editorial. Still, an advertising message cannot succeed if its appeals are thin.

Keep these persuasive structures in mind as we examine two broadcast messages, both of which have definite sales functions.

Looking at the broadcast style

Writers in the electronic media are well aware of the role the senses play in the reception and translation of a message. The television audience may be more passive because the message is "fed" to it, but that does not mean that the audience is uninvolved. Sound is a stimulus; moving images provide a deeper and more dynamic dimension than the graphic monotone of print.

However, such apparent advantages do not ensure the automatic success of the message. Form (presentation) cannot cover for weak function (content). Let's examine part of the broadcast style by reviewing a radio commentary and a radio advertisement. Read them aloud and then have a friend read them to you; do the words you can't see have the power to persuade?

The commentary

It took commentator Russell Sadler less than two minutes to deliver this opinion piece. Because no special graphics are needed for this presentation, his radio script would remain unchanged if he also delivered his message on television—the only difference is that he'd wear a coat and tie on TV. Here is his script for a radio delivery. Note his use of sarcasm in attacking what he considers a silly and illogical bill:

INTRO: THE U.S. HOUSE OF REPRESENTATIVES APPROVED A BILL REQUIRING UNIFORM POLL-CLOSING HOURS IN PRESIDENTIAL ELECTIONS BY A NARROW MARGIN. RUSSELL SADLER OBSERVES CONGRESSMEN HAVE THE WRONG PRESCRIPTION FOR THE WRONG PROBLEM.

SADLER: WE NEED UNIFORM POLL-CLOSING HOURS, ACCORDING TO WASHINGTON CONGRESSMAN AL SWIFT BECAUSE THE MEAN, NASTY, EVIL MEDIA ARE TELLING US THE RESULTS OF THE ELECTION BEFORE THE POLLS ARE CLOSED IN THE WEST, BASED ON THE RESULTS OF VOTING IN THE EAST. TO PREVENT THIS DASTARDLY DEED, THE BILL PASSED BY THE HOUSE WILL CLOSE THE POLLS AT 9 PM IN THE EAST, 8 PM IN THE CENTRAL TIME ZONE AND 7 PM IN THE MOUNTAIN TIME ZONE. FOLLOWING THIS FORMULA, IT WOULD CLOSE POLLS ON THE WEST COAST AT 6 PM. BUT MANY CONGRESSMEN COMPLAINED THAT WOULD CAUSE PROBLEMS FOR WEST COAST VOTERS CASTING THEIR BALLOTS AFTER WORK. SO THE MEASURE EXTENDS DAYLIGHT SAVINGS TIME FOR THE WEST COAST AN EXTRA TWO WEEKS—BUT ONLY IN PRESIDENTIAL ELECTION YEARS—SO THE WEST COAST POLLS CAN CLOSE AT 7 PM. GOT THAT? YOU'RE RIGHT. IT'S CONFUSING. FOR ABOUT TWO WEEKS EVERY FOUR YEARS, THE WEST COAST WILL BE TWO HOURS BEHIND THE EAST COAST, WHICH WILL HAVE SWITCHED TO STANDARD TIME.

CONGRESSMAN SWIFT AND HIS FRIENDS HAVE THE WRONG PRESCRIPTION FOR THE

WRONG PROBLEM. PEOPLE DID NOT LEAVE
THE POLLS IN 1980 BECAUSE THE
TELEVISION NETWORKS PROJECTED
REAGAN THE WINNER OVER CARTER. IT
WAS CARTER'S PREMATURE CONCESSION
SPEECH THAT PROMPTED PEOPLE TO SAY
THERE WAS NO POINT IN VOTING THAT DAY.
THE DEMOCRATS COULD SOLVE THIS
PROBLEM BY NOMINATING A MORE
COMPETITIVE CANDIDATE FOR PRESIDENT.
IN A CLOSE PRESIDENTIAL RACE, VOTERS
ON THE EAST COAST WILL HAVE TO STAY UP
LATE TO FIND OUT WHO WON.
ALASKA AND HAWAII ARE EXEMPT FROM
THIS BILL BECAUSE THERE WAS NO WAY TO
FIDDLE AROUND WITH THE TIME ZONES TO
MAKE UNIFORM CLOSING HOURS WORK IN
THOSE TWO STATES. ARE ALASKANS AND
HAWAIIANS LESS SUBJECT TO THE
INFLUENCE OF THE MEDIA? NO, THEY JUST
KNOW THE VIRTUE OF BEING LEFT ALONE
TO COPE WITH THE PROBLEM THEIR OWN
WAY. THAT'S THE WAY TO SOLVE THIS
PROBLEM. PEOPLE WHO FEAR THEY MAY
BE INFLUENCED BY EARLY PROJECTIONS
CAN ALWAYS VOTE EARLY IN THE DAY.

With a little sarcasm ("mean, nasty, evil media," "dastardly deed"), Sadler introduces the problem and proceeds to show the weaknesses behind the proposed solution. Knowing that radio cannot hold audience attention the way television can, Sadler is brief. He uses inflection and emphasis to give his words personality and force. For example, when Sadler asks, "Are Alaskans and Hawaiians less subject to the influence of the media?" he makes points with an audience that has been following the argument so far.

Writing for radio requires an ability to predict how the audience will *hear* the message. Sentence length, punctuation, use of subordinate constructions and selection of colorful and descriptive words are important in helping the audience *see* the images and concepts you are trying to present.

Let's look at another radio message, a 60-second commercial for a well-known health insurance plan. Health coverage is a serious topic, but the ad agency of Borders, Perrin and Norrander chose a light-hearted theme with which to explain the flexibility of their client's health plans. Note the use of music and sound effects (shown as S/FX) to hold audience interest. All sound effects and instructions are listed in italics.

(Slightly tongue-in-cheek announcer delivery over whimsical music. Open on sound of man rowing.)

MAN SINGING: Row, row, row your boat. . . .

ANNOUNCER: This is a story about two Oregon businesses. One is a very small boat builder who builds very small boats . . .

(Bring up rowing S/FX and singing.)

ANNOUNCER: . . . the other, a very large boat builder, who builds very large boats.

(Fade out rowing, cue sound of sailboat on high seas.)

MAN SINGING: Sailing, sailing, over the bounding main. . . .

ANNOUNCER: Normally, you wouldn't expect these two very different companies to have much more than the water in common. But unfortunately, they have the very same kind of health plan. So, the large boat builder felt that his coverage was going to leave him high and dry.

(Bring up rowboat singer.)

ANNOUNCER: And the small boat builder thought he might get sunk any day. But now, Blue Cross/Blue Shield has a new, more personal kind of health plan. One that boat builders can customize to fit their needs perfectly.

(Bring up sailboat singer.)

ANNOUNCER: So the very large boat builder will have a policy that's ship-shape.

(Rowboat singer up.)

ANNOUNCER: And the very small boat builder will be able to have coverage without any holes

in it. Your very own personal insurance company. Blue Cross and Blue Shield of Oregon.

With the use of several voices, realistic sound effects and easy-to-
follow copy, this advertisement both entertains and informs. Entertainment often is the "hook" that grabs the audience for an advertisement. However, the message must be brief, and the entertainment
must not overpower the thrust of the message. The use of sound
effects in radio is equivalent to print's use of graphics and design.
These effects give variety and rhythm to the message—clearly, they
are part of the ad copywriting process. The lighthearted play on
words ("policy that's ship-shape," "coverage without any holes in it")
may seem fanciful, but this technique can support a serious message.
In the case of this campaign, you might even say it is seaworthy!
(Sorry.)

Television's special requirements

Mastering the radio format is helpful in understanding the particular
needs of television. For example, a commercial selling raisins as fun,
healthful food can be more effective and entertaining in a visual medium. That's what the Raisin Growers of California discovered when
they enlisted the aid of clay animation expert Will Vinton to create a
scene with dancing raisins singing the rock classic "I Heard It
Through the Grapevine." The visual impact of this unlikely song-and-
dance team promoting "raisins made in the California sunshine" was
so strong that the advertisement led to the marketing of various raisin
novelty items, including a cassette tape of rock standards done by the
singing raisins.

Working effectively with the visual medium requires the ability to
substitute images for words. The words often play a secondary role to
those images, which have the responsibility to attract attention and
hold audience interest. The words must be used strategically to identify the product or service, to make the pitch and to close the
presentation.

However, understanding the principles of persuasive writing remains the first step in effective presentation for any medium. Students
should focus on these principles until they master this foundation.

To help in understanding techniques of persuasion, let's turn to
an examination of various stylistic devices in editorials, advertising
and speeches.

Persuasion's varied styles

$\mathbf{W}$e don't have enough space to list all the writing approaches used in the persuasive style, but we can examine several commonly used forms. We'll look at repetition, understatement, word play, humor, comparison and contrast, and straight talk.

Repetition

Repeating key words and phrases not only creates emphasis, but it also alerts the audience to a certain rhythm in the argument or sales effort. You'll note its effectiveness in the last sentence of the Gettysburg Address (page 262), in which Lincoln repeated the conjunction *that* to create a series of hopes and promises. In the following example, syndicated columnist Carl Rowan uses three words to announce several thoughts at the beginning of his column. (We have underlined for emphasis.)

WASHINGTON—The acquittal of Bernhard H. Goetz of charges of attempted murder and assault says a lot more about what has been happening to America than about either Goetz or the jury that cleared him.

It tells us that because of a frightening increase in crimes, and demagogic exploitations of that fact, the crazy passions of vigilantism are as alive in America today as the AIDS virus.

It tells us that a public outcry over violent crimes can make the majority of the U.S. Supreme Court do a flip-flop on the meaning of the Constitution, unleashing in state after state the drooling operators of the electric chair, the gas chamber, the deadly injection, the firing squad.

It tells us that in this atmosphere, juries succumb easily to the mindsets of "Rambo," "Dirty Harry" and that celebrated "Death Wish" vigilante created by Hollywood's Charles Bronson. . . .

Like so many factors in writing, repetition suffers when it is over-done. How much is enough? That's hard to say, but you should be able to recognize when the rhythm of the repetition is slowing the piece down. In Rowan's column, beginning three paragraphs with the same words after setting up in the lead paragraph what the Goetz case says seems just right.

Repetition is especially effective in speechwriting. The speaker can add inflection and gestures to the emphasis created by the selective repetitions.

Understatement

Sometimes, a direct, no-punches-pulled approach won't work. A more subtle—and more surprising—technique is needed. It's meant to be low-key, but the results can be startling. Consider this approach by the Partnership for a Drug-Free America (see page 288) as it gives some advice to people who want to try the lethal street drug known as crack.

Although this is a shocking presentation, the impact actually is created by understatement. It's another way to gain attention, this time by saying in effect, "If no other approach has worked to fight this drug, let's see whether we can salvage some body parts." The message is clear, the impact frightening.

Understatement requires either a sophisticated audience or a simple, unmistakable theme. It can be effective in all forms of persuasive writing.

The advertisement on page 288 is an example of how a bold headline leads the audience into the message. It also shows how a strong visual—in this case, an organ donor card—is the anchor for a message awash in white space. Like the ad for the hotline for battered wives (page 32), this message depends on little copy, yet its impact is undeniable.

Self-deprecation

A relative of understatement is the "devaluing" of self. Writers do this by deliberately shying away from their accomplishments and good points and instead understating those factors. To make an attempt at *serious* self-deprecation, the writer should ensure that enough information is already known about the subject so that the audience can see that understatement is at work.

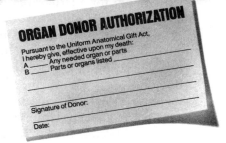

When *USA Today* editor John Quinn received the annual William Allen White Foundation award in 1987, he used part of his speech to poke fun at himself and his newspaper. Such a technique can put an audience in a friendly, receptive mood:

This 38th annual William Allen White National
Citation Luncheon puts us all in great danger

of being struck dead by an editorial thunderbolt from the heavens.

Consider the peril, in William Allen White's own words:

"Frank Munsey contributed to the journalism of his day the great talent of a meat packer, the morals of a money changer and the manners of an undertaker. He and his kind . . . (I emphasize his kind) . . . have succeeded in transforming a once noble profession into an eight percent security."

Is it not likely, then, that the editor of the *Emporia Gazette* would inflict the same "May he rest in trust" epitaph on this year's recipient of the citation bearing his name?

First, Frank Munsey was a New Englander; your 1987 recipient talks funny, too.

Second, Frank Munsey was involved in acquiring newspapers at a great profit; your 1987 recipient is a groupie, a bona fide member of a chain gang, a media-merging monster.

And third, Frank Munsey launched an illustrated general circulation publication; your humble honoree today is the editor of *USA Today,* which he helped launch as The Nation's Newspaper. It has been acclaimed far and wide by professional colleagues for bringing new depth to the definition of shallow.

Consider other accolades heaped upon this latter-day version of *Munsey's Weekly*:

—The titan of tidbits.
—The explosion in a paint factory.
—The nearbeer of newspapers.
—The flashdance of editing.
—The junkfood of journalism. . . .

Self-deprecation is most successful when it is done for a lighthearted purpose. Using it to create an image of true humility in a serious message can be quite a gamble.

Word play

One of the many wonders of our language is its playfulness. Taking a word or a phrase and stretching it to an unusual use can be both inventive and humorous. Advertising copywriters especially enjoy this technique because it generally elicits positive reactions. Here are three examples:

A new twist on an old idea.

(From a 15-second TV commercial on the Skil power screwdriver)

Never stuff another turkey. Or cram a ham. Or squeeze a melon.

(From a magazine ad on a new and larger General Electric refrigerator)

Learn to prepare this dish in 30 minutes.

(From a magazine ad for the U.S. Army, seeking recruits for its signal corps. It is looking for people to assemble high-tech satellite dishes in the field)

Word play is not as common in editorial writing because it could detract from the seriousness of the issue. However, it can be used in a humorous piece or when satire or sarcasm would be effective. In any case, word play stops working when it gets outrageous.

Humor

We all like to laugh. It makes us feel good. Norman Cousins has written that laughter helped improve his health. It's not surprising, then, that humor in the proper doses and at the right times can enhance the effectiveness of persuasive messages. Humor can be present in understatement and in word play, but it also works in direct expression when the writer pokes fun or presents images that we're not quite ready for. When we are surprised, we often laugh.

Consider, for example, the political candidate who explains his non-photogenic qualities on TV by saying,

I have a great face for radio.

Dow Chemical's corporate communications director began a speech by explaining that he was a last-minute substitute for the scheduled speaker. A little humor helped:

Just 12 days ago, I got one of those "good news, bad news" phone calls. The good news was that there was an unexpected opening for a speaker today. Then the caller added that the fellow who canceled was an expert in his field and was probably irreplaceable.

The manufacturer of Isuzu cars succeeded with outrageous humor in a series of print and broadcast ads in which the spokesman was portrayed as a liar. By admitting to untruths, the company humbles itself, and then it "fesses up" with some impressive facts. In this ad the spokesman is leaning out of a sports car with a speed-braking parachute at the rear. He provides the headline, and the manufacturer responds, in this segment of the print form:

"I just broke the land speed record. 956.39 mph in a stock Isuzu Impulse Turbo."

He's lying.

The Isuzu Impulse Turbo will not go 956.39 mph.

In fact, we've never had one go even 900 mph. But on the test track, its fuel-injected, intercooled, turbo charged engine powered the Impulse Turbo to an honest 130 mph.

And, unbelievable as it may seem, it'll go 0–60 faster than a Porsche 944, BMW 325es or Aston Martin Volante.

As long as we're being honest, there's something else we should tell you about. . . .

This humorous treatment that poked fun at the manufacturer was an instant hit. Its lack of seriousness and its low-key presentation of facts caught audience interest. And in sales, getting attention is half the battle.

Of course, humor can go awry. It's a sad sight when it happens. Consider your audience: Will it understand your intention? Consider unintended meanings: Are you aware of certain information or contexts that will cause a misunderstanding?

Comparison and contrast

Juxtapositions are important in writing. We play words and ideas off one another in order to create images. For example, we can use *implied comparisons* (metaphors) to paint a more complete picture.

Consider the television commentator who expresses her concern about a U.S.-Soviet nuclear treaty by claiming that the accord would "strip away Europe's security blanket"—a reference to that continent's concern about losing Cruise and Pershing missiles in NATO countries. Comparing that concern to the loss of a security blanket says in a few words what direct analysis would take longer to do.

In a syndicated column, George Will targets the "antiseptic arithmetic of arms control," colorfully suggesting that merely trying to match numbers of nuclear warheads ignores military realities. Such a comparison, which likens a peace treaty to cold, clean numbers, provides the audience with a startling and persuasive image.

Juxtaposing through *contrast* is another effective way to gain attention and to make a point.

In a campaign to secure donations for public broadcasting, the announcer says:

We're here every day for you. We ask you to be
here twice a year for us.

In these two sentences, *every* is contrasted with *twice; day* with *year;* and *you* with *us.* In addition to creating emphasis, such juxtaposition also has a pleasing rhythm, especially when the constructions stay simple.

In a magazine ad warning about cocaine, one sentence uses contrast to show adverse health effects:

Like speed, cocaine makes you talk a lot and
sleep a little.

In a newspaper ad promoting an athletic club during the winter months, the writer fashions a "Come on over!" headline:

Now that it's cold, dark and rainy, why not join
us at Courtsports where it's warm, bright and
dry!

Comparisons and contrasts are especially effective in speeches because the speaker can emphasize pointed and colorful juxtapositions.

Straight talk

Sophisticated word games, understatement and humor aren't always appropriate. In the midst of the 1987 stock market crisis, the firm of Merrill Lynch didn't keep its televised message of money management (with its strong, silent bull symbol) on the air. Instead, it televised its chief executive officer looking directly at the camera, giving this reassuring message:

America's economy is the greatest in the world. The stock market provides capital that creates jobs. And Merrill Lynch is still bullish on America.

Straight talk from an authoritative source: Sometimes that's what it takes to be persuasive. In the midst of such a crisis, using comedian Eddie Murphy to make bull-and-bear jokes won't do the job.

When manufacturers of birth control pills looked for ways to counteract adverse publicity about their product's side effects, they turned to the Association of Reproductive Health Professionals for straight talk. Here are segments of the association's magazine advertisement, beginning with the headline:

TRUTHRUMOR
. . . When the topic is the Pill, they're hard to separate.

It's good for you. It's bad for you. It causes cancer. It prevents cancer. It makes you more fertile. It makes you less fertile. You should get on it. You should get off it.

All the conflicting information floating around about the Pill is enough to make you contemplate abstinence. We recommend a far less drastic measure: educate yourself. Gather all the information you can from reliable sources and, together with your doctor, make the decision that's right for you.

Here are a few facts to start you off. First, the Pill is actually many pills. Since its introduction in 1960, it's evolved from one high dosage product into many much lower in dosage. From 150 mcgs. of estrogen in 1960, down to 35 or less today. Yet, it's still the most effective form of birth control available to you other than sterilization. . . .

When the world was shocked by disclosure that a subsidiary of the Japanese electronics giant Toshiba had sold the Soviet Union some machinery that the U.S.S.R. ultimately used in development of a nuclear submarine with a silent propeller, Toshiba turned to a Washington law firm to help present some straight talk. It took the form of a full-page advertisement in many of the top U.S. newspapers. The ad was so startling that its copy was widely quoted in print and broadcast stories all over the country.

Not only was this information intended to be persuasive to the public, but it also was directed at Toshiba employees, to help calm their fears and concerns. Here is a portion of that ad, which was so unusual that it also became an item of international news:

TOSHIBA CORPORATION EXTENDS ITS DEEPEST REGRETS TO THE AMERICAN PEOPLE

Toshiba Corporation shares the shock and anger of the American people, the Administration and Congress at the recent conduct of one of our 50 major subsidiaries, Toshiba Machine Company. We are equally concerned about the serious impact of TMC's diversion on the security of the United States, Japan and other countries of the Free World.

Toshiba Corporation had no knowledge of this unauthorized action by TMC. And the United States and the Japanese governments have not claimed that Toshiba Corporation itself had any knowledge or involvement.

Nevertheless, Toshiba Corporation, as a majority shareholder of TMC, profoundly apologizes for the past actions by a subsidiary of Toshiba.

As a measure of personal recognition of the grievous nature of TMC's action, both the chairman and the president of Toshiba Corporation have resigned. For the Japanese business world, this is the highest form of apology. . . .

An open apology and voluntary resignations of powerful people—this is persuasive stuff. The impact of such direct language is even greater when the stakes are high. Straight talk requires both an authoritative source and an authoritative tone.

On a much lesser scale, when the facts and statistics are in their corner, car manufacturers like to use the straight-talk technique to present a side-by-side comparison of competing models and their car. If the statistics (price, mileage, warranty, speed, braking distance) favor them, then straight talk is a solid ally.

All of these persuasive techniques work only when they fit. To decide when they are appropriate, the writer must consider:

— The *thesis* of the message. What is being advocated or sold, and how can that persuasion be best accomplished?

— The *intended audience*. How will *this* group react to humor? To straight talk? While editorial writers may have a good sense of their community, advertisers reaching out for larger markets often pre-test their message to determine whether it has its intended effect.

— The nature of the *argumentation*. Is the message aggressive or low-key? Is logic a key feature, or does the message depend on psychological appeals?

In short, you tailor your persuasion to the concept (product) and the audience (buyers). As you have seen, there are many ways to be persuasive. But our message remains the same, regardless of format, style or medium: Be accurate, be logical, be concise.

It's a great way to start—and it often will carry you to the finish.

Persuasive Writing

**Recognizing the similarities,
remembering the differences**

Persuasion is a tough-minded business. It demands success from messages that want attention, that present arguments and that hope for action from audiences whose needs and attitudes are far from universal or predictable.

At its core, all persuasion is information. It grows from seeds of facts and spreads its influence over those who are sensitive and responsive to its subject matter. Persuasion may be hard-hitting or subtle; it may be grounded in logic or it may dance, fancifully, with audience desires that defy reason.

It's tough. It's challenging. And for many writers, it's fun and rewarding.

As we have done in previous sections, let's examine the basic similarities and differences of the persuasive technique.

Similarities

Whether a media writer is preparing an editorial, an advertisement or a speech, the writing will share some common characteristics, including:

— *A deliberate "sales" function.* Persuasive writers present slanted information—that is, they choose information as part of a strategy that will result in the audience's immediate or eventual action. Persuasion is not throwaway information. Whereas news may be disposable, persuasive writing tries to linger in influence.

— *Organization that highlights arguments and appeals.* Most persuasive messages focus on the pitch and then ask the audience for a response. In most cases the response is not sought until the arguments and appeals have been successfully established.

— *Organization that tries to keep the audience involved.* Most newswriting is done with the assumption that readers and listeners will "fade" from the message—some sooner than others. In an editorial or speech, the writer tries to present as cohesive a package as possible, moving from announcement of issue, to position statement, to argumentation and then to a call for action or resolution. The advertisement generally has the same format, but the presentation may be more informal and often more daring in style.

Understanding the common characteristics of persuasive writing is the key to understanding and mastering persuasion itself. If you accept the notion that all persuasion is a form of selling, then you can also see that an audience isn't going to buy an argument or react favorably to an appeal if the information doesn't create the proper desires and attitudes.

Differences in approach and style

The editorial

Whether it is intended for print or broadcast use, the editorial is the most analytical and news-oriented of all persuasive forms. Because it focuses more on issues and on commentary, the editorial does not share the same aggressive sales function of the advertisement or the long-term, parochial aims of the public relations project. Its closest relative in terms of organization and style is the speech. Unlike the advertisement, the editorial does not use humor or satire frequently and instead aims at expanding both the information and perspective of its audience, for use in short- and long-term decision making.

The advertisement

The most inventive and visually stimulating of all persuasive forms, the advertisement is our media's sales force. It will try to sell any-thing—from suppositories to political candidates. It packages prod-ucts, issues and services with words, images and appeals. Although it has been known to do this with thin organization and condescending style, the advertisement can be both powerful and sophisticated with its information and appeals. Humor, understatement, irony and straight talk are common stylistic features of this form. Because it also is a costly form (after all, it subsidizes our news and entertainment media), it is also the briefest. The advertising copywriter faces the challenge of attracting and holding the attention of an audience that is constantly bombarded by sales messages on television, radio and billboards, and in newspapers, magazines and direct mail. Competi-tion is fierce, but the rewards are great for the copywriter whose messages hit home.

The speech

The most peculiar characteristic of speechwriting is ghostwriting—the practice of having a professional writer put words in others' mouths. Consider the busy chief executive officers of large corporations. They don't have time to write each of the 30 or so speeches per year they may be called upon to deliver. So, in consultation with the CEO, a staff writer (usually a member of the public relations department) prepares a speech that reflects in content and personal style what and how the CEO thinks and speaks. Such work requires a knowledge of the person who will deliver the speech, the makeup of the audience, how the message will be delivered and, of course, the subject matter itself. A speech is the opportunity to make not only a personal state-ment, but perhaps an institutional one as well.

The public service announcement

Combining the organizational brevity of the news burst and the promotion of an advertisement, the PSA depends on the community spirit of media outlets to disseminate these messages free of charge. Most often done for broadcast, the PSA must not abuse the generosity of its host by being overly long or too obviously commercial. The PSA is an important tool of the public relations practitioner, who uses it as "promotion with a news peg."

The public relations project

Public relations is a media hybrid. It trades on both information and persuasion and deals with a wide variety of audiences. Although its title may imply otherwise, public relations does not serve the public *first*. It has masters who pay the bills. The information released through the PR function is both limited and controlled; however, such information also provides important insight not easily gained by the news media. The activities of the Tobacco Institute, as described in Chapter 16, comfortably fit within the definition of a public relations project. In fighting a ban against tobacco advertising, the institute does research, prepares position papers, writes speeches and lobbies on behalf of manufacturers of tobacco products. This is long-term work, aimed at creating attitudes in favor of the tobacco industry. It is advocacy, and it uses many persuasive forms.

As we said at the beginning of this section, persuasion is a difficult and challenging writing form. It requires knowledge of subject, audience and technique. Like a debater, the persuasive writer must be well-prepared. Weak argumentation, loose logic, faulty transitions from a position to a call for action: They all will signal defeat in a highly competitive race for the minds, hearts—and money—of an unpredictable audience.

Responsibilities of the Mass Communicator

Media writers don't work in a vacuum. They perform their jobs in two overlapping environments—professional and societal—both of which impose responsibilities and offer guidelines for action and conduct. Now that you have a broad understanding of what media writers do, it's time to consider the larger context in which they operate.

The professional environment

As skilled, white-collar workers, media writers are, in the most general sense of the word, *professionals*. They are members of a working corps that can be considered a *profession*.

What does it mean to be a professional?

Regardless of their profession, *professionals* behave in a certain way. When they make appointments, they keep them. They are punctual. They are prepared. They don't waste other people's time. They follow simple rules of business etiquette, from basic phone manners to civilized interpersonal contact. Professionals know what they're doing. They carry out their business with assured competence. They have high personal standards of excellence for their own performance. They respect others without kowtowing to them.

This last point is especially relevant for media professionals. Basic respect for others is a virtue in a harried, fast-track world. But in the context of mass communications, it is not impolite—and it is certainly not unprofessional—to be aggressive. Media writers often must be assertive, forceful and insistent as they do their jobs. This does not mean trampling on other people's rights, invading their privacy or being insensitive to their feelings. Being aggressive does not mean being belligerent and hostile. It means being vigorous, energetic and enterprising.

Aggressiveness is thus appropriate behavior for media writers. Like professionals of all stripes, they react appropriately to whatever situation they find themselves in. In a hushed meeting room, they don't talk in stage whispers to their colleagues. As observers, they make themselves as unobtrusive as possible. When meeting a client, they don't wear cutoffs and a T-shirt. These are matters of common sense and personal maturity.

It is the sum of this appropriate behavior—from telephone manners to standards of excellence, from punctuality to assertiveness—that makes someone a professional. By their attitude and conduct, professionals both demand and give respect.

Seeing yourself as a member of a profession

Acting professionally and *being a member of a profession* are not synonymous. Any competent, mature worker—short-order cook, lifeguard, welder or media writer—can (and should) act professionally. But media writers, along with others who consider themselves members of a profession, such as doctors or architects, do more than that. They have a broader view of who they are and what they do. These are some of the characteristics that separate media writers from other workers who, although they conduct themselves in a professional manner, are not members of a profession:

— They see their job in a larger context. They understand that what they do for a living is bigger than the job they happen to hold at the moment or the organization they currently work for. They see themselves as part of a larger (worldwide) community of media writers.

— They see themselves as part of a long tradition of people who have done similar work. Their field has a history, and they know something about it.

— They believe that their field has certain standards of performance, and they want to maintain or exceed them.

— They believe that their actions reflect not only on themselves but also on their colleagues everywhere.

— They share goals and ideals with their colleagues everywhere.

The profession of journalism

Not everyone believes journalism is a profession. Some say it should not be admitted to the exalted ranks of The Professions (law and medicine, for example) because it lacks certain characteristics basic to traditional professions. For example, members of a profession are specially trained. Doctors must go to medical school in order to practice; lawyers must go to law school. But journalists need not graduate from journalism school. In fact, they need not graduate from college or even high school. It is possible for a bright, well-read, determined person to learn journalistic skills on the job; it is not possible for the same person to master the techniques of open-heart surgery on the job.

A profession not only demands special training, argue some people, it also maintains its standards by licensing its practitioners. Lawyers must pass the bar exam; doctors must pass medical boards. Journalists, however, must only pass muster with their bosses. Professions also maintain their standards by creating umbrella organizations that devise enforceable codes. A lawyer who violates an American Bar Association code can be officially censured and expelled from the bar. That lawyer will be prohibited from practicing law anywhere. But a journalist who commits an unacceptable act is merely fired and may continue working in the field for another boss.

A profession also creates a secret language (jargon) that reflects a body of specialized knowledge its members alone possess. ("This neonate presents with necrotizing enterocolitis," says one doctor to another.) The cumulative effect of jargon, special knowledge and training, licensing, and enforceable codes is to insulate a profession from the public. "Only we understand what we do, and only we are qualified to monitor our own actions" is the message a profession sends to the public. "We can take care of our own" is the profession's generally respected attitude. But journalism is anything but insulated from the public. The work and language of journalists is understandable to a wide variety of non-specialists.

Nonetheless, there are powerful arguments *for* journalism as a profession: The field has a long history and tradition; it has standards of excellence; its members share goals and ideals; it imposes accepted codes of behavior. These codes address the responsibilities and obligations basic to all who work in the media industry. They suggest the broad moral purposes of mass communication and define standards of behavior. These guidelines—although not enforceable like the codes developed by some other professions—unite all mass communicators under an umbrella of professional and social responsibility.

Print reporters, broadcast journalists, public relations practitioners and advertising professionals are all guided by their own codes of ethics. Although the codes differ somewhat, reflecting the differences in medium and intent of message, they have many common characteristics. A media professional, say all the codes, should be:

— truthful

— accurate

— fair

— responsible

— honest in his or her dealings with others

— free from conflict of interest

All the codes stress the media worker's responsibility to the public and to the profession. They emphasize human dignity and integrity, staking out high moral ground. All point to the fundamental value of free speech. All define dubious behavior, from lying and bribe taking to breaking confidences and invading privacy.

But the codes also reflect the separate concerns of those who inform and/or analyze and those who persuade. Guidelines devised by the Society of Professional Journalists, the Associated Press Managing Editors, the American Society of Newspaper Editors and the Radio-Television News Directors reflect the interests of those who present news and information. In these codes the public's right to know is paramount. "The public's right to know of events of public importance and interest is the overriding mission of the mass media," states the code devised by the Society of Professional Journalists. "The primary purpose of broadcast journalists—to inform the public of events of importance and appropriate interest in a manner that is accurate and comprehensive—shall override all other purposes," says the broadcaster's code. For those involved in news (including, of course, in-depth writers), factual, impartial treatment is presented as the ideal.

The goal of those who persuade for a living is obviously not impartiality. Nor is the public's right to know considered a vital ingredient. Codes written by the Public Relations Society of America, the American Association of Advertising Agencies and the American Advertising Federation instead stress the importance of dealing fairly with clients, adhering to accepted standards of good taste and avoiding misleading statements and exaggerations.

It is true that the directives in these codes may be too simplistic to be useful. For example, it's fine to ask (and expect) journalists to be "truthful," but what in fact does that mean? It is also true that the codes may be superficial. In most cases they do not provide answers to tough ethical questions, pointing only to obvious vices like bribe taking while avoiding stickier, more important concerns like the difference between presenting facts and reporting truth. And it is true that these codes have no teeth. While an individual boss may fire an individual employee for behaving inappropriately, no broad-based national association demands that journalists stick to the codes in order to keep practicing their profession.

Yet for all these shortcomings, the codes illustrate that media workers take their jobs seriously. They think about their responsibility to the people they serve and the colleagues they serve with. They view their work in the larger context of their profession and want that profession to have high ethical standards and widespread credibility.

Toward a system of professional ethics

Dissatisfied with the superficial approach to ethics provided by the codes, some have sought to define a system of journalism ethics. One of the most articulate advocates of this approach is University of Missouri Professor Edmund Lambeth. In his important book, *Committed Journalism,** Lambeth discusses what he sees as the five principles of ethical journalism. Although he is primarily concerned with the news and analysis functions of the media, note that the final three principles are applicable to media writers of all stripes—from news reporters to advertising copywriters.

1. *The principle of truth telling.* Journalists must not only develop a "habit of accuracy," they must also seek the larger truths behind the facts.

2. *The principle of justice.* Journalists must maintain a daily concern for fairness, and news organizations must help create a climate conducive to high ethical standards. The news media must take its watchdog role seriously, guarding against abuses of power by other societal institutions.

3. *The principle of freedom.* The individual media writer must be free, unencumbered by divided or conflicting interests. As a representative of the mass media in a functioning democracy, the media writer should guard the constitutional freedom afforded the press.

4. *The principle of humanness.* The media writer, like all human beings, should do no direct, intentional harm to others, instead giving assistance and preventing suffering where possible.

5. *The principle of stewardship.* The media writer is a caretaker or steward of free expression. He or she "manages . . . resources of communication with due regard for the rights of others, the rights of the public, and the moral health of [his or her] own occupation," writes Lambeth.

---

*Edmund B. Lambeth, *Committed Journalism*, Bloomington: Indiana University Press, 1986.

The societal environment

Just as individual media writers work within the broad context of their profession, the mass media profession as a whole exists within the larger societal environment. Have you ever stopped to consider just how odd the position of the mass media is in our society?

With the notable exceptions of public broadcasting and a smattering of foundation-supported periodicals, the American mass media are *for-profit* organizations. Like cosmetic manufacturers or soft drink corporations, they are businesses with a great interest in maximizing revenues. They want (and need) to keep owners, investors and perhaps stockholders happy. They want (and need) to increase sales. Like other companies, they produce a product for a price. The difference—and it is a big one—is that the media's product is *the message*. And this product, unlike shampoo or cola, has been revered by Americans since the founding of the country. This product has a special place in our society.

Free speech is considered a basic right in the United States. Protected by our Constitution's First Amendment, it has generally been upheld through more than 200 years of legal and legislative actions. Americans consider the dissemination of information throughout society (via various channels of mass communication) necessary for the functioning of a democracy. Most people—even those momentarily angered by a sexist advertisement or a biased news story—would agree that media messages help them participate in the political, economic and cultural life of the country. The media of mass communication are therefore involved in both a higher calling—the spread of information—and the everyday world of business.

For the news media particularly, this is a precarious position. On the one hand, those in the business of presenting and analyzing current events are performing a vital societal function. At their best, these writers and the organizations they work for function as keen-eyed, fair-minded watchdogs. They guard against abuses of power by other societal institutions, placing the people's right to know above all else.

On the other hand, the news media are for-profit organizations. Many newspapers and magazines are owned by megacorporations with hundreds of other "properties" and thousands of stockholders. Most broadcast stations are affiliated with one of the three major networks (which, in turn, are owned by parent companies with scores of other business interests). As business organizations, the media have a primary responsibility to their owners and investors. As news organizations, they have a primary responsibility to the public. Can they simultaneously seek the truth and a profit? Not always. There is a deep and often unresolvable conflict between the goals of doing good and making money.

For those who practice persuasion, the conflict may not be as deep, but it exists nonetheless. Advertising copywriters, editorial writers, public relations practitioners and advocacy journalists perform many important societal functions. Their messages present a range of available options that help us make decisions. True, some decisions are unimportant, like what brand of toothpaste to buy. But others may have great impact on our lives or the lives of others, like which candidate to support or what charity to contribute to.

Persuasive writers must feel a sense of responsibility toward those they are trying to influence and the society they will—in big and small ways—affect. But members of advertising agencies and public relations firms must first serve their clients, not the public. The difference between what's good for the public and what's desirable for the client creates tension that the persuasive communicator must either live with or resolve.

In short, the mass media occupy an uncomfortable niche in American society, somewhere between public service and private enterprise. But regardless of their business orientation, they perform vital public functions that give them elevated status and impose weighty responsibilities on those who create their messages.

Rights of the media writer

Along with the weighty responsibilities a media writer must shoulder come some certain basic rights that underlie the operation of our mass media. Most fundamental, of course, is the right of free speech guaranteed by the Constitution. Those who drafted the First Amendment were primarily interested in protecting *political* communication (news, analysis and opinion related to current events and issues). But over the years, other kinds of public communication—*corporate* and *commercial* expression, for example—came under the First Amendment umbrella.

Hand in hand with free speech comes another tenet basic to a democracy: the right of the public to discover the public's business. The public has a right to know how its money is spent and how the people it elects perform their duties. The public has a right to know what goes on inside public institutions, from the U.S. Senate to a local community college. To exercise this right, the public needs access to accurate, timely information. Thus the public's right becomes the mass media's mandate.

These fundamental rights form the basis of federal and state legislation that helps media writers do their jobs and live up to their professional and societal responsibilities. Without delving into legal details, let's take a brief look at two broad areas of legal rights relevant to the media writer:

— *The right to gather information.* The right to communicate information (the First Amendment) means little if not accompanied by the right to gather information. Like all citizens, media writers have the legal right to attend public meetings (which must, by law, be announced in advance) and the right to examine public records. On the federal level, media writers (and anyone else) have a right to see any unclassified document produced by any arm of the government.

— *The right not to be coerced by the government and its laws.* Free speech, the public's right to know and the right to gather information are enjoyed by all citizens. But journalists, by virtue of their special place in American society, have acquired additional rights. If the news media are to act as effective watchdogs over societal institutions (including government), then the government should not be able to coerce journalists into withholding information from the public, breaking confidences with sources or handing over information legally gathered in the course of a story. Journalists need this protection to operate freely and in the public interest.

Mastering the message

Mastering the message means more than learning and perfecting the techniques of media writing. It means practicing them within the broader context of the mass communication profession and the society it serves. We believe that creating media messages is an art. We believe that it takes hard work, dedication, perseverance—and talent—to do it well. We also believe that this art, like all others, exists within the larger sociocultural environment. To be a skilled media writer, you must appreciate the philosophical, ethical, legal and professional framework in which you do your job. Only then will you do your job well; only then will you master the message.

Index

Acknowledgments

We gratefully acknowledge permission to use the following:

Ann Keding and The Los Angeles Commission on Assaults Against Women (p. 32)

The Rockport Company (p. 99)

Excerpt from "Growing Pains," by Brian Gard (p. 100)

Los Angeles Times, Copyright 1987 (p. 151)

Greenpeace (p. 155)

ABC News (p. 158)

Northwest Magazine (p. 172)

CBS News (pp. 198, 204)

Scott Simon/National Public Radio (p. 209)

Lauren Kessler (p. 211)

Tom Hager (p. 220)

Farrar, Straus and Giroux, Inc., for "Under the Snow," from *Table of Contents* by John McPhee. Copyright © 1980, 1981, 1982, 1983, 1984, 1985 by John McPhee. Originally appeared in the *New Yorker*. (p. 225)

"In Time of War," by Lauren Kessler (p. 227)

Milwaukee Journal (p. 254)

Charles A. LeMaistre, M.D. (p. 262)

George Gladney (p. 274)

Philips Consumer Electronics Company (p. 278)

Russell Sadler (p. 282)

Blue Cross and Blue Shield of Oregon and Borders, Perrin & Norrander (p. 284)

keye/donna/pearlstein (p. 288)